MAKE WORLDS

Minka Maria Izida

When We Are On Hormones

europe books

www.europebooks.co.uk | info@europebooks.co.uk

ISBN 9791256971862
First edition: November 2025

When We Are On Hormones

I dedicate this book to you, dear women.
I want to help you understand your body.
And I dedicate this book to you, dear men,
because you must deal with both your own hormones
and with the hormones of the women around you.
It is easier when you understand.

With love, Minka Maria

Contents

Acknowledgements

A book is like a child. At first, it is a tiny idea that grows and grows. Then it is born. And that you cannot do alone, you need the help of experts.

We are guided in our lives. I believe there are no coincidences. I meet many wonderful persons, who helped me through the period of this book, but special thanks is going to my teachers.

I am grateful to the company NeoLife, with which I have been working for several years. The knowledge I have gained through the expert lectures by their Scientific Advisory Board is invaluable. I am also grateful to many other great minds who contributed their knowledge and help in raising my awareness: Louise L. Hay, Dr Alex Loyd, Dr Bruce Lipton, Doreen Viture, Harv Eker, Anita Moorjani, Lorna Byrne, Dr Wayne Dyer, Rhonda Byrne, James Redfield, Don Miguel Ruiz, Vladimir Megre, Sanja Lončar and Marija Merljak. You are all my mentors through your books. Thank you!

I would also like to thank everyone who has given me a bitter experience in life. Because of you, I am what I am today. It is not easy to go through bitter experiences, but they are necessary for us to grow. You were sent to me as personal emotional trainers. Thank you!

Finally, I want to thank my family. Firstly, my mother, who encourages me with her motherly love and prayers. Mum, thank you for your knowledge about herbs – you have contributed to the diversity of this book. And thank you, dad, for supporting me in all decisions I make.

And thank you, my three daughters! Your views on life are unburdened, brave, swift and sometimes very direct. I love you – Sara, Pia and Anja!

Minka Maria Izida

Introduction

My 44th birthday was coming up. Considering I already had three children, I panicked. My period refused to come. What if I am pregnant? A friend of mine, Tatjana, had given birth a few months earlier - her third child at nearly 44. I did a pregnancy test - nothing. But my period still did not come. Panic!

As I was thinking about the possibility of being pregnant, I was horrified at the thought that I would once more have to go through a period of severe hunger and weight gain, when you feel like an elephant, and you simply cannot control your eating. I was horrified at the thought that after the baby was born, I would once more have to lose all the weight. I thought about how I would again not feel good in my body and how nothing would fit me. The next thought was: where can I find a book that will help me through this period, where there are the daily meal plans I can follow so that through my pregnancy I can easily control my hunger and so that after the baby is born, I can regain my body and wellbeing without any great problems?

And because I knew that there was no book to guide women through the times when their hormones go wild - when hormones have a party - i.e. puberty, pregnancy, infertility, breastfeeding, and menopause - I decided to write such a book myself.

I am convinced I can help you! The book offers solutions which will make it easier for you to build a new self-image and confidence, to persist on the path you have chosen and to reach your goal.

You can seek a solution outside yourself, you can seek it with psychiatrists, psychologists, voodoo witch doctors, etc. But they all treat the symptoms, while the cause stays the same. You can compare this to a field of weeds - if you cut the weeds down, within three weeks they will grow even stronger and denser. If you want to get rid of the weeds, you have to pull them out together with the roots and throw them on the compost heap. This applies to all problems: if you want to get rid of the symptoms (the weeds), you must do away with the causes (the roots).

Chapter 1. Hormonal balance and love

You cannot be happy when you are unhealthy

What can you do when hormones cause problems? Hormones have to be lively, not wild or lazy.

Hormones connect feelings, thoughts and body. Hormones are the communication system in your body. When you are in harmony, your hormones are in harmony, you feel wonderful, and you have a feeling that you are invincible and that you can do anything you want. But what do you do when your hormonal balance is out of sync, when your hormones start controlling and dictating how you feel? One minute you are ecstatic, the next you are floored; one minute you are losing weight, the next you are putting it on uncontrollably; one minute you are in a good mood, the next you cry over the smallest problem; one minute you feel like sleeping all day, the next you lie awake all night long. It feels you are on a roller coaster, which takes you high up one minute and then the next thing you know, you are hurtling at deathly speed toward the ground.

There are over 400 types of hormones. They are produced by the endocrine glands, which are directly connected with the body's energy centres - chakras:

- hypothalamus,
- pineal gland,
- pituitary gland,
- thyroid gland,
- thymus,
- pancreas,
- adrenal glands,
- reproductive glands.

Life energy centres – chakras

The word *chakra* means a circle, or a whirlpool of light and chakras are strong, magnetic centres:

• The **first chakra** is the root chakra and is connected with the reproductive glands - sex hormones and reproduction (*who I am, I trust in life*). It is blocked by fear and guilt.

• The **second chakra** is connected with the spleen and the adrenal glands. This is where the stress hormone, cortisol (which ages you) and DHEA (which regenerates you) are produced (*I feel peace*). It is connected with the feeling of satisfaction and blocked by disappointment.

• The **third chakra** lies above the belly button and influences the pancreas - and the hormone insulin - i.e. the ability to "digest" life (*I can, I go with the flow*). It is blocked by anger.

• The **fourth chakra** is in the heart area and influences the thymus - the heart chakra influences the immune system, heart, lungs and breasts (*I feel love*). It is connected with forgiveness and blocked by bitterness.

• The **fifth chakra** lies in the throat area and is connected with the thyroid gland; it is also known as the throat chakra (*I express and talk the truth*). It is blocked by hatred and a feeling that you are a victim in life.

• The **sixth chakra** influences the pineal gland and is connected with the third eye - the centre where the growth hormone is produced (*I see truth*). It is blocked by self-criticism.

• The **seventh chakra** influences the hypothalamus and the pituitary gland, where the hormones of happiness are produced - the crown chakra is connected to everything divine, to creativity (*I trust in the divine guidance - I know that everything will be as it should*). It is blocked by fear.

The energy centres are also connected with each other:

• The first and seventh chakra* act in tandem - when a person is in a state of calm, aligned with nature and God, the sex chakra functions normally.

• The second and sixth chakra - when you are under stress, the sixth energy centre, which produces the growth hormone, does not function well and consequently there is no regeneration, a person ages quickly and puts on weight. When you calm down, the regeneration process is set in motion again.

• The third and fifth chakra - the third energy centre is connected with the pancreas, which influences the excretion of insulin. The more you feel disappointment and that everything is in vain, the worse is the functioning of the third chakra. When in addition you feel that you cannot speak the truth and you suppress your feelings, you are also blocking the functioning of the thyroid.

• The fourth chakra - the heart chakra - does not have a pair. It is an energy centre in the middle of the body and a conductor of our emotions, feeding all the other energy centres. From it, the messages go to the hypothalamus, which is like a control board that conveys all the information to the other hormonal centres. Recent research at the HeartMath institute confirms that the heart acts like a sensor - it is a refined information centre that sends information to all the other energy centres. When we feel the joy of life, the heart chakra informs all the other centres of this. It represents the ability to give and receive love. Did you know that heart energy radiates in a radius of over a metre around us and that it is 5000 times stronger than that of the mind and the magnetic field of the brain? This is also the answer to the question why within a moment we can sense who we are dealing with.

**A great deal has been written about the chakras. In many sources, the first chakra is connected with the adrenal glands and the second chakra with the sex glands. In my description of the chakras, I am using Peter Kelder's book 'Ancient Secret of the Fountain of Youth'. Besides, since the first chakra is closest to the genitalia it seems logical that it is connected with the sex glands. It acts in tandem with the crown chakra. The second chakra is closest to the adrenal glands and works in tandem with the sixth chakra. Both these centres produce regeneration hormones.*

Because I had no knowledge about the chakras and only began to discover these energy centres when I started doing the 'Fountain of Youth' exercises, I first wanted to recall the colours of the chakras. I knew that they were the colours of the rainbow, but what was the order?

It is very simple! People are energy. When light gets refracted through a prism, rainbow colours appear - red, orange, yellow, green, blue, indigo and violet. And these are the colours of our energy centres and the order they appear in.

I firmly believe that we can influence our energy centres through the colours we wear. If you are having problems with your genitalia, you should be wearing red underwear; those who have frequent digestive issues should wear orange or yellow vests or t-shirts. If you have diabetes, liver or heart problems, you should wear as much of the enlivening light green and emerald as possible. Those with throat and thyroid issues should wear blue clothes or blue scarves around their neck. And if you often get headaches or have problems with your sight, you should wear purple clothes. It has been proven that every colour has its own frequency - and this frequency also has a healing effect on our body.

Observe your body: if there is something wrong, it gives you gentle warnings that can easily be ignored. Your body wants to let you know that there is a hormonal imbalance in the following ways:

- changeable moods,
- hunger attacks,
- nervousness and irritability,
- fear,
- a tight feeling in the throat,
- lack of concentration,
- restlessness,
- lack of joy, indifference,
- chronic sadness and wanting to cry,
- lack of motivation,
- tiredness,
- spottiness,
- dizziness,
- weight gain and inability to lose weight,
- hot flushes or attacks of shivering,
- weakening of the libido,
- weak immune system.

All these are caused by a heavily burdened emotional state, which is reflected in the functioning of the hormonal centres. When we are drowning in negative feelings, our hormones function badly. Just the opposite happens when we are filled with good emotions: then, our cells produce even more chemicals that make us feel even better.

Emotions influence physical processes

Love

Hope Bliss

Faith Happiness Peace Pride

Joy Being in love Passion Gratitude

Enthusiasm Respect Calm Satisfaction Excitement

FORGIVENESS

Anxiety Irritation Disappointment Worry Revenge

Criticism Anger Sadness Envy Superstition

Guilt Despair Jealousy

Shame Hatred

Fear

You feel either positive or negative feelings. The predominant feelings decide the direction your life will take. Hormonal balance issues, particularly those connected with the thyroid gland, originate in the feeling that you are always only looking after others, that you are never taken care of, that you come last, that you are not heard or understood. Since all healing begins inside ourselves, these problems are only the body's reminder that it is time to start valuing oneself.

When you say:

- “No one understands me,” this is your soul’s message, saying: “I don’t understand myself.”
- “I always come last,” is your soul telling you: “I always put myself last.”
- “No one values me,” is really telling you: “I don’t value myself.”
- “I count for nothing in this household,” in fact means: “I don’t value myself enough.”
- “No one listens to me,” is your soul’s way of telling you: “I don’t listen to myself, and I ignore the messages sent by my body and my soul.”
- “No one cares about me,” really means: “I don’t care about my body and about how I feel.”
- “Everyone is progressing faster than I am,” means: “I’m not good enough.”

This is why you should begin by repeating the following healing statements: “I’m starting to love myself. I value myself. I know how to take care of myself.” Say this 100 times a day, say it so many times that your body becomes saturated with the sentence “I love and value myself.” In the evening, before going to sleep, hug yourself and give yourself all the love you wish to feel and that you feel for yourself - after all, you will be living with yourself for the rest of your life.

Loving self-care and forgiveness should become daily habits

You should respect your body. The commandment: "Love your neighbour as yourself," means that if you do not love yourself, you cannot love other people.

Repeat to yourself: "I love and value myself, therefore:

- I want to consume healthy food;
- I exercise every day - I take time for myself;
- I talk about my feelings;
- I socialise with positive people,
- I listen to useful information;
- I can stand up for myself in a loving way."

Because you love and value yourself, you know how to take care of yourself. In his book *'The Monk Who Sold His Ferrari'*, Robin S. Sharma says:

"[...] self-mastery and the consistent care of one's mind, body and soul are essential to finding one's highest self and living the life of one's dreams. How can you care for others if you cannot even care for yourself? How can you do good if you don't even feel good? I can't love you if I cannot love myself."

Loving care for yourself is a habit, it is a daily practice. In the beginning, when you are just learning to love and appreciate yourself, read the following sentences to yourself every day:

Deep within my being, there is an infinite wellspring of love.

I now allow this love to surface, filling my heart, my physical being, my thoughts, my consciousness, and radiating outwards in all directions, returning to me amplified.

I permit myself to love my body. I nurture it with care and attention, and in return, it flourishes with vitality and robust health.

By valuing myself, I create a comfortable environment that fulfills my needs and brings me happiness. I imbue each space with the essence of love so that everyone who enters, including myself, feels nurtured by this affection.

By valuing myself, I engage in work that brings me true joy, utilizing my creative talents and collaborating with individuals I love and who reciprocate that affection, all while earning a respectable income.

By valuing myself, I interact with others in a kind and loving way, knowing that the love I give is returned to me manifold. My surroundings are filled only with those who reflect love back to me.

By valuing myself, embracing each moment positively, with the belief that my future is bright, joyful, and secure. My world is harmonious and filled with goodness.

Listen to yourself

Listen to the hidden messages from your soul: "Please, take care of yourself." Ask yourself: "Where am I? Am I happy? What do I feel at this moment?"

When you are stuck in your job or in your relationship, which exhausts you, "sucks you dry" so that you need a few hours a day to put yourself together again, it is right to stop and ask where the path you are on now is leading you. You should ask whether there is any point in continuing on it. If at work or in your relationship old grievances have been going on for a long time, your life energy starts to weaken. If your relationship is such a burden that you are having health problems, it would perhaps be sensible to think about where you see yourself in the future and what makes you happy. If you are having health problems now, in a few years you will be of no use to anyone anyway - you will be on your own, ill and without money. When you lose your freshness of spirit, you lose your strength.

The message is very simple: "Listen to your feelings, listen to your emotions! Stop shutting your eyes to things and stop lying to yourself!"

I hear you say: "But what about security? I have to survive!"

Of course, we have to survive - we all have our monthly bills to pay.

A few years back, I left a safe job because my health started sending me warnings. Every day my stomach hurt. On Sunday night, at a mere thought about work, it started hurting and it hurt - or at least I was aware of my stomach - until Friday afternoon. When I saw that my energy was weakening and I was only just over 20, I made a decision. I left the safe embrace of a permanent job and set off into the unknown. I had no idea what I would do, all I knew was what I did not want. I did not want to spend 8 hours or more in a team where the atmosphere was stale. It is like in your home - if you do not air it for a while, first there is a musty smell you do not even notice because you live there, but with time mould starts to grow. And mould leads to illness.

When I left my job, I felt elated about having freed myself. Then I started looking. I found work that within six months led me to what I do now - help people to better health.

It sounds really simple - you make a decision, you find something else to do and there you meet someone who opens the door to something else again. It would be so simple if we were not plagued by fearful thoughts - fear of failure, fear of what other people might say, fear of being alone; then there are also comments by those who love us, but do not believe in us. All change is initially a little uncomfortable.

Someone we respect might say to us: "Think about it carefully. I don't think you're making the right decision. Just think how many people would be happy if they had your salary/home/husband/boss/office/car. Just put up with it, it'll get better." People who love us should give us faith, strength and courage, not fear. People who want good things for us should say: "I believe in you. You can succeed in anything. The only important thing is that you're happy, the money will come and there will be even more of it when you radiate happiness. I wish you to succeed and I'll help you as best I can because I believe in you!"

If the people around us do not say this to us because they are infected with the energy of fear, then we must tell these things to ourselves. Let the following statements be our mantra:

• I believe in myself. I believe the Universe supports me. I believe that I'm completely safe here and now.

• My soul is filled with the divine love. God loves me. Through me there is a constant flow of God's love, peace, harmony and success in all areas. God is my eternal source. All my spiritual, emotional and material needs are fulfilled at all times and everywhere.

• I accept new ideas; new doors are opening for me and I can move on.

When one door closes, another one opens. Perhaps at this moment you cannot see the way ahead. But have trust. You are not alone. Ask all the forces in the Universe for help and you will see that there is something better for you. Give in to the flow of life. You will feel alive again. You will have hope again that all will be well, hope for better times. You will have a desire for creativity. Suddenly, there will be a twinkle in your eye again and you will feel energy in your body. First thing in the morning, when you wake up, you will be glad of the new day. Once more, you will feel Life, Freedom and Joy!

Life is supporting you when you dare to leave apparent safety. When you dare to start taking steps, life follows. But until you take even the smallest steps, life cannot support you. When you are stuck, you are killing yourself, your energy and your soul. Freshness, enthusiasm and faith in a bright future are the driving forces of success.

Follow your bliss and the universe will open doors for you where there were only walls.

Joseph Campbell

Just the fact that you have a desire, means that you have the necessary ability to realise it. When you set off on a journey to happiness, you will find a way to survive. Think how you can serve people and contribute towards the big picture of a happier planet. But the first step starts with you - what do you have to do to be more satisfied and happy? And what you learn you can then teach others. **Make a decision!**

When you are doing what you really like, you will definitely feel deep satisfaction. And your feeling of satisfaction will bring serendipities into your life. Believe that feeling - a tiny voice that speaks to you - and follow it. Love yourself and go forward. Leave fear behind! When you dare start, life follows!

The only thing that is constant is change.

Heraclitus (535 BC - 475 BC)

If you want to calmly go through the changes, you have to take care of your own peace. Create a distance between you and the events and people that sap your energy. Be peaceful in your soul, do not let them suck you into a whirlpool of negativity.

Tell yourself: "My soul is calm. I'm safe here and now. All is good. My emotional state is always balanced. All the forces of the universe are supporting me."

When you need additional strength, go out into the natural world as often as possible. Allow nature to fill you with new energy; allow yourself to be enchanted by the sounds of the forest, to be calmed by the sound of a stream. Just sit down, look at the water and breathe. Allow your soul to be filled with new energy. Allow tears to flow. Do not be ashamed of them, tears wash your soul; they are like a "car wash".

When you are worried about something, when something is pulling you down, when you are drowning in negative emotions, throw all the negative thoughts into the water and allow the water to carry them away and cleanse them. You can throw stones into the water or snowballs in the winter, or leaves - let every stone represent a negative thought, every snowball a feeling you no longer wish to feel. Fear, even anger, resentment, etc., let all the negative feelings flow away from you. The water purifies them, washes them and you do not harm anyone - either yourself or others.

Is our life not like a flowing stream - connected with the eternal source that never dries up? There are periods in our life when everything flows calmly - the flow slows down and we think that it will always remain calm. But it does not. Rapids appear, the flow of life speeds up, usually changes happen in many areas of our life simultaneously. These rapids give us a good shake, life pulls us under, sometimes we can barely breathe. And although we try as hard as we can, it seems that there is no end to problems. But sooner or later we overcome them and reach a calmer period again.

The power of love and forgiveness

It is easy to hate, easy to be negative, easy to find excuses. Love, compassion and forgiveness require a big heart, an exceptional mind and constant work on oneself. When something bad happens to us, we are angry, upset, disappointed. We resent people's words and actions.

Forgive all the people who did something bad to you, who have hurt you. They did the best they could. They are incapable of doing it better, they don't know how to. If they knew how to do it better, they would.

Repeat this sentence until you feel relief: "Let God's love for (the name of the person who has hurt you) fill my heart."

You are on the right path!

How do you know that for sure? Your nearest and dearest will tell you that you have become strange, that you are different because you are reading "strange" books, you go out into the countryside, you listen to gongs, you pray, etc.

Does this sound familiar? You are not strange; you have just set off on a path of personal growth. On a path of freedom. When your friends and family see that you are changing, they get scared. They want the old you back; they want nothing to change; they want to squeeze you back into the "box" you were in before, where they could control you, where you never talked about your feelings, where you kept quiet and suffered, where you accepted everything just to keep the peace.

They are scared. But who are they scared for? You or themselves? They are scared for themselves, which is why they want to keep you where you used to be, because that is how they can easily sap your energy. They want you quiet and obedient - just like you used to be for years and years. Because you are moving forward, they are deprived of your energy. But you must carry on courageously! You are on the right path.

The only sticking plaster that really helps is forgiveness

Look inside yourself and begin to put plasters on your emotional wounds, plasters of love, forgiveness, compassion and understanding. No one has hurt you deliberately. Your parents or your partner did the best they could and if they are still with you, they are still doing the best they can. Forgive them, they were children once, too, brought up by their parents who did their best. By the age of five, children have accepted the programmes transferred to them by the people who brought them up. Perhaps your parents or partner experienced lack of love, perhaps they were frequently punished. How can a person who has not experienced love, give love? What you do not have, you cannot give.

This is why you should first forgive your parents - be grateful for the gift of life, for your first year when you were unable to even wipe your own bottom. Not one of us could have survived on our own. And this is a sufficient reason for being deeply grateful to the people who looked after us during our first year. Tell your parents you love them. Write them a letter, let them know that you are grateful. Write to them that you forgive them for all the conflicts between you through the years, because you understand and know that they tried their best. Write to them that you love them.

If they are not with you anymore, you can still tell them that you are grateful. Love does not die. Love is an eternal emotion that can be felt by the souls of the dead.

Then forgive your family and those close to you.

Be aware that if people are mean to you (because of your appearance, your work, your family, your way of thinking), they have a problem with themselves. If a remark hurts you, it means that they have scratched an open emotional wound. In that case, you have a problem, too. People around us are our teachers, our personal emotional trainers. Ask yourself: "What do I have to learn? What do I feel? What is life's lesson for me?"

If you keep playing in your mind the film of how someone hurt you, what they said or did, you are hurting your soul, and this reopens the wounds so that they start to bleed again. That is not what your soul has come here to learn. Your soul has come here to learn forgiveness and love. When you are able to take care of yourself in a loving way, what needs to happen will happen.

> In my work, I deal with people a lot. And every person has their own story. When I listen to these stories, I can draw a simple parallel: if you cannot stand up for yourself in a nice way, life gives you a slap. And if that is not enough, it puts you on an edge and pushes you over so that you have to act. But not by attacking yourself - you have to act with love for yourself. My friend Mima says: "After overcoming cancer, I became a little egoist. I take care of myself now, I do what I enjoy, I'm full of enthusiasm. I have peace in my heart."

I recommend that you read James Redfield's book *The Celestine Prophesy.* The sixth insight talks about clearing the past (summarised):

> *Interrogators create aloof people. Intimidators create the "poor me" drama or another intimidator. There's no end to these dramas. Usually, we can recognise them in other people but think that we do not have them. It is necessary to transcend this illusion, otherwise we cannot move on. Nearly all of us have at some point been stuck in a drama for a while, therefore we have to step away and look at ourselves until we find it.*
>
> *We must see our life as a long story. You have to glance at all the key events in your life from birth to the present moment. You have to recognise and understand the meaning of all the events. Answer the following questions: "Why was I born to my particular parents, my particular family? What purpose is behind this? What was the point of everything that happened to me within my family? What you would like to change in your parents is part of what you are striving for.*
>
> *As soon as we discover the truth and the higher purpose of our life, it becomes clear who we really are, it explains the path we are on and our behaviour.*

And I started to look: What bothers me in my mother? This is there for my education - that which bothers me, I have to transcend. What bothers me in my father? This is also there for my education. The people around us only place a mirror in front of us, showing us what we have to do. We notice drama in other people, but not in ourselves.

Family members are what they are. And that leads to conflicts. The family offers us an opportunity for growth, for becoming a better person. Ask yourself: "Do I hold grudges in my heart? Has someone closest to me hurt me and I can't forgive them?"

"I can't forgive him for what he did and said to me." When the beloved person has hurt you in the past, betrayed you, or if she or he disappointed you again and again, it is hard to forgive, hard to love again. There is a bitter aftertaste. If you saw your emotional body, you would see your wounds that have not healed yet; the scabs that hurt and bleed at the slightest touch.

Grudges lead to a blockage at the energy level and consequently to illness.

Cancer is directly tied to old grudges buried deep inside your subconscious. The only cure for when someone disappoints you and wrongs you, the only cure that liberates you, is forgiveness. Forgiveness is a selfish act. By forgiving we liberate ourselves.

Imagine that you have an emotional vessel inside. All the unresolved emotions are deposited in it: inferiority feelings, anger at your parents and your partner, resentments towards your work colleagues, etc. The heap of unexpressed emotions keeps growing. We were not taught to talk about it, we were taught to be quiet and put up with it. But when the vessel is full, a crack appears somewhere. Some people are constantly angry, some use drugs, some alcohol, some food, others the computer or television. All this in order to escape reality.

If you often reach for unhealthy food, alcohol or have another addiction, answer the following questions:

- Who do I want to protect myself from, who has hurt me so that I need protection around me?
- Which emotions do I suppress?
- Why am I punishing myself?
- What do I long for?

Learn to talk about your feelings: "At this moment I feel ___________." Say it out loud or, even better, write it down. When single words won't do it, write a letter, feelings that are written down are easier to understand. Do not accuse. Do not write: "You're unfair, you said ..., you're hypocritical, you're deceitful, you're dishonest, etc." If you notice all this in others, you have to ask if all these accusations do not apply to you at least to some extent. People around us place a mirror in front of us. Everything that bothers us in others is there for our education. We can always only change ourselves, never others.

The magic words

I'm sorry …

Forgive me …

Thank you …

I love you …

A letter, i.e. feelings written down, is more understandable to men. Women experience the world through the spectrum of emotions, men through logic. When feelings are put on paper, a man can analyse them in peace, read them a few times, think about it in peace, put himself in our shoes. He does not feel under attack.

Women often moan that they are victims, that they have to do everything themselves, that no one does anything, that they are like a single mother who is alone for everything. This used to be my monologue once, too, charged with anger, disappointment and silent grudges. Everything can change when you begin to value yourself, when you start to share the work and when you state clearly that you need help. Tell the people around you what you need! Tell them where you need help. If you keep saying to yourself: "I'm alone for everything," and just throw anger around you, how are they supposed to know what you need? Everyone withdraws because you are grumpy again, because you are menopausal, because it is that time of the month, because it is full moon, because … Your supressed emotions are shouting inside you, while externally you show a face that is not yours.

Tell the world around you what you feel and what you need!

A friend was just about to get a divorce. With three children, a job and a household she moaned that she was alone for everything. Dissatisfaction burned inside her, disappointment, anger and resentment because no one had noticed what she needed. Because of all this, she comforted herself with food. Slowly, her weight grew. All traces of the happy, playful girl that her husband had married were gone. She was submerged by fat, constantly angry and exhausted, and she nagged.

When we talked, I advised her to start with healthier food and a few positive affirmations and to write a list of what she did and what her husband did at home. She wrote a list and, on her side, the sheet of paper was covered to the bottom, while her husband's side was practically empty. She did not have the strength to negotiate with her husband but helplessly left the list next to the computer. Her husband must have seen it because the next morning, he washed the dishes. A few days later, she came to me with tears in her eyes and a wide smile on her face and said that miracles were happening. Her husband had rung her at work and said kindly: "I see there's a pile of dirty washing. Please tell me how to put the washing machine on."

This story has a happy ending. Even though they were on different banks of the river, and it seemed that it would be impossible to rebuild the burnt bridges, they succeeded. They now have another baby that is the fruit of their love. Everything is possible, even if it seems that all is at an end, a miracle can happen in your life. Believe in the power of love! And love starts with you, in your heart!

Love is patient, love is kind and is not jealous; love does not brag and is not arrogant, does not act unbecomingly; it does not seek its own, is not provoked, does not take into account a wrong suffered, does not rejoice in unrighteousness, but rejoices with the truth; bears all things, believes all things, hopes all things, endures all things. Love never fails.

The Bible - First Letter to the Corinthians, 13.

Every relationship teaches us a very simple lesson, the lesson of love. If we do not learn it in a nice way, we experience it through the blows given us by life. And blows often have a stronger effect than caresses. If we cannot learn to love ourselves in a better way, our body gets sick; if we cannot learn about love in a relationship, the relationship dies. All that is left in the end is fear and darkness.

Love is always kind. Fear is always unkind. [...] We feel victimized by everything; we feel angry or sad or jealous or betrayed.

Anger is nothing but fear with a mask. Sadness is fear with a mask. Jealousy is fear with a mask. With all those emotions that come from fear and create suffering, we can only pretend to be kind. We are not kind because we don't feel good, we are not happy. If you are in the track of love, you have no obligations, no expectations. [...] Everything is going well for you and that is why that smile is always on your face. [...] Love is always kind, and that kindness makes you generous and opens all the doors. Love is generous. Fear is selfish; it is only about me. Selfishness closes all the doors.

Love is unconditional. Fear is full of conditions. In the track of fear, I love you if you let me control you, if you are good to me, if you fit into the image I make for you.

[...]

*In the track of love, you are giving more than taking. And of course, you love yourself so much that you don't allow selfish people to take advantage of you. You are not going for revenge, but you are clear in your communication. You can say, "I don't like it when you try to take advantage of me, when you disrespect me, when you are unkind to me. I don't need someone to abuse me verbally, emotionally, physically. I don't need to hear you cursing all the time. It's not that I'm better than you; it's because I love beauty. I love to laugh; I love to have fun; I love to love. It's not that I am selfish, I just don't need a big victim near me. It doesn't mean that I don't love you, but I cannot take responsibility for your dream. If you are in a relationship with me, it will be so hard for your Parasite, because I will not react to your garbage at all." This is not selfishness; this is self-love.**

*Don Miguel Ruiz: The Mastery of Love

How much you love yourself can be seen in the very basic things, such as hunger, thirst and needing to use the toilet.

Our body sends signals we have to respond to:

• **Hunger**: take a minute of your time and eat something healthy, e.g. a bit of low-fat cheese, a handful of almonds, etc. (more about healthy snacks that don't increase hunger later).

• **Needing to go to the toilet**: you delay and your body gets used to keeping toxins inside. Toxins must come out or you will get ill, not while you are still working, but later, when you retire, when all your bodily functions are completely confused. That is only the result of neglecting your body.

• **Thirst:** you don't drink enough. Get a bottle of water ready so that you know how much you have drunk. Drink at least ten 2-decilitre glasses, or even better, 1 litre of water per 25 kilograms of bodily weight.

Tell yourself as many times as possible:

"It is time for me to increase self-love. I acknowledge that I am a cherished creation of the universe. I recognize the presence of love within me. I can fully embrace my feminine form. I can unconditionally accept all aspects of creation. Love flows freely through all my connections.

I am presently planting the seeds of love.

I forgive myself and allow myself to be forgiven. I realize that everything good belongs to me. Let the healing energy flow through all my relationships.

May the love of the divine fill my heart towards ________ (the person who caused me pain).

Love fills all my relationships. I allow new energy to flow into my life, bringing spring to all areas. I permit and welcome miracles.

I am aware that my consciousness is expanding to a higher level. Because I want to progress, I take care of myself with love. I know it's time to change my diet. I allow myself to enjoy healthy food. I realize that foods that contain white flour and refined sugar slow down my brain and my spirit. I feel and perceive what is really good for my body. I do all this because I love myself more every day and because I appreciate myself more and more.

Every part of my being is pure. I am aware that my body is a sanctuary, it is a temple, and therefore I support it with healthy food and beautiful thoughts. I feed it, dress it, take care of it and touch it with love. All that depletes my body, all relationships that drain my soul - I let go of all that burden. I reach for healthy food and healthy relationships.

I don't need to beg for love because I am a reflection of divine love - I am love."

Opinions about yourself

In the morning, you walk past a mirror and say: "I look awful." Then you take a shower, see your stomach and the rest of your body and you criticise yourself again: "This horrible stomach - I'm fat, my fat legs, I don't want to see them again." Then you dress and find it difficult to do up your belt. You criticise once more: "I must lose weight. I look terrible."

I say this from my own experience. I used to say this to myself. Every day, I would offer myself such negative statements and criticisms. Every time I walked past a mirror, I criticised. I was unable to say anything nice to myself. Even before breakfast I consumed a big portion of criticism.

Learn to love yourself by respecting your body. When you wash, be as gentle with yourself as if you were washing a baby; when you feed yourself, pay attention to the taste of the food that will break down into the cells of your body and become a part of you. When you have been doing this for a while, your love will start to grow stronger. Repeat several times: "I love and value myself." In the evening, hug yourself, tell yourself in front of the mirror that you are glad that you are here and now, that you are safe here and now. When you love yourself, all your relationships get sorted out. Don't let yourself be exploited. Sometimes it is necessary to say "No."

Love for yourself is also reflected in making love. When you love yourself, you can see yourself enjoying it. You can even see yourself naked without being disgusted. You touch your partner's body with the same love you feel for yourself, and you no longer have to hide in the dark. You accept every bit of your body; you accept your thoughts; you accept your shortcomings.

Satisfaction with your body is reflected in all areas of life. If you reject yourself and feel "disgusted" with yourself, how can you relax at the sight of your body? Sooner or later, you will blame your partner for your dissatisfaction and accuse him of not finding you attractive anymore. The truth lies somewhere else - you are rejecting yourself and you no longer find yourself attractive, so you began to avoid intimacy. You have accused your partner, but it is your truth that speaks out of you.

When you do not love yourself, someone else may really love you, but you will accuse him of insincerity. When you do not love yourself, you punish yourself, you are mean with yourself and with others. When you do not love yourself, you cannot build a solid happiness - either with yourself or with your partner.

The background responsible for the negative programmes is hidden in your early childhood. Many people are told by their parents:

- Be quiet and put up with it!
- He who flies high, falls low. But what they did not tell you is that he who flies high can land high.
- You don't deserve this. You're not good enough.
- Genitalia are ugly.
- You'll come to no good.
- If you don't do as you're told, you're a naughty girl. (If you don't do as I tell you, you don't deserve love.)
- You mustn't trust people.
- Be modest - modesty is a virtue.
- Money and honesty don't go together.
- You're so clumsy.
- You're so stupid.

With time, a child will forget all these claims, but they are still stored in her unconscious mind - in her subconscious. They are written in her heart. And what is written in your heart, what is sunken in the subconscious is a million times stronger than what is in your conscious mind.

Do you know how they tame elephants? When they are still very small, they tie them to a tree with a rope or a chain. The baby elephant resists, tries to save himself, tries to be free. But after a while, he stops trying, he accepts that the rope cuts into his legs and that it is better to be obedient for the rest of his life.

The baby elephant grows into a strong elephant. He is still tied, he can be tied with only a thin thread to a small tree, which he could break with a single sway of his leg, but his beliefs are still at the level of the baby elephant. The rope and the tree are part of his subconscious. This mighty animal limits his current capacities with limitations from his childhood. This is called the "baby elephant syndrome".

Here is a quote from the book *The Honeymoon Effect* by Bruce H. Lipton, Ph.D., so that you can more easily understand how in the early years the "programming" of the subconscious takes place:

> *In the womb and through the first year of life, the human brain predominantly operates at the slowest brain-wave frequency, .5 to 4 cycle per second (Hz), known as delta waves. This isn't surprising because babies sleep a lot; in adults, delta waves predominate during our deepest sleep, when we dream and we're hardest to wake up.*
>
> *From two to six years old, a child's predominate brain wave is theta (4 to 8 Hz), a vibrational frequency associated with the state of imagination. This is the stage of development when a child's delightful imagination runs wild. When you see a child with a broom and he says it's a horse, don't tell the child it's only a broom! It's a horse in the child's mind, because at this wonderful stage of life theta waves dominate brain function, a state in which imagination and reality become entangled. In the child's mind, the broom has become a horse.*
>
> *[...]*
>
> *For the first six years of life, children do not express the quality of consciousness associated with alpha, beta, and gamma EEG activity as predominant brain states. Children's brains primarily function below creative consciousness, just as adult brain activity drops below consciousness in sleep and during hypnosis. In their highly programmable theta state, children record vast amounts of information they need to*

survive in their environment, but they do not have the capacity to consciously evaluate the information while it is being downloaded.

Around the age of six to seven, children become less susceptible to hypnotic programming as their developing brains start to function increasingly at higher-frequency waves (8 to 12 Hz). Alpha wave activity is correlated with states of calm consciousness.

Once a lady said to me that when she was young, she was often told: "The fatter you are, the stupider you are." What do you think her thought pattern is now, when she is well over 60 and a grandmother several times over? The statement still reverberates in her subconscious.

I don't know who said this to her, but it is a lie. The lies you heard when you were young have to be replaced with thoughts of love and forgiveness. We are valuable! Each and every one of us came into this world with special talents and abilities, everyone has something they are really good at, with which they can add value to this world.

When I observed my patterns, I realised that I had the following belief: "If I'm a good enough girl, they'll love me," and "I always come last." Recently, my mother told me that when she was pregnant with me, she had the feeling that if she was able to do more, she would have been accepted by her husband's (my father's) family. Now I understand why I had that belief - within five years, she had 4 children, had to work on a farm, had a job, had to save money, etc.

I carried my negative beliefs into all areas of my life. I needed to take care of everyone else before myself – however bad I felt, it was still good enough for me. I could wait. I took care of the children, the family, the business, but not of myself.

Putting myself last was also reflected in my eating. When the children were little, I was caught in the trap of a "rubbish bin". All the food that was left on everyone's plate was put away by me. The children would have porridge for breakfast and what was left landed in my tummy. Morning snack - the children would have cottage cheese with fruit, I would eat the leftovers. The same happened with lunch, afternoon snack and dinner. I took care of myself as I went along. Although I watched how much I ate, the kilogrammes failed to melt away - because I was a rubbish bin.

The patterns from our childhood that do not serve us:

• "Surely we can't throw food away!"

• "Eat it all up! Think how many hungry people there are in the world. They'd gladly have this!" If you eat all the food that is left, you certainly will not be contributing to the world's wellbeing. Just think how many people in Africa will get full if your stomach hurts because you have just put away everything left on the plate?

Negative beliefs about yourself, health, money, age, sex, people, etc. keep you in the same spot. Even though you are trying hard, there is no progress. It is as if you keep stepping in the same spot.

Negative beliefs are like mantras we repeat every day. The more we repeat them, the more firmly they get rooted in our life and the more chance there is that we will experience the same thing again. They are like a curse. When again and again you feel the same feeling, you ask yourself: "What do I need to learn? What is the point here? What am I doing wrong?"

Those who are convinced that fat people are happier people, will never lose weight. They will automatically not do anything because they don't want to be less happy.

Nobody wants to be unhappy. If you have this belief, you may be able to lose a few kilos with great effort, but they will soon come back.

You can replace the negative belief with a positive declaration:

"I admire thin people and I'm becoming thinner myself. I feel endless happiness because of this."

Imagine yourself happy as you dance effortlessly or wear a summer dress that is fluttering in the breeze, and you feel ever so attractive.

Several times a day, say this affirmation out loud - in this way, you will free yourself of the negative belief about happiness and fatness. When your belief about happiness being connected to fatness dissolves, the excessive weight will also gradually fall off. Every day, feel satisfaction with what you are as often as you can.

Another belief that does not benefit you is that chocolate makes you happy. You have to find pleasure outside of food, outside of sweet things. If you always tie your pleasure and your happiness to food, you will torture yourself indefinitely. Find pleasure elsewhere. You can find satisfaction and happiness in activities, such as:

- a massage
- soaking in a bath
- going for a walk
- exercise - cycling, swimming, skiing, dancing
- listening to good music or reading books
- listening to good news
- gardening
- acquiring new knowledge.

You can find pleasure in so many things, not only chocolate and other sweet things. Chocolate is like a drug - an addiction which can give you short-lived pleasure, but in the long term it gets you into its claws and you can no longer do without it. No addiction is healthy.

The belief that you are not sufficiently beautiful, smart, persistent, decisive, educated, attractive, thin, etc. is keeping you in the past.

The most sensitive period and at the same time the most important for the construction of a healthy self-image is adolescence - the time of growing up. In order to build a healthy attitude to yourself it is important to hear from the parent of the opposite sex that you are wonderful, beautiful, clever, wanted and accepted.

If you don't hear this, you grow up having a feeling that you are not beautiful enough, clever enough, intelligent enough, wanted enough, worthy enough, etc.

- What have your parents never told you?
- What did your parents keep telling you?
- What would you like to have heard, but never did?

I know that these are emotional wounds that can persevere throughout your life, but now it is time to heal them. You cannot change the past. It is what it is. Now it is up to you. I have noticed that after the age of forty, all the subconscious programmes, all the negative feelings (particularly those that have really shaken us) that we felt in early childhood and early puberty, i.e. between 10 and 13, develop to the extent that we can no longer push them aside. These are the seeds that have turned into what is now perhaps a fully grown tree, throwing a shadow over our happiness. The more we pretend not to see them, the greater the problems they create. This is why the only solution is to remove all the negative programmes and feelings from childhood and replace them with new ones - the feelings of safety, being accepted and loved. A feeling of lack cannot be filled by anyone else - partner, children, job, your own business, lovers or friends - no one. No one else can give you value - only you can. It is time you cut down the tree of negative beliefs and sow some new seeds, the seeds that will make you happy in the future. Now the ball is in your court - either you remain sitting in the shadow of the tree that bears nothing but bitter fruit, or you cut down the tree, sow some pretty grass and flowers that will decorate your consciousness - life is beautiful!

Recognise your unconscious beliefs that are written in your heart

In his book *The Honeymoon Effect,* Dr Bruce Lipton says that one of the greatest obstacles to creating lasting happiness is the programming that says we do not deserve love. It is true, when subconscious programming is assessed with muscle testing, most people's subconscious mind rejects the statement: "I love myself."

> *I learned about the effectiveness of muscle testing the first time I went to a chiropractor after a serious motorcycle accident. The chiropractor demonstrated muscle testing as a means of communicating with the subconscious mind. He asked me to hold out my arm and resist the downward pressure he applied to it. I had no problems resisting the light force he put on my arm. Then he asked me to hold out my arm and resist him again, this time while saying, "My name is Bruce." Again, I had no trouble resisting his pressure.*

Then he told me to hold out my arm and resist his pressure while saying, "My name is Mary." To my amazement, my arm flopped down, despite my strong resistance. "Try that again," I said. "Apparently, I wasn't ready." So we did, and this time I concentrated even more forcefully on resisting. Nevertheless, after I repeated, "My name is Mary," my arm sank like a stone. That's because when the conscious mind makes a statement that conflicts with a belief stored in the subconscious mind, the resulting disharmony is experienced as weakening of the body's muscles.

In my lectures, I often ask the audience to muscle test the phrase "I love myself". When the majority of arms sink, I ask them to think about how their subconscious belief that they are not lovable impacts their relationship. If you don't love yourself with both minds, what is the chance that other people will love you? Very low, because your subconscious mind does not believe you are lovable. If someone claims they love you, how worthy can they be when even you don't find yourself lovable?

This was the first time I came across a way of recognising subconscious programmes. Curiosity led me to Theta Healing. This method is so simple that everyone can recognise their subconscious beliefs.

The body responds like a pendulum. Now, stand up. Let your arms hang loosely by your body and either silently or out loud say a statement and let your body sway; if the statement is true for you, your body will sway forward and if it is not true, backward. When I say: "I'm Minka," my body in relaxed, upright position sways forward, but when I say: "I'm John," which is something I am not, my body sways backward, even though I try to stop it. If you resist, clenching your fists and refusing to relax, your body will not cooperate, so use this method of finding out your subconscious beliefs only when you are fully relaxed.

This is a way in which everyone can check their subconscious beliefs:

- I have a right to happiness.
- I love myself.
- I deserve love.
- All good opportunities pass me by.
- If you're honest, it hurts.
- It's difficult for me to love because I've been so disappointed in the past.

- I'm a woman who loves too much.
- The person I love always leaves me.
- I always come last.
- People are dishonest.
- People always use me.
- People always disappoint me.
- Whenever I start something, I fail.
- I'm afraid to leave my regular job.
- I'm always in debt.
- I'm spiritual, money ruins everything.
- It's too late to follow my dreams.
- Money is the root of all evil. It's better not to have it, so I can avoid evil.
- The growing-up period is difficult.
- When you're in the menopause, you have lots of problems.
- Men like young and beautiful women.
- It's hard to lose weight after having a baby.
- Men always disappoint me.
- I'm afraid he'd break my heart.
- I know how to say NO.
- I can always stand up for myself.
- I'm too lenient.
- If you show your feelings, people hurt you.
- Jealousy is a proof of love.
- If I'm good, people will like me.
- In my family, we're all on the fat side. It's in our genes.
- In my family, everyone has problems with __________.
- I'm prone to _________.
- I get every virus that's going around. Every cold gets me.
- Love passes quickly.
- Love is blind.
- Happiness and brains rarely meet.

Always use a positive statement, do not use the word "not." In this way, you can check if you still blame anyone for something. Just get up, relax your arms and say: "I forgive my mother for everything she ever said or did. She did the best she could." Your body will respond, and you will know. Do the same for your father, partner, children, brothers, sisters, superiors, subordinates, etc., for everyone who has ever hurt you in any way.

Mahatma Gandhi said:

Your beliefs become your thoughts,

your thoughts become your words,

your words become your actions,

your actions become your habits,

your habits become your values,

your values become your destiny.

Sticking bits of paper on the fridge doesn't work

Repeating affirmations that are based on what you believe gives you an impetus, new energy and calm, while affirmations that you say without believing them only give you more stress.

Dr Alex Loyd and Dr Ben Johnson in their book *The Healing Code*, says:*

For about two years I've been experimenting with forms of manifestation that work on the principle of: "Tell me what you want and you will receive it." I monitored people with the heart rate variability testing device (a medical appliance for measuring stress) while saying claims like "My new car is getting closer" or "My cancer is disappearing right now."

You know what? Almost every time the heart rate variability test results were horrible, the people experienced an enormous amount of stress just making statements. Remember that stress is the main cause of most harm we know. I was excited when I learned that the Canadian University of Waterloo in 2009 did a similar study. This was a leading news around the world. The result of the study shows that this kind of manifestation is not working. Even more, it makes things even worse.

This is why I, for several years now, rather advocated another method that uses "statements focused on the truth" Yes, the statements are positive and about a thing you are certain is true. Instead of claiming "My cancer is disappearing.", the statement you don't believe, rather use a statement* *focused on the truth like "I want to beat the cancer. I am certain I can, and I beg for God's help to succeed."*

When people repeat statements focused on the truth while connected to the heart rate variability testing device, their stress levels improve. Where is the difference? It is a similar situation as a placebo versus the real deal. One statement you believe in, and is positive, the other you don't believe, and you are lying to your heart.

*On the following pages there are a few statements that are based on truth.

Positive Transformation

All negative images can be nullified, allowing you to fill your heart with light.

The Healing prayer of decoding unconscious emotional patterns

The process of clearing subconscious programmes can be compared to working with a virus affected computer. When a computer has viruses, its system at first works slower than usual, some functions may not respond to our clicks as we would wish them to. Over time, if we don't get rid of the viruses, our computer becomes unresponsive and useless, or it can even shut down completely. A computer is supposed to work as we command it to. This is the same with our life: it is supposed to respond to our will, but sometimes it can't serve us in the right way because of subconscious programmes. They manifest first as a dysfunctionality in a specific area of our lives and over time, if we don't get rid of the virus, it can make our life completely fall apart in all areas.

It's a good thing we can take our life in our hands, get rid of the viruses and make our lives responsive to our will again.

The Healing Prayer of decoding is a great tool we can use to point out a specific virus and clear it from the screen of our lives. If we want to solve a problem, first we must point it out. This is the first step. The second step is the command 'delete' - just like with a computer virus.

We do this by putting our hands into the 'mudra hakini' position (look at the picture), placing them on our face, with the tips of our index fingers touching the forehead and the tips of the thumbs touching the chin, then taking a deep breath in through the nose, through the ‘mudra hakini’, and then placing our hands, still holding the mudra, to our heart chakra and breathing out through our mouth there.

Now we have cleared the subconscious programme, the computer virus. What follows is the software repair, so we must recover. Literary re-cover the space which we had a virus deleted from. We fill this space up with new energy, coming from the Healing light of God. We point it to the four main points of self-healing (look at the picture); the forehead - the third eye chakra, the throat at the Addams apple - throat chakra, right by the ears; here we have two small energy canters, connected to the adrenal glands, which impact the lowering of stress, and to the temples, which are connected to the pineal gland - a tiny part of the brain, which affects our feeling of happiness.

1. The first step - pointing out the virus - discovering our programming

Sit upright with a straight spine and our hands open upwards, resting on our thighs.

Say:

“I am calling in all healing light forces.”

Then take a deep breath in through the nose, inhaling the light forces presence into your heart. Feel the presence. Slowly exhale out of the mouth. Breathe in the light forces as many times as you need to feel your heart completely filled with healing light.

Let us pray:

“All loving God, The Creator *, if it is in tune with the holy laws of Love, may my soul be freed of all conscious and subconscious codes, in all dimensions of time and space, that are connected to this subconscious programme: ______________”. (We put in the previously discovered programme, for example: 'I must punish myself', or we can put in a problem we have, for example: With the feeling of abandonment).

“I command all levels of my soul to be filled with the Healing Love of God.”

* You can use the term Love, Universe - use the term which resonates most with your own heart. Remember, that you yourself are Love. You are God. You are the Creator. So, you are free to pray simply as your spirit feels is right. You are free to use your own words, or simply to feel the process of the space in yourself getting cleared of the blockage and being filled with pure Love. *

2. The second step - clearing of the virus

We place our hands into the 'mudra hakini' - a mudra for new power, lay them on our face, breathing in the new power through the mudra, feeling it travel down and fill our lungs with new energy, with Love. As we exhale, we place our hands, still holding the mudra, to our heart chakra and in feeling this space we say:

«I am receiving Healing. All levels of my soul are filling with the divine healing light.»

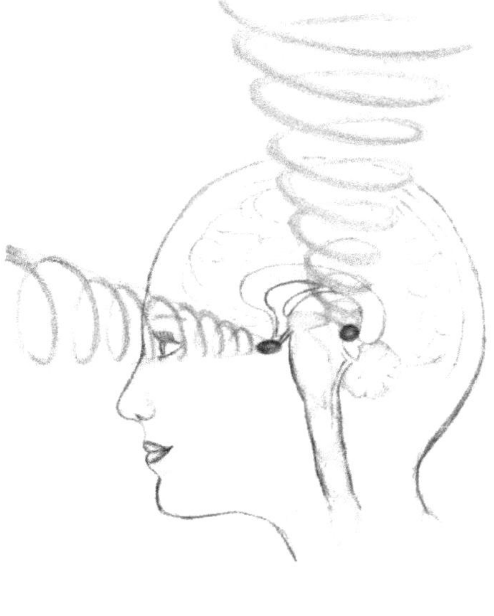

3. The third step: Healing harm on a physical and mental level

After you have said the prayer, for the following few minutes sit and repeat the positive statements you believe (you can find them below) and use the power of your hands to "shine a light" on the healing centres.

Four healing centres (as per book *The Healing Code* by Dr Alex Loyd and Dr Ben Johnson);

• **The bridge of your nose** – between the beginning of your nose and the middle of the eyebrows, if they met in the middle. This part influences the pineal gland and the pituitary gland, which controls all the most important hormonal processes in the body.

• **Adam's Apple** – directly above the Adam's Apple. This part influences the spinal cord and the central nervous system, as well as the thyroid gland.

• **Jaws** – at the extreme end of the jawbone on both sides of the head. Here you can influence the emotional brain, including the amygdala (the centre that in a stressful situation triggers the fight or flight response, speeds up the heart and ensures that high quantities of stress hormones are released into your blood system) and the hypothalamus, the spinal cord and the central nervous system.

• **Temples** – a centimetre and a half above your temples and a centimetre toward the back of your head on both sides. When you direct energy to this part, you influence the cerebellum (left and right hemisphere) and the hypothalamus.

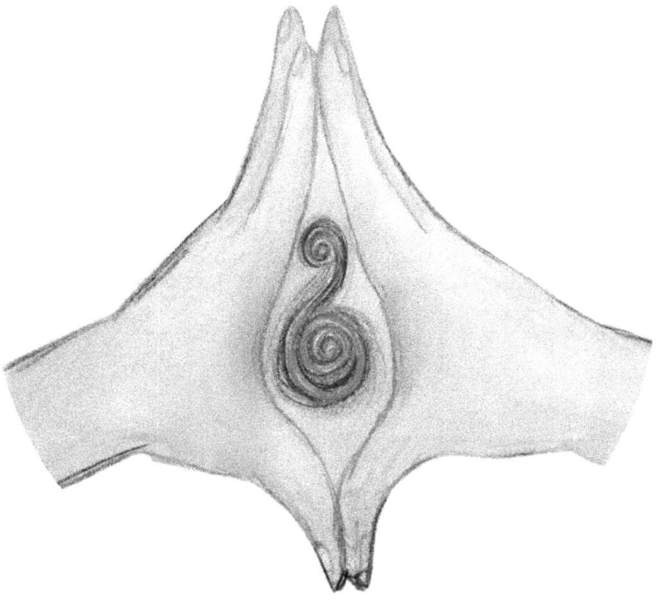

4. The fourth step: Visualization of the happy future

We place our hands in the blessing mudra, in front of our chest. We feel into the new energy we have created in our space. We visualise and feel ourselves in the desired state – Full of Love, glowing from happiness, completely healthy and glowing from abundance. We allow ourselves to already be at our destination. Feel how this version of yourself feels in as much detail as you can. We visualise at least one other person that is positively affected by our new energy. We feel and see ourselves happy with our family, going about life lightly, doings tasks lightly, and completely enjoying who you are now.

When we finish, we place our palms on our chests and say:

«Thank you, Divine Love, for healing.»

Here are some positive statements that we can believe:

- I allow myself to love and value myself. This is why I drink enough water, exercise every day, eat healthy food, read positive news, choose healthy relationships and socialise with positive people. I am worthy of love.

- I am guided in my life. I can trust myself and others.

- I am safe here and now. I am a loved child of the Universe and am always taken care of.

- Love belongs to me. I am learning how to give and receive love.

- I am filled with the richness of the infinite. All my needs are taken care of now and to the end of my days. God is revealing to me new creative ideas, which will benefit humankind in many areas. God's wealth runs to me in streams of abundance.

- I can relax completely because I know that I am guided by God's hand.

- I am always kind to myself and others. I choose love.

- I am worthy of love. I express this love firstly to myself by completely accepting myself. I am compassionate and kind with myself.

- I deserve a partner who loves me, is patient, loving, attentive, generous, joyful.

- I send thoughts of gratitude to my family.

- God always shows me the right path. In my life, I can do what I enjoy, and I am richly awarded for my work. All the forces of the Universe support me.

- I choose peace. I can always be calm, irrespective of where I am and what is happening.

- For me, money is a divine substance since everything is one. Matter and spirit are one. Money comes to me joyfully and in an endless flow. I am richly awarded for my work.

- God is my eternal source. God's abundance circulates in my life. There is more than I need. Every day and every night I advance; I am developing spiritually on all levels.

- My emotional state is always in balance. My heart is full of God's love.
- I am safe here and now. I and my family are always taken care of. Everything is happening for the highest good of all involved. Even though I can't see it yet, I know only good things await me.
- I am grateful for all the good in my life.
- Life supports me. I am a beloved child of the creation. I and my family are always taken care of.
- Everything is as it should be. I am calm. The infinite inside me cannot fail. My life is ruled by God's order and peace. My spirit is suffused with God's love. In all areas I am guided by God's intelligence.
- God's love flows through my cells. With every day, I grow more beautiful. God has a beauty salon.
- I accept people around me. I choose to see their good characteristics instead of looking for something to criticise and disapprove of.
- I send love to all the people around me. Everything I give returns to me in abundance.
- In me there is infinite intelligence, I am God's child, I am a daughter of infinity. My soul is filled with God's love. God loves me. Through me God's love, peace, harmony and success in all areas are constantly flowing. God is my eternal source. All my spiritual, emotional and material needs are fulfilled at any moment and everywhere.
- All I need to know comes from the infinite presence inside me. The infinite intelligence works through me, revealing to me what I need to know. My thoughts, words and actions radiate love, peace and good will for all people. I know that what I give comes back to me.
- God knows all the answers. I am receiving the full answer now, because God is the eternal now. All the decisions are made through me by God's wisdom. All my decisions and all my actions are right. My spirit is calm. I move in the light of belief and confidence. I trust in the only force that exists.

• I choose positive thoughts. Through me flows the light that shines from me.

• I trust that my children are completely safe everywhere. They are always in God's care. There is peace in my soul.

• Positive energy touches everyone who comes in contact with me.

• My work blesses, greets, inspires, cheers and ennobles people's spirit and heart. For this I receive a wonderful compensation from God.

• I feel peace. My home is a home of peace, love and harmony.

• I always decide what is right and good – both for myself and others. I believe in God's guidance.

• In me there is strength. With every breath, I am stronger. I am accompanied by angels who open the way forward.

Read these truths at least twice a day. Allow them to sink into your subconscious and do not give up. Even when your conscious mind tells you that you know it all, if you have not achieved what you want, then persist and carry on. With repetition, everything you want will show up on the screen of your life. Believe and you will see!

Explanation of the fourth step:

Visualization is imagining yourself on the inner screen of consciousness. It is the feeling of emotions and sensations opposite to the problem we have decoded.

Put your hands in front of you - in the position of blessing. To activate the power of your palms, press the thumb of the opposite hand in the middle of one and then the other palm. You may feel the heat in the middle of your palms if you have a strong energetic flow.

When visualizing, imagine the screen raised about 20 degrees with your eyes closed - as if you were looking up. When we visualize, we can 'see' the screen in front of us, or the film screen - as if we were watching a movie. It is important to see the final result. Research has shown that if you look upward with your eyes closed, you can reach a relaxed alpha state of consciousness more easily. In the alpha state, the brainwaves slow down. It is a state of calmness, mild hypnosis, artistic and intuitive creation, and creative visualization. When we perform the Healing Prayer of Decoding, we breathe in through our nose, and when we put our hands against our forehead, we subconsciously turn our head upwards. By doing so, we instantly calm the brainwaves and 'move' them into a state susceptible to (self)hypnosis.

For example, when we visualize health, we can imagine swallowing a miracle pill that begins to radiate and fill cells with healing energy. We can imagine angels removing blockages in our bodies. We can imagine our palms glowing - we put them on the part of our body that needs healing. When we visualize a dream job, we can imagine being invited for an interview and having a relaxed conversation with the new employer; We can also imagine our wallet being filled with the golden light of abundance. Anyone who wants a beautiful relationship can imagine angels sprinkling the magic dust of love on an existing relationship or imagine what it feels like to walk hand in hand with their (new) love and be overflowed with happiness.

If it's easier for you, you can keep a diary of visions. Sometimes, especially for people who are a visual type, it helps to write everything down. For hearing (auditory) types of people, it helps to record their vision and listen to it at least twice a day. While listening, imagine vividly how you feel. People who need mobility (kinaesthetic type) should imagine themselves in motion. Let yourself create vivid images of how satisfied and loved you feel with a loved one during a walk, on vacation, in a new car, and in a nice apartment, and how you enjoy being at work and actively participating in new projects.

The subconscious needs only 21 days to adopt a new truth

We all know how a computer functions. When we want a new program to start working, we load it. In the case of some programmes, this happens very quickly, while with others we have to wait a little. The subconscious needs three weeks to load a new programme.

The subconscious adopts a new programme most quickly in a calm state, in alpha state - that is five minutes before sleep and in the morning, when you are waking up. When your conscious mind is calm, you have direct access to your subconscious; that is when the conscious mind, which is like a guard, is still turned off. The negative voice inside you is still quiet then.

Your subconscious will adopt a new truth only through repetition. How did you learn how to ride a bike? In the beginning, you were terrified, but then riding a bike became automatic. How did you learn to swim? How did you learn the multiplication tables? How did you learn how to drive a car? With repetition. The same applies here.

Every evening and every morning, read the above positive statements aloud in front of a mirror. Or you can simply record them with a voice recorder (all smart phones have one) and play them just before sleep and in the morning during waking up. So that your partner does not think you have gone crazy, he should do the same. Your subconscious will adopt the statements as the truth - and the new truth will help you to greater happiness in all areas.

> These truths will sink into your subconscious. They will transfer from your consciousness to your subconscious like the seeds you put in the soil. Your thoughts about love, peace, joy, success, abundance, safety and goodwill are planted in the garden of your spirit. That is God's Garden. Believe me, your garden will bear rich fruit. With your thoughts you create your destiny. Believe that the force that created everything is supporting you. Persist in the belief in the good. Live expecting the best, because expectation speeds up the process. In your thoughts about the good is God's power. These are the seeds of goodness, truth, beauty and abundance. God's glory and beauty will be expressed in your life. From now on, express life, love and truth. Glow with happiness and joy in all areas and God will joyfully multiply your inner wealth! *

*Summarised from: Dr Joseph Murphy: *The Power of Your Subconscious Mind.*

Note: if the word God gives you a negative vibration, use another expression - Light, Universe, Creation… Find an expression that fills you with trust. I have noticed that many people find it easier to say the word 'angel' or 'angels' than God. It does not matter which you use, what is important is that the words leave good vibrations, i.e. a good feeling in you.

"Scientists at the Institute of HeartMath in California have shown that feeling love, gratitude, and appreciation in your heart boosts your immune system; increases vital chemical production; increases physical vitality and vigor; reduces stress hormone levels, high blood pressure, anxiety, guilt, and burnout; and improves glucose regulation in diabetics. Feelings of love also create a higher degree of harmony in the rhythm of your heart." *

*Rhonda Byrne: *The Power*.

Start telling yourself that you are a beloved child of the Universe!

Now that you love yourself, you feel alive first thing in the morning. Even if others don't give you hugs, you give yourself one and feel the warmth that warms you like the sun warms the morning sky; even if no one tells you that you are wonderful, you say it to yourself. You need encouragement like that in order to come alive. Now you don't have to compete with others, now you don't have to prove yourself or do something to deserve love, now you know that you deserve love just as you are.

Irrespective of your weight, you are worthy. Even if your weight is 20 or 50 kilogrammes higher than it should be, you deserve love, respect and approval. From yourself first. When you have built the feeling of worth, no one can hurt you anymore, not even yourself, because you know that you deserve nothing but good; because you know that nothing but good belongs to you!

You don't have to hide from the world anymore. You don't need padding around your body to hide the feeling that you are not good enough. You are perfect inside - your soul is perfect, and you don't need a mask in front of others. It is time you shine in all your glory, because you are magnificent. It is time you throw away the black clothes that hide your curves, it is time you discard all the surplus weight that has been weighing you down all these years and made you walk through your life with your head bent low - it is time you became YOU!

As we observe nature, we can learn a lot. For nature to wake up after a cold winter, it needs the sun; warmth is required for buds to swell. When something is not going right, people get angry, disappointed and unsupportive. It is a bit like if God sent colder for nature to wake up. You cannot make a positive shift with cold feelings. When we want a change, love is needed. Are we loving enough when we want to change something? Do we send more warmth into a relationship that is not yet how we want it to be?

Love is the answer and the solution for everyday relationships. Those can't be improved with negativity. Make a list of everything you like or love and talk about it. Envision you already have a perfect relationship, envision it on the highest level, and feel in your heart you already have one. If you are having trouble feeling the relationship, in that case, try to focus on everything related to it and ignore all negativities about it.

Envision you have a perfect health. Make a list of everything that brings you joy, as you would already have perfect health, perfect weight, and perfect energy. Feel the life energy flowing through you with all your heart. Take a deep breath and feel that you are alive. Exhale all bad energies that are hidden in your body. Embrace your body and be grateful. Be grateful for living, for being here, and simply for being alive.

Whenever you give love through your feelings, words, and actions, you bring love into your field. The more love you emit, the bigger, and more powerful your magnetic field becomes. Whatever is there, attracts more of the same. The more love is in your field, the greater is your power to attract even more things you love into your life. You can reach a point where things you like simply appear in your life.

Mind is a powerful and excellent tool, but it must be controlled. Don't allow it to confuse you with thoughts of fear but direct it to help you with giving out love. The mind can be quickly trained to focus on love with questions like: "What do I like about myself? What is beautiful? How will I feel when I have my ideal weight? How will I feel when I have as much money as I need? How will I feel when I am in a loving relationship?" *

*Per Rhonda Byrne's book *The Power*

When you begin "practising" love for yourself, within a few weeks you will notice that you are calmer; that you perceive the beauty of nature; that you drive more calmly and that you smile more frequently. You will no longer attract agitated people - either on the road or at work. Life at home will also become calmer. You will notice that people "fall in love" with you - because you are in love with life!

"Spread love wherever you go: first of all, in your own house. Give love to your children, to your wife or husband, to a next-door neighbour ... Let no one ever come to you without leaving better and happier. Be the living expression of God's kindness, kindness in your face, kindness in your eyes, kindness in your smile, kindness in your warm greeting."

Mother Teresa

Go with the flow of life. Nothing that must come into your life, is against this flow; everything that has to come into your life will come easily - with the flow. Life will bring you everything you need. When you go with the flow, you notice that life is joyful, that there is energy everywhere, that nature is brimming with life.

It is time you feel the kind of passion and enthusiasm for life that you felt when you were young. Start moving and walking with enthusiasm. Sit upright, breathe consciously and deeply, feel the energy of life flowing through you. Abandon all 'old-people's' habits - from the way you walk and talk to 'moaning' about life. Feel the passion and fervour, smile and life will fully return all this to you.

Let a glow fill your eyes as you observe nature; a cloud being chased by the wind; the sun sliding behind the horizon and reappearing the next morning in all its beauty; the rain that shows abundance; the stream rushing and murmuring across the rocks; the new shoots in the spring; the ripe fruit inviting you in the summer to taste their energy. Allow yourself to feel the wind in your hair as you drive through a field of wheat and each ear greets you separately; allow yourself to shout with excitement on top of a hill - when you are alone with nature, just you and God; allow yourself to jump into the sea and taste the salt in your mouth, to float on the water and just be; allow yourself to be filled with beauty and gratitude by the autumnal leaves and colours; allow yourself to feel the joyfulness of snowflakes gently falling down; allow yourself to play excitedly in the snow, shrieking with joy; take the time to observe children and notice the glow in their eyes. Allow yourself to feel life, because You are a beloved child of the Universe and God wants to let you know that you are on this Earth so that you can love. Love yourself and love everything and everybody around you - no one can take that away from you!

May God bless you on this path of learning to love yourself!

Chapter 2. Cortisol, the Stress Hormone

What do I feel? Do I dare admit my true feelings?

Burnout is a message from the soul, calling for change!

When cortisol is within the normal range, we are quick, organised and our thoughts are clear.

Cortisol is produced by the adrenal glands. It is necessary for coping with everyday life: when you are in a hurry to get to work, but have to drop the kids off at the nursery or school on the way, or when you are stuck in a traffic jam, but urgently need to be somewhere else, etc. This type of stress is supposed to be short lasting and, above all, not occur every day. If the stress hormone levels are constantly raised, this is reflected in your health.

Nowadays, time seems to go very quickly. Tied to the wheel of our everyday lives, we become tense. This is called chronic stress. The human body was created for living in harmony with nature. At one time, people experienced stress only when attacked by a dangerous animal or when there was a natural catastrophe; now every day is filled with tasks, the phone ringing, deadlines, monthly bills, rushing to work and back home again, pressure from those above us at work and from competition, shortage of time for our children, partner, rest; the result is a feeling of helplessness and dissatisfaction with life. All this is caused by stress.

Chronic stress basically means that we are doing nothing to change the negative circumstances and that our life is out of balance.

In their book "The Healing Code," Dr Alex Loyd and Dr Ben Johnson explain that the central nervous system is responsible for managing stress levels. Physiological stress is triggered by the hypothalamus-pituitary-adrenal gland axis. While it was previously believed that both the hypothalamus and the pituitary gland were equally significant, it is actually the pituitary gland that acts as the conduit for hormones into the bloodstream. The hypothalamus functions as the brain's central processing unit, intricately linked to the limbic system, which governs emotional responses. Through nerve cells, the hypothalamus is connected to various brain regions and the entire body via hormones released by the pituitary gland. Notable functions under the control of the hypothalamus include regulating blood pressure in arteries, body temperature, water balance through thirst and kidney function, uterine contractions, lactation, emotional responses, growth hormone production, adrenal gland activity, thyroid hormone regulation, and sexual organ function.

From a physiological standpoint, stress causes alterations in the functioning of all the organs mentioned above. The outcomes of elevated cortisol levels and decreased levels of the DHEA hormone, responsible for repairing damage, can be severe:

- reduced effectiveness of the immune system and frequent inflammation:
- bad digestion and a frequent desire for something sweet;
- irritability and quick anger, or even depression;
- sleeping problems and insomnia;
- chronic tiredness;
- a need for sedatives and sleeping pills;
- proneness to cardio-vascular diseases, heart attacks and strokes;
- elevated blood pressure;
- faster than normal heartbeat, or even palpitations;
- raised values of bad cholesterol and an increase in triglycerides in the blood;
- fat gathering on the stomach;
- raised sugar levels and diabetes;
- migraine or frequent headaches;
- backache;
- stomach ulcers;
- water retention in the body;
- tinnitus;
- worsening of the memory and reduced concentration, confusion;
- slow weight loss or inability to lose weight;
- the body becomes more susceptible to toxins and finds it more difficult to excrete heavy metals and other toxins; this leads to the acidity of the body;
- the appearance of allergies;

- brittle bones and osteoporosis;
- reduction in the functioning of the thyroid gland, which lowers the metabolism and body temperature, as well as vitality;
- irregular periods, or even loss of periods;
- infertility – women under constant stress do not ovulate regularly, may have irregular periods or regular periods without ovulation;
- the growth hormone levels fall; this hormone ensures regeneration in our sleep, if the levels fall, our mental and physical regeneration is reduced, which leads to ageing;
- the metabolism of protein lowers and the breakdown of muscle tissue increases, which leads to the loss of bone collagen and to wrinkles, arthritis, muscle loss and physical weakness;
- stress destroys interhuman relations, causes fear, anger and general dissatisfaction.

Research has shown that over 95 percent of all diseases and health problems are connected with stress.

Cortisol ages and causes disease

Raised levels of the stress hormone cause the breakdown of skin, muscle tissue and bone; it makes us overreact and tense. Cortisol is at its highest level in the morning, while in the evening it should be at the lowest level. If it is too high all day long, you cannot calm down and relax. It triggers a desire for carbohydrates (chocolate, biscuits, white bread, doughnuts, etc.) and for fat. This leads to a fall in energy and the blood sugar level, the body demands "tasty" food; you can quickly fall into a vicious circle – the more stress you have, the greater your desire for unhealthy snacks, the quicker you put on weight and get even unhappier.

Often, we get stuck after the age of forty. The first hormonal changes occur, a woman goes for a regular check-up, complains a little and she is given "mild" hormonal tablets, which will help her feel more balanced. Of course, she doesn't read about the side effects in the leaflet that comes with the tablets, where it clearly says that there is a greater possibility of depression occurring or of thrombosis (a blocked blood vessel). After a few months, she finds herself crying after the smallest effort and goes to the doctor again; of course, she is told that her mood swings are normal in her condition and is given an antidepressant. And then she doesn't worry anymore. Her world becomes numb, her feelings are frozen, and this goes on for a week, a month, a year. And she gets more and more unhappy.

In their book "The Healing Code," Dr Alex Loyd and Dr Ben Johnson mention that The HeartMath Institute has been at the forefront of conducting exceptional alternative clinical research globally for many years. One particularly remarkable study involved placing human DNA in a test tube and asking participants to hold it while focusing on painful thoughts or recalling destructive memories. It is impossible to remember painful memories without also experiencing the associated devastating emotions. Subsequently, when the researchers examined the DNA after this exercise, they found it was damaged. The same DNA was then returned to the test tube, with participants instructed to hold it again, this time while thinking about positive and happy memories. This task naturally evoked positive emotions. Upon re-examination, the researchers discovered that the DNA had undergone a healing effect due to the influence of positive thoughts. This experiment indicates that negative memories can harm DNA, while happy memories and positive emotions have a reparative impact on it.

If you keep forgetting about yourself, you will not be able to cope!

Perhaps you are feeling the quick tempo of life yourself every day? Do you fall into bed in the evening exhausted and then wake up next morning to a day that is no better than the previous one? In this haste, you are perhaps not aware enough of the fact that you have to first take care of yourself and your health if you want to be effective in all other areas. Never before have we been under such a heavy burden. In addition to the family, which only a few decades ago was the only worry for most women, today's women also have to look good, earn a lot of money, be happy, smile all the time and feel well rested.

Cells that are in harmony regenerate every day

The human body consists of fifty billion cells, which form the skin, muscles, bones, organs, blood, etc.

These cells grow and regenerate. Within a few years, they get completely renewed. This process is taking place all the time and is not controlled by thoughts (it is automatic and is controlled by the autonomous nervous system) – cells are constantly born, they grow and then die. The body must be focused on growth and development, since this is the only way in which it can replace the lost cells.

According to Dr. Bruce Lipton, a cell that grows and regenerates is said to be resilient against disease. In his book, “The Honeymoon Effect”, he explains that the body's response changes drastically when it is stressed and facing a life-threatening situation, such as the need to "fight or flee."

Picture yourself walking in the woods when suddenly, you hear a rustling nearby, and a large, roaring animal emerges from the bushes, charging towards you.

Instantly, the body recognizes the threat and reacts by adjusting its biology to cope with the new circumstances. Energy is swiftly directed to the vital organs for defence, while the extremities receive essential nutrients. In a flash, both the mind and body are focused and prepared for either confrontation or escape. Essentially, the body is given precise instructions on how to respond.

This survival mechanism has evolved since ancient times and has been crucial for our continued existence.

Imagine a walled town by the sea 500 years ago. When there was peace, everything ran according to a settled routine. Merchants came through the town gate, the markets were lively, the women cooked and looked after their family, while the men were craftsmen or artists or shoemakers or bakers, etc. Sometimes, a person died, and new members of the community were born. The inhabitants looked after the town and ensured that it looked good.

But when the town was under attack, the situation was completely different. The town gates were closed so that nobody could get in or out. Food supplies were interrupted. Everyone capable of fighting, fought. It was a state of war. A few babies were born, but many people died in the fighting. This was not a time for doing repairs – now everything was focused on survival.

Dr Alex Loyd and Dr Ben Johnson in their book "The Healing Code" compare the state of stress with a ship under attack:

The cells literally close up, like a ship battening down the hatches in a time of attack. Nothing is going in or out. You don't see a tender ship coming up beside a battleship to give it food or to unload the garbage during a battle. In the same way our cells don't receive nutrition, oxygen, minerals, etc., nor do they get rid of waste products and toxins while under stress. Everything stops except what is necessary to survive.

When the human body is under stress, it uses the following vitamins, minerals, amino acids and fats as a priority in the creation of the stress hormone:

- fat soluble vitamins A and E,
- vitamin C, flavonoids from coloured fruit and B-complex – especially vitamins B1, B2, B5, B6 and B12,
- the minerals magnesium, calcium, zinc, manganese and selenium,
- the amino acid tryptophan,
- omega-3 fatty acids.

If the body does not get sufficient of the above nutrients, a desire for specific food appears. The body keeps telling and warning us. Brittle nails tell us that there is a vitamin B deficiency; muscle cramps and twitching tell us that there is a shortage of magnesium and vitamin B1; a desire for very specific food is a way our body tells us what nutrients are missing.

Your body is talking to you. Listen to it!

Below is a list of foods most often reached for by people who are short of the essential vitamins and minerals:

- **Bananas** – If you keep reaching for bananas, this may be your body telling you that it is short of potassium. This often happens with people who are taking diuretics, as diuretics deplete the body of potassium. Potassium binds to calcium, which is necessary for the binding of vitamin

B12 – if there is a shortage of this vitamin, you feel irritated, sad and anxious.

• **White bread** – if you cannot resist white bread and rolls, your body is warning you that you are short of chromium, which controls the incessant desire for simple carbohydrates. The easiest way to consume chromium is pickled mushrooms and egg yolk. This way you will also consume protein, which will reduce your desire for white bread. Chromium binds with iodine, so it is also possible that your body is telling you there is a shortage of the thyroid hormones.

• **Paint and dirt** – children often want to eat paint or dirt. This may be a sign of a shortage of calcium and vitamin D. Examine the child's diet. Remove from it all the pasteurised dairy products. Buy farm-produced fresh milk, eggs and cottage cheese.

• **Onions** – a desire for sharp tasting food can be a sign of problems with lungs or sinuses. It indicates a silent inflammation in the body. Allicin, the smelly substance in garlic and onions, acts as a natural antibiotic.

• **Chocolate** – the most common food addiction is that to chocolate. An incessant desire for chocolate also points to a lack of vitamins B, mainly B3. Chocolate raises serotonin levels, thus giving a quick feeling of happiness. If you have this desire, your body is telling you that you are short of magnesium, vitamins B and protein. If you cannot live without chocolate, try eating dried carob, walnuts, peanuts or almonds, which contain protein, magnesium and B vitamins.

• **Fizzy drinks** – this points to addiction to sugar and caffeine. Chromium will be a great help with this; you can get it from egg yolk, mushrooms and nuts.

• **Eggs** – you may be short of choline, which dissolves cholesterol and improves the functioning of the brain. Choline – vitamin B8 is necessary for overcoming emotional stress.

• **Apples** – contain many beneficial substances. Perhaps you are eating a lot of food that contains saturated fats and the pectin in apples has an effect on these fats. In order to establish a good balance between good and bad fats, add the beneficial omega-3 fatty acids.

• **Pickled cucumbers** – if you are not pregnant and still reaching for pickled cucumbers, it could indicate a shortage of potassium. Potassium binds to natrium. Add a little more salt to your food. Use sea salt.

• **Sour fruit** – a persistent desire for sour fruit often means problems with the gallbladder or liver.

• **Peanut butter** – this is a rich source of vitamins in the B group and protein. Have you been under a lot of stress recently? If you are constantly hungry for peanut butter, it may make sense to take vitamins B. You can get most vitamins B from brewer's yeast.

• **Fatty foods** – if you crave bacon, your body is telling you it needs calcium and magnesium. Calcium is also present in almonds, which have an excellent proportion of calcium and magnesium, ensuring better absorption. You can get even more calcium from cottage cheese and other dairy products.

• **Mayonnaise** – a craving for mayonnaise indicates lack of good fat in your diet – especially omega-3 fatty acids. Fatty sea fish is an excellent source of omega-3.

• **Milk** – a craving for milk indicates lack of calcium, vitamin B12 and/or protein. The amino acid tryptophan, which you get from milk, has a calming effect.

• **Olives** – people with an underactive thyroid often reach for olives. A lazy thyroid can be stimulated with a multivitamin supplement. More about the thyroid hormones on page 157.

• **Cheese** – if you cannot resist cheese, your body is telling you it needs calcium and phosphorus. A replacement for cheese is broccoli, which also contains calcium and phosphorus but no saturated fats.

• **Ice cream** – if you crave ice cream, there is a strong chance you have problems with high sugar excretions – your body is trying to tell you that it is short of chromium, which controls the release of the "hunger hormone" insulin.

• **Salt** – if you add salt to already salted food, your body is telling you that your thyroid may be sluggish. Research has shown that a desire for salt can be triggered by lack of calcium, iodine, iron or potassium, but they bind only under the condition that there is enough natrium.

• **Ham** – if you are frequently craving ham, you must be short of omega-3 fats and protein. Have you been under a lot of stress recently? Are you maybe also on a diet and/or eating monotonous food, which is empty of nutrients? Your body is not getting enough omega-3 and fat-soluble vitamins – A, E and K, as well as protein, which is the cornerstone of new cells.

See also: Signs of vitamin and mineral deficiency on page 252.

*Summarised from: Earl Mindell: *Vitamin Bible for the 21st Century*

Your body's messages – where do you store fat?

James Duigan says that the wrong food, hormonal imbalance, stress and toxins in the body determine where the excessive weight is stored. *

*Summarised from: James Duigan: *Clean & Lean Diet: The Bestselling Book on Achieving Your Perfect Body.*

Fat on your stomach indicates a raised level of the stress hormone

The most common reason for weight gathering around your waist is stress, which causes a high level of cortisol in your blood. Another reason is an imbalance in the intestinal flora. The food does not disintegrate into smaller fragments and nutrients do not get absorbed into cells.

Even if you lose a few kilos, but you still have a "beer belly", this indicates bad metabolism of proteins, fats and carbohydrates. And this, in turn, points at a lack of group B vitamins, particularly B6, vitamin C and magnesium. These are metabolic vitamins and minerals, which contribute to food turning into energy rather than fat. If you wish to get rid of the fat on your stomach, you need good omega-3 fats.

The good news is that you can get rid of the fat on your stomach without heavy exercise, since intensive exercise also causes the release of the stress hormone. It is recommended that you do activities that calm you, such as yoga, Pilates or the Fountain of Youth exercises. Of course, you also need to change your diet – white bread, pasta, sweet things and alcohol feed the wrong intestinal bacteria, so they should be strictly limited or best avoided altogether. Your diet should consist of good protein (fish, cottage cheese, eggs), vegetables and nuts.

The external fat on your stomach, which makes it somewhat difficult to do up your belt and gives you a "Baroque" appearance, is a warning that there is also fat inside your body. Your heart is probably padded with fat, as is your liver and digestive organs; often, your blood pressure will also be raised, as well as the fat in your blood – triglycerides, while there will often be a lower level of the good cholesterol – the HDL cholesterol. All these problems are a sign of the metabolic syndrome. People with this syndrome are prone to atherosclerosis (blocked arteries) and consequently cardiovascular diseases (heart attack or stroke, gangrene of the lower limbs, etc.). The metabolic syndrome means that, due to a shortage of nutrients, you are not metabolising fats and carbohydrates very well. The only thing your body is capable of is turning food into fat, not into energy.

How do you know that you have bad metabolism or that you may have the metabolic syndrome? It is simple – measure yourself. The circumference of your waist should always be smaller than the circumference of your hips and should not be greater than 88 cm in women and 102 cm in men. A waist circumference of more than 80 cm in women and 94 in men indicates that there is a great likelihood that the metabolic syndrome will occur.

Strong calves

If your calves are as big as your thighs, this could be the consequence of the following:

- not enough rest, insomnia,
- lack of vitamins B,
- too much salt (natrium) and not enough potassium. See also: Fluid retention in the body on page 184.

In order to sleep better, avoid sugar, sweet things and caffeine before bed. You can get vitamins B by eating sea food, meat, nuts, yoghurt and eggs. Your evening meal should consist of protein and vegetables. This way, your body will be able to make the sleep hormone, you will sleep better and your body will reshape while you sleep. See also: Meal plans for losing weight on page 126.

Back fat

Women often find fat collecting on their back and around their armpits. This type of fat indicates the slowed down metabolism of carbohydrates. Carbohydrates first get digested in the mouth and then in the small intestine.

A question: if you have fat on your back and around your armpits, are you perhaps eating very quickly? Do you often eat on the way to somewhere, do you not take the necessary time for your meals, and do you swallow your food whole because you are always in a hurry?

Take time for your meals. Turn off music and the telephone. Chew your food so that it is easier to digest, give up white bread and pasta and replace them with wholemeal versions. Eat more vegetables and protein.

In order to encourage the digestion and metabolism of the food you eat, you need good probiotic bacteria and metabolising vitamins and minerals: vitamin C, vitamins B – mainly B6, and magnesium.

In order to reduce back fat, it is also good to do exercises for your arms and back – lifting weights or simply the Fountain of Youth exercises. More about the Fountain of Youth on page 224.

Fatty arms

Fat collecting on upper arms shows toxin retention in the body, resulting from consuming food and drink in plastic packaging. Start with detoxification and avoid heating up food wrapped in plastic. You can speed up the detoxification by sweating and drinking nettle, dandelion or goldenrod tea, and consuming calcium and magnesium, which help toxins leave the body faster. More about calcium and magnesium on page 280 and 282.

Bloated face

If your face is round and bloated, you have a double chin and the excessive weight immediately goes to your face, you may be retaining fluid in your body. A frequent reason for fat collecting on the face is alcohol, as it dehydrates the skin. Reduce the consumption of alcoholic drinks and speed up the circulation in your face with massage – begin with the nose and massage outwards towards your ears. Herbal teas made from elder, parsley and nettles will help with the release of fluids from your body. More about fluid retention on page 184.

Saddlebags

It is possible that you have a genetic predisposition for saddlebags. From the point of view of your health, this fat is not problematic as it does not burden your heart and vascular system. But fat on the thighs is a storage space for toxins and indicates that your lymph system is not functioning as it should. The best help here is regular exercise. Take your legs for a walk – every day!

You can also use the following herbs:

- camomile,
- nettle,
- green tea,
- cambogia, which is one of the best natural appetite suppressants and fat burners – garcinia cambogia increases thermogenesis and the use of consumed calories, as well as the use of the already stored fat,
- ginseng,
- chilli.

The following herbs help with microcirculation and movement of the lymph. First, answer the following questions:

- What is your digestion like? If it is bad, toxins remain in your body and because of this you cannot lose weight.

- Do you sit a lot? Roughly massage your thighs in the morning and evening and do a few stretching exercises at least in the morning.

- Do you drink enough? If you do not drink enough fluid (water or herbal teas), toxins stay in your body.

- Do you eat enough protein? Protein is necessary for building muscle mass, which determines the firmness of your thighs. More about protein on page 233.

The Slovenian monk Simon Ašič recommends the following herbal teas:

When too little cortisol is released:

- wild strawberries, goldenrod, centaurium,
- elder, absinth, milfoil.

You drink 2 cups of this tea 3 times a day, always before meals.

A low level of cortisol is a consequence of a long period of stress and a long period of an increased release of cortisol. It shows in the form of chronic tiredness and inability to feel like you are getting enough sleep even though you are sleeping enough; you lack energy and strength in your muscles, you are exhausted and without mental sharpness. In the morning, you are barely able to get out of bed and your will to live is reduced. If you do nothing at this point, you may lead your body into a state of complete burnout.

When cortisol is raised:

- tea made with young blueberry leaves, raspberry leaves and St John's wort,
- viola tricolour, nettles and bramble leaves – cover 2 tablespoons of the herbal mixture with half a litre of boiling water.

Raised cortisol can cause health problems

When there is too much cortisol, you experience the world as hostile, difficult and aggressive. You respond heatedly, angrily, you feel anxiety, you may feel like crying and that you cannot cope with life.

In addition to psychological consequences, cortisol also causes physical changes. There can be raised blood pressure, elevated heart rate, disturbed heartbeat and even your immune system may become impeded. You may get headaches, sometimes migraines; you feel tired and "washed out" so you begin to reach for stimulants and sedatives. Stress uses a lot of vitamins C and B. A 20-minute period of emotional stress uses as much as 300 mg of vitamin C, an amount found in six freshly picked oranges. Research has shown that this condition can be simply improved by adding vitamins C and B and magnesium. Take a multivitamin that contains a lot of vitamins B, calcium and magnesium, as well as omega-3 fats. This is a combination of nutrients that is effective against hidden inflammation, helps eliminate toxins and helps with metabolism. Vitamins B, magnesium and vitamin C are metabolic vitamins, which increase energy and calm down violent reactions. Natural vitamins B will not make you put on weight.

Adrenal glands can be fatigued by food.*

It may be hard to believe that you have the power to impact adrenal fatigue through your diet. What you eat and when you eat both play a crucial role. The key principle is to avoid letting yourself get extremely hungry. Low blood sugar triggers a stress response in the body. Consider the consequences of skipping breakfast and then consuming inadequate food later in the day; this constant pattern places a significant strain on your body. Your body requires a continuous supply of energy, even during sleep. Cortisol regulates your blood sugar levels around the clock. Prolonged fasting forces the adrenal glands to work overtime to produce more cortisol (to maintain optimal blood sugar levels and energy levels throughout the day) and adrenaline. The most effective way to support your adrenals is to have three balanced main meals each day, along with two smaller meals in between, to provide essential nutrients for organ function. By following this approach, you can stabilize your blood sugar levels throughout the day, minimize fluctuations, and lessen the burden on your adrenals.

*Adapted from an article published in the Slovenian magazine Jana by Milka Krapež.

Lack of sleep makes you put on weight

We all know how we feel after a sleepless night. Not only do we not have any energy, everyone around us knows that we have not slept enough. Everything makes us tetchy; we raise our voice without any reason, we cannot focus, we are tense behind the steering wheel and at home nothing pleases us. When we don't sleep enough, we stress our body.

Cortisol converts all food into fatty deposits

Raised cortisol ensures that the body is in constant tension, all the food is converted into sugar reserves, which leads to accumulating fat and not being able to lose it. If you are constantly under stress, cortisol makes you retain fat mostly on the stomach. If the stress hormone is too high in the evening as well, you cannot calm down and go to sleep. When you sleep your body regenerates, but if you do not sleep, this cannot happen.

In addition, people who don't sleep enough, eat more. Research carried out by the American Heart Association showed that women who sleep only four hours a night, eat considerably more than when they sleep the normal eight to nine hours. Women in the study ate more and more often reached for food rich in carbohydrates.

Not getting enough sleep makes you hungrier!

If you don't sleep enough, this sets off processes in your body that cause weight gain. Lack of sleep influences the hormones leptin and ghrelin. The former lets the brain know how much energy is available and how to use it, while the latter increases appetite. If there is more ghrelin in the body, hunger appears. As lack of sleep influences energy levels in the body, too much ghrelin is automatically produced. At the same time, there is not enough leptin, which lets your body know when you have had enough food. This is why people who don't sleep enough eat up to 30 percent more food during a meal.

Another interesting study showed that those who eat healthily but do not sleep enough lose muscle mass rather than fat. The study involved healthy, but slightly overweight people, who were offered healthy food. The first group slept 7 hours and a half and the second 5 hours a night. The results were astonishing. In both cases, the participants lost about the same amount of weight. But the first group lost fat, while the second group lost muscle mass.

Research has shown that lack of sleep and the resulting release of ghrelin stops the burning of stored fat and increases the desire for sweet snacks. Ghrelin is thus released when you:

- do not get enough sleep,
- miss meals,
- eat food with a high glycaemic index.

So, look at the number of hours you sleep and your weight. On average, a person should sleep eight or at least seven hours a night. A study on 30 young, slim people showed that those who slept only 6 hours, began to put on fat, while those who slept at least 8 hours kept normal weight. To begin with, you should go to bed an hour earlier and at least from time to time sleep longer in the morning. At night, your body undergoes the process of regeneration. After two hours of solid sleep, your body begins to release the growth hormone, which reshapes your body while you sleep.

See also: The growth hormone regenerates and rejuvenates you and makes you lose weight on page 199.

The opposite hormone to the stress hormone cortisol is DHEA, which regenerates and makes you younger

Like cortisol, DHEA is a hormone produced by the adrenals. DHEA and cortisol oppose each other. DHEA regenerates and rejuvenates, while cortisol degenerates and ages. For optimal health, the two hormones should be in balance. When we are under stress, cortisol is released and when the stress passes, the body reduces the production of cortisol and increases the release of DHEA, which repairs the damage during sleep. This process takes place when the body is exposed to a short period of stress.

Long-lasting stress destroys the balance

Ray Grauber in his book "The Single Cause and Cure for Any Health Challenge" describes a study done on mice:

> *When mice are placed on an electric grid and given very mild shocks, they are unaffected as long as they are given enough time to recover from the stress and the shocks. But if these mild shocks are too frequent, the mice are not able to recover from this harmless stress and they die from old age within a few short days. Even though each electric shock itself was harmless, the accumulative effect of frequent stress without enough recovery time causes the body to just give up and die.*

What we can conclude on the basis of this study in connection with people is plain to see: when we don't have enough time to recover after each stressful event before a new one comes along, our cells remain out of action, our body ages and we may die before our time.

Lack of DHEA can be the result of stress and nutritionally poor food. It shows up as:

- chronic tiredness,
- anxiety and panic attacks,
- gaining fat on the stomach,
- depression and despondency,
- joint pain,
- weak immune system,
- reduced libido,
- bloated face and bags under the eyes,
- dry and split hair,
- appearance of cellulite,
- bloated stomach.

When your body is exposed to long-lasting stress – this includes bad relations in the family or at work and a long-lasting inflammation in the body – ever increasing quantities of the stress hormone are produced and ever smaller quantities of DHEA. One study has shown that after 28 days of uninterrupted stress, cortisol levels increased by as much as 240 percent of the starting value, while DHEA levels fell by 15 percent. What is worse – even after stress is reduced, the body sometimes doesn't recover. The hormonal balance doesn't return to the starting level, instead the high level of cortisol and low level of DHEA persevere. In this case the body must be helped to recover.

The first form of help is a calmer life. We can get upset about the state of affairs in our country, about politics, about our boss, about our ageing parents, about our partner and children. If we want, we never run out of excuses for stress. But it is us who choose our thoughts!

We can decide to have a calmer life. It is better to ignore the things we cannot change and employ our thoughts with something beautiful. There is plenty of beauty around us.

I also warmly recommend that you perform the healing prayer of decoding (page 43) in order to heal your cell memory, to make it easier to focus on something beautiful and to bring peace, love and divine harmony to your cells.

DHEA – a hormone responsible for the regeneration of the body and for reducing fat on the stomach

DHEA is released copiously when we are young, reaching its highest level at the age of twenty-one; after the age of thirty, the level starts falling gradually and by the age of sixty there can be as much as 60 to 80 percent less of this hormone than in our twenties. Those who have a sufficient level of this hormone are more vital, have an excellent memory and can think quickly, they have stronger bones, firm muscles, a tight behind and a flat stomach. In addition, DHEA makes the skin younger, eases the symptoms of depression, the effects of stress (nervousness, tension), lowers body fat percentage and even eases menopause symptoms. It is also responsible for the sex hormones. When we have enough DHEA, we have a feeling that we can cope; and we have calm nerves. We feel more vital and younger by the day and our skin looks younger as well.

DHEA has the following beneficial effects on your health:

- increases vitality and strengthens the immune system,
- improves the memory function and the speed of thinking,
- enables a calmer reaction to stress,
- stronger bones,
- increased muscle mass,
- younger, firmer skin,
- depression prevention or reduction,
- alleviation of the effects of stress (nervousness, tension),
- hinders the release of cortisol, the stress hormone,
- accelerates regeneration during sleep,
- lowers body fat percentage,
- eases menopause symptoms and influences the sex hormones,
- increases libido.

In the desire for profits and eternal youth, experts have created artificial DHEA, which is connected with a number of cancers. Thus, playing with artificial DHEA is not worth it.

The body can produce DHEA on its own – every night!

It is simple – while you sleep, your cells are happily making hormones, regenerating you, ensuring that your joints remain flexible and rejuvenating you. And the fat around your stomach melts away.

In order to accelerate the production of DHEA and fat burning, you need the following nutrients:

- vitamins A, B, C and E,
- minerals calcium, magnesium and selenium,
- amino acids – all 22 of them (more about proteins on page 236),
- omega-3 fatty acids. Without good fats, your body cannot produce hormones.

As you can see, your body needs the same nutrients for producing hormones that age you and make you put on fat, as for releasing the hormones that regenerate and rejuvenate. When you are under stress, cortisol "burns up" all the vitamins and minerals stores, and you do not have enough components for regeneration.

Six food substances that contribute toward burning the fat on your stomach:

1. **Sauerkraut juice** (the water sauerkraut is fermented in) contains probiotics. When we are under stress, nutrient absorption in the intestines is reduced. This can be helped with a good probiotic supplement.

2. **Fish** (sardines and salmon) is full of good protein and fat, which influence the balancing of cortisol that keeps the body ready for sudden activity. You should consume fatty fish at least 3 times a week; if you use tinned fish, it should be sardines.

3. **Lemons** contain vitamin C, which is of key importance in the cortisol balance. Did you know that during 20 minutes of stress your body uses 300 mg of vitamin C? This is the equivalent of six oranges.

4. **Brewer's yeast** contains lots of vitamins B. During stress, there is an increased need for the vitamins from this group as they are necessary for the preservation of a healthy nervous system.

5. **Almonds** contain the best ratio of calcium and magnesium. These two minerals are necessary for the transfer of nervous signals. During stress, the need for these two minerals increases and consequently the metabolism slows down. Magnesium is the key mineral in activating cell metabolism. If there is not enough of it, you lack energy and motivation, while the scales show an ever-increasing number.

6. **Avocado** contains good fats, vitamin E, which increases concentration, vitamin C, which prevents ageing, potassium, which acts against depression, magnesium, which influences your energy level, proteins, and as many as 18 essential amino acids – mostly tyrosine, which is a component used in the production of the growth hormone and DHEA, which are the opposite of cortisol; avocado also contains lots of vitamins B, necessary for calm nerves.

If you want to get rid of the fat on your stomach, then supplement your diet with good omega-3 fats! You fight like with like – add the omega-3 fatty acid in the evening. For more about good fats, see page 262.

The evening meal is the most important meal – it decides whether DHEA will be produced

The evening meal should consist of protein and vegetables:

If you like prosciutto, add a little bit of cheese, a few olives and almonds. In the evening, avoid bread, sweet things and alcohol, since all these contain a considerable amount of sugar – they have a high glycaemic index. This results in excessive levels of insulin, which "locks" the fat cells for the next few hours, preventing the use of energy from the fat cells, which slows down regeneration during sleep. More about suitable foods to eat in the evening for the production of regenerative hormones on page 124.

Foods with low glycaemic index are a solution for many health problems

This is such a simple way of eating that it is suitable for the whole family. It is not a diet, but a lifetime solution. When you have mastered the glycaemic index, you will no longer be in a battle with your stomach and have a constant desire for something sweet; you will be energetic and filled with enthusiasm; you will rid yourself of surplus weight, sort out your digestion, speed up detoxification and help your body to create a hormonal balance.

Those who have been thin all their life don't know what a severe attack of hunger feels like. These people can eat at any time and anything and their bodies do not change.

I am sure you know someone who can eat what they want and always stay slim; you, on the other hand, just have to walk past the fridge and put on some weight. This is not fair! Sometimes people tell me: "I put weight on at a mere sight of a glass of water!"

People differ. Do the following test and find out whether you are sensitive to carbohydrates. Respond with a yes or a no.

Are you sensitive to sugar in food?*

*Adapted from Dr Richard F. Heller and Dr Rachael F. Heller: *The Carbohydrate Addict's Lifespan Program: A Personalized Plan for Becoming Slim, Fit, and Healthy in Your 40s, 50s, 60s, and Beyond*

1. After I have eaten a full breakfast, before it's time for lunch I get hungrier than if I had not had any breakfast or had just had a cup of coffee.

2. In the middle of the afternoon, I get tired and/or hungry.

3. After a big meal, I become very lazy and tired.

4. Sometimes I have to put off the evening activities because I lose motivation after the evening meal.

5. Once I start eating food full of starch, snacks or sweet things I cannot stop; stopping is a lot harder than not eating at all.

6. Approximately two hours after a meal I sometimes become tired, hungry, irritable, confused and start trembling, I lose motivation and get a headache. Sometimes I feel better after I have something to eat.

7. When I'm under stress, I want to eat, either immediately or as soon as the tension has eased a little.

8. Food that contains white sugar, fructose or artificial sweeteners is part of a number of my meals.

9. As I get older, I have a feeling that I put on weight more quickly.

10. At least one of my blood relatives is fat.

11. My way of life is inactive.

12. At home or at work I am regularly under a certain amount of stress.

13. I was told that I have some of the following health problems: high blood pressure, high level of fat in my blood (high cholesterol), high level of triglycerides, low level of HDL, high level of LDL, or age-related diabetes.

14. One or both of my parents have (had) at least one of the following diseases: high blood pressure, high level of fat in their blood (high cholesterol), high level of triglycerides, low level of HDL, high level of LDL, or age-related diabetes.

15. I am (have been) under hormone replacement therapy, I constantly have to take laxatives, I take (OTC) medicines for one or more of the following problems: high blood pressure, high cholesterol.

Scoring (add only the points for the questions you have answered with a "yes")

1. .... 6 points
2. .... 2 points
3. .... 1 point
4. .... 4 points
5. .... 5 points
6. .... 3 points
7. .... 3 points
8. .... 1 point
9. .... 3 points
10. .... 3 points
11. .... 3 points
12. .... 3 points
13. .... 5 points
14. .... 4 points
15. .... 4 points

Highest possible number of points: 50

Levels of sugar sensitivity:

13 points or less – doubtful addiction to carbohydrates

14 to 22 points – mild addiction to carbohydrates

23 to 35 points – moderate addiction to carbohydrates

36 to 50 points – severe addiction to carbohydrates

Doubtful addiction to carbohydrates

If you wish to lose a few excessive kilos, you don't have a problem with this. You eat a little less and this solves it for you.

Mild addiction to carbohydrates

Occasionally you consume greater quantities of snacks, sweet things or starchy foods than you intend to. Sometimes you find that you cannot control yourself and resist this type of food. Foods rich in fat and carbohydrates, such as ice-cream, chocolate, pizza, bread or Chinese food, seem incredibly tempting to you.

Even just the sight of food and its smell stimulates you to start eating when you would otherwise have been able to control yourself.

You may be one of those people who simply likes eating. You have a few excessive kilos. In the rest of this book, you will find out which foods will stop the desire for frequent eating or the need for excessively large meals. This desire will simply vanish, while the natural ability of your body to use the energy obtained from food will increase, stopping this energy from being stored as fat.

Moderate addiction to carbohydrates

You have battled excessive weight several times and quickly regained it. Sometimes you persisted and tried to completely resist the food you craved. On other occasions, although you tried to keep control over the size of the meals and the choice of food, the results of stress, cessation of smoking, menopause, tiredness or ageing robbed you of the ability to effectively control your eating habits and weight.

Sometimes you feel that you cannot resist foods rich in carbohydrates and fat, such as ice-cream, chocolate, bread, pizza and Chinese food. Even when you manage to show a "superhuman" measure of self-discipline, you are awarded with minimal weight loss, or sometimes even no weight loss, in spite of your efforts.

In the rest of this book you will see how within only a few days you can control the cravings for the above-mentioned foods. When your insulin (hunger hormone) levels normalise, your need for "cheating" will probably disappear. When your blood sugar level is balanced, your energy will increase and with it your motivation and ability to think clearly.

You will be able to lose weight and keep the new weight!

Severe addiction to carbohydrates

You sometimes feel strong addiction to foods rich in fat and/or carbohydrates, such as ice-cream, chocolate, pizza or Chinese food. When you consume these foods, you quickly gain weight.

When you were young, you moderately craved foods rich in carbohydrate, but now that you are a little older, you gain weight with this type of food much more easily and quickly. You start losing weight, but as soon as you return to your old eating habits, you gain the weight back, and with it the feeling of guilt.

The sudden rises and falls in your blood sugar levels can cause mood swings, irritability, nervousness and fear, tiredness, apathy and lack of motivation. If you are severely addicted to carbohydrates, then only you know how very hard you have tried and how difficult the struggle is.

In the rest of this book, you will find out how to get rid of the unstoppable desire for food and stop gaining weight – this is not a diet that requires sacrifice and going hungry, but one that involves fixing the hormonal imbalance, which is what is actually causing your problems with eating and weight.

Chapter 3. Insulin – the constant hunger hormone

Can I digest life; can I go with the flow?

GLYCAEMIC INDEX

Eat to live, do not live to eat!

Cicero

In the morning you have a coffee, with sugar of course, and a biscuit – just so you don't have an empty stomach. Great! You go to work and at around ten you already feel like eating something – the saliva is collecting in your mouth, your blood sugar has fallen and you eat something close to hand: a little bit of chocolate. Then comes lunch. The food served in the canteen tastes so good! You feel great, but after lunch you wish you were near your sofa. You become tired, without energy, sometimes irritable. And this goes on for the rest of the day (the blood sugar swings through the whole day are shown in the graph).

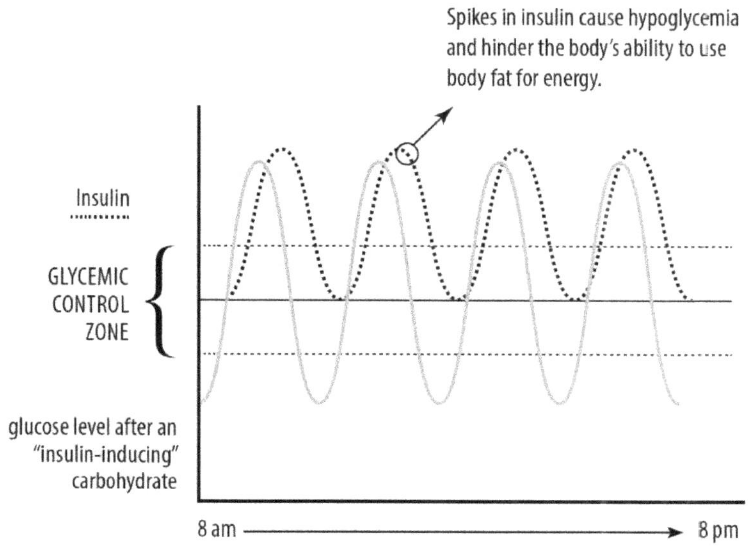

The glycaemic roller coaster

High insulin levels cause hypoglycaemia and prevent the body from using fat in the production of energy

Glucose level due to consuming carbohydrates, which "encourage the production of insulin"

What's wrong? Why do you feel so bad every day? Why such fluctuations?

The answer lies in glycaemia. The glycaemic index of foods tells you how quickly and to what degree food turns to blood sugar. Most of the food you are consuming (white flour, sugar, various snacks, etc.) has a high glycaemic index, which means that your blood sugar rises too rapidly and excessively. Your body (pancreas) then sends insulin in order to sort out this imbalance in your blood. But, because there is too much sugar, there is also too much insulin released, which then lowers your blood sugar too much. As a result, you feel tired and without energy. We are all familiar with the statement: "My blood sugar has fallen."

A diet that takes into account the glycaemic index of foods is based on this finding: it encourages the consumption of foods with a low glycaemic index and limits the consumption of foods with a high glycaemic index – the foods after which you feel hungrier.

Advantages of a diet that takes into account the glycaemic index of foods

Optimal insulin and glucose levels that help with the breakdown of fats in the body

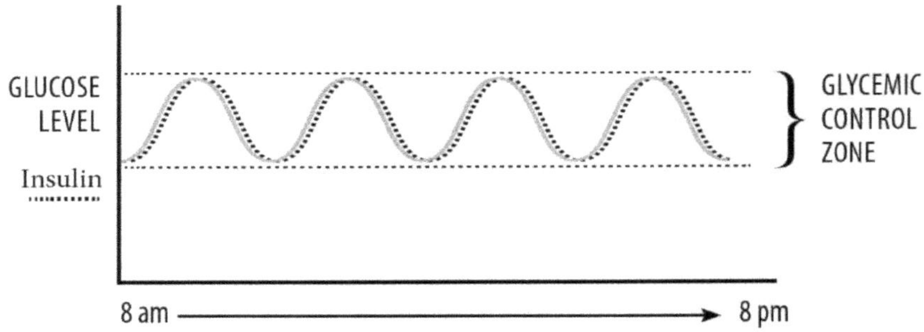

The advantage is that you learn how to eat properly. This way of eating does not take you to extremes, where you have to omit whole groups of foods from your diet.

The only shortcoming is that it is sometimes difficult to see whether a specific food has a low or high glycaemic index, because salt and/or fats are added to packaged food.

Ask yourself whether food like this was eaten 50 years ago. Eat rye or buckwheat bread instead of white; consume plain yoghurt without anything added; if you want yoghurt with fruit, add the fruit yourself. This way you will avoid all the added sugars and preservatives.

The glycaemic index diet doesn't put a burden on your kidneys and doesn't raise your cholesterol. Because it is rich in vitamins, minerals and fibre, it helps to prevent many diseases. Your general wellbeing is improved, and you also have energy for the things that previously seemed completely out of reach. The chart above shows the blood sugar level that is within the glycaemic control value, which means that throughout the day you have enough energy, and your cells are given the order: **"BURN THE STORED FAT!"**

Balance you blood sugar levels with the correct combination of foods

You have probably already established that a constant struggle with your feeling of hunger leads nowhere. I know from my own experience how you feel since I used to struggle, too. In the following pages you will find how to "tame" that constant hunger.

Important:

All the foods with a glycaemic index over 51 make you put on weight.

These foods include white bread, white rice, rice pudding, popcorn, cornflakes, jam and marmalade with sugar, white pasta, puffed rice cakes, bananas, pizza, energy drinks and all potatoes.

Foods with a glycaemic index between 35 and 50, prevent weight gain, but do not allow you to lose weight either.

These foods include brown rice, whole grain basmati rice, wholemeal pasta, white spaghetti cooked "al dente", wholemeal bread, kiwi, grapes, roasted nuts.

Foods with a glycaemic index under 35 make you lose weight

These foods include: cabbage, cauliflower, broccoli, aubergine/eggplant courgettes/zucchini, spinach; fruit: peaches, cherries, fruits of the forest (e.g. blueberries); and grains, legumes and nuts.

A table showing foods according to their glycaemic index (GI):***

***Summarised from: Michel Montignac: *The Montignac Method.*

High GI – above 60 (the foods you should eat as little of as possible):

115 – corn syrup

110 – beer

100 – glucose syrup

100 – modified starch

100 – wheat and rice syrup

95 – potato starch

95 – potatoes (fried)

95 – potatoes (roasted, without skin)

95 – rice flour

91 – crispy rice cakes/biscuits

90 – gluten-free bread (from white flour)

90 – mashed potato (instant)

90 – potato flour (starch)

90 – rice (parboiled rice, sticky rice)

90 – rice with gluten

85 – bread, sliced

85 – bun for hamburger

85 – carrots (cooked)

85 – celery (cooked)

85 – corn flakes

85 – corn mush

85 – corn starch

85 – popcorn

85 – potatoes (microwaved)

85 – pretzels

85 – rice (instant, overcooked)

85 – rice cake/pudding

85 – rice milk

85 – rice pudding cooked in the oven

85 – tapioca – cassava root flour

85 – turnip (cooked)

85 – white wheat flour (suitable for cakes and confectionary)

80 – crisps

80 – mashed potato (freshly cooked)

80 – pancakes made with white flour

80 – pizza margherita

75 – biscuits, savoury

75 – doughnuts

75 – graham crackers

75 – lasagne made with white flour

75 – pumpkin

75 – waffles with sugar

75 – watermelon

75 – white flour (for bread and pastries)

70 – baguette

70 – bread crumbs

70 – brown sugar

70 – chocolate

70 – chocolate bars with caramel and nuts

70 – corn bread

70 – corn flour

70 – corn pudding

70 – croissants

70 – dates (dried)

70 – fizzy drinks

70 – gnocchi

70 – grains (refined)

70 – kohlrabi (cooked)

70 – millet

70 – molasses

70 – polenta

70 – potatoes (boiled, peeled)

70 – rice (instant, non-sticky)

70 – rice bread

70 – risotto (white rice)

70 – sugar (sucrose)

70 – sugary drinks

70 – tacos

70 – toast

70 – tortellini (filled with spinach)

70 – wheat pasta

70 – wheat semi-white flour (for semi-white bread)

70 – white bread

70 – white sugar (sucrose)

67 – hazelnuts (roasted)

65 – apricots (tinned, with syrup)

65 – beetroot (cooked)

65 – bread (brown with seeds)

65 – bread from wholemeal flour

65 – chestnut flour

65 – chestnuts

65 – chocolate bread

65 – coconut milk with chocolate

65 – corn (raw, steamed)

65 – corn (tinned)

65 – couscous

65 – flakes – muesli with sugar or honey

65 – grape juice

65 – instant oat flakes

65 – jam (with sugar)

65 – marmalade (with sugar)

65 – macaroni cheese

65 – maple syrup

65 – mushroom soup

65 – orange juice (industrially-produced)

65 – pineapple (tinned)

65 – potatoes (boiled in their skins)

65 – quince jam

65 – raisins

65 – rye bread (30% rye)

65 – sorbet (with sugar)

65 – wheat flour (for brown bread)

60 – banana (very ripe)

60 – French barley

60 – blueberry tart

60 – bran

60 – chocolate powder with sugar

60 – ice-cream (vanilla with a cornet)

60 – mayonnaise (industrially-produced)

60 – honey

60 – melons

60 – pineapple juice (no added sugar)

60 – pizza

60 – pizza, cheesy

60 – ravioli

60 – rice, long-grained (white)

60 – semolina

Medium GI between 40 and 60:

57 – pizza dough

55 – apricot jam

55 – biscuits with butter, pastries with sugar

55 – chocolate spread

55 – corn

55 – fruit salad

55 – ketchup

55 – lasagne, wholemeal

55 – mustard with added sugar

55 – oat biscuits

55 – papaya

55 – pasta, white (well cooked)

55 – peaches (tinned, with syrup)

55 – pineapple (fresh)

55 – soup noodles

55 – spaghetti

55 – strawberry jam

50 – buckwheat bread

50 – crab sticks

50 – cranberry juice (without added sugar)

50 – couscous (wholemeal)

50 – fruit tea with sugar*

50 – persimmon

50 – kiwi

50 – lychee (fresh)

50 – macaroni made from durum wheat

50 – mango (fresh)

50 – muesli bar (energy bar, without added sugar)

50 – pancakes (made with buckwheat or spelt flour, with sugar)

50 – quinoa bread

50 – rice (unrefined basmati)

50 – soya yoghurt (with added fruit or fruit-flavoured)

50 – sweet potato – Jerusalem artichoke

50 – tortellini (filled with cheese)

50 – wholemeal flour

50 – wholemeal pasta

55 – wide noodles (well cooked)

48 – grapefruit juice

45 – banana (less ripe)

45 – buckwheat flour

45 – buckwheat mush

45 – cereal flakes with a lot of fibre

45 – cranberries (dried)

45 – cranberry juice

45 – couscous flour

45 – custard, industrially produced

45 – grapes (all varieties)

45 – jam (without added sugar)

45 – kamut bread

45 – lentil soup

45 – orange juice (freshly squeezed, unsweetened)

45 – pasta (cooked "al dente", wholemeal)

45 – peas (tinned)

45 – rye brown bread

45 – rye flour

45 – spaghetti (spaghetti, cooked “al dente”, without sauce)

45 – spelt bread

45 – tomato sauce (tinned)

45 – wholemeal bread roll

45 – wholemeal bread with bran

45 – wholemeal muesli

40 – apple juice (no added sugar)

40 – apricots (dried)

40 – beans – red (tinned)

40 – beans (roast)

40 – carrot juice (no sugar added)

40 – coconut milk

40 – figs (dried)

40 – freshy squeezed fruit juice with no sugar added

40 – ice-cream (vanilla flavour)

40 – kamut flour (Egyptian wheat)

40 – muesli without sugar

40 – mulled wine (Martini)

40 – must

40 – oat flakes (raw)

40 – oats

40 – pancakes made with buckwheat flour (no sugar)

40 – peanut butter with no added sugar

40 – pears (Williams)

40 – prunes

40 – quinoa flour

40 – rye

40 – sorbet (no sugar)

40 – spelt

40 – wholemeal couscous

40 – wholemeal wheat pasta ("al dente")

40 – yogurt (light, with added sugar)

37 – tomato soup

A low GI is under 35 (foods for healthy slimming):

35 – cranberries (fresh)

35 – broad/fava beans (shelled and cooked)

35 – peaches (fresh)

35 – chickpeas (tinned)

35 – chickpea flour

35 – wild rice

35 – energy bar with protein and nuts

35 – figs (fresh, ripe)

35 – shelled beans (cooked)

35 – mustard

35 – peas (dried or fresh, cooked)

35 – pomegranate

35 – pears

35 – cashew nuts

35 – dried apples

35 – cooked apple (without sugar)

35 – coconut

35 – quinoa

35 – yeast

35 – quince (fresh)

35 – apricots (fresh)

35 – tomato sauce (natural)

35 – tomato juice

35 – orange (fresh)

35 – sesame seeds

35 – ice cream with fructose

35 – sunflower seeds (roasted)

30 – garlic

30 – chickpeas (cooked)

30 – apples (fresh)

30 – yogurt (plain, with 3.2 % fat content)***

30 – Chinese noodles made from beans or soya

30 – carrots (raw)

30 – lentils (all varieties, except green)

30 – desert wine (all varieties, e.g. white Muscat)

30 – mandarins

30 – almond milk

30 – cow's milk (full-fat or semi-skimmed)

30 – milk, powdered

30 – nectarines (fresh)

30 – oat milk

30 – tomato

30 – beetroot (raw)

30 – turnip (raw or pickled)

30 – cottage cheese

30 – plums

30 – soya milk

30 – string beans (with dressing)

25 – blueberries

25 – pumpkin seeds

25 – cherries

25 – grapefruit

25 – strawberries (fresh)

25 – barley

25 – gooseberries

25 – goat's milk (fresh)

25 – lentils – green

25 – raspberries (fresh)

25 – almond butter (no sugar)

25 – redcurrants

25 – blackberries

25 – soya flour

25 – dark chocolate (over 70 % cocoa)

23 – fructose

22 – Chinese noodles (soya variety)

20 – acerola

20 – bamboo shoots

20 – dark chocolate (over 85 % cocoa)

20 – aubergine/eggplant

20 – cocoa powder, unsweetened

20 – swede (raw)

20 – limes

20 – lemons

15 – agave syrup

15 – peanuts

15 – artichokes

15 – Brazil nuts

15 – courgettes/zucchini

15 – pumpkin seeds

15 – kale

15 – broccoli

15 – Brussel sprouts

15 – cauliflower

15 – onions (all kinds)

15 – chilli

15 – blackcurrants

15 – mushrooms

15 – horseradish

15 – ginger

15 – aniseed

15 – yogurt (plain, with 1.3 % fat)

15 – sprouts

15 – sauerkraut

15 – cucumbers (fresh or pickled)

15 – hazelnuts

15 – lemon juice

15 – almonds

15 – olives

15 – walnuts

15 – bran (oat or wheat)

15 – peppers (red, green)

15 – pesto

15 – pistachios

15 – leek

15 – rhubarb

15 – duck liver

15 – radishes

15 – carob flour

15 – sweet paprika

15 – soya

15 – soya yogurt (plain – without added sugar or flavourings)

15 – soya sauce (no sugar)

15 – sunflower seeds

15 – string beans (young, without seeds)

15 – shallots

15 – button mushrooms

15 – asparagus

15 – spinach

15 – celeriac

15 – celery

15 – green salad (all kinds)

15 – cabbage

10 – avocado

10 – tofu (soya cheese)

5 – vinegar

5 – crabs (lobsters, spiny lobsters, crabs)

5 – herbs (oregano, parsley, basil, thyme, cinnamon, vanilla ...)

0 – alcohol – spirits**

0 – white meat (poultry, turkey, rabbit, fish)

0 – mayonnaise (natural – eggs, oil, mustard)

0 – butter, lard, olive oil, pumpkin oil

0 – seafood (prawns, mussels, oysters, octopus, squid)

0 – eggs

0 – coffee

0 – sour cream (1 tablespoon a day, as a condiment)

0 – oils

0 – red meat (beef, pork, veal)

0 – fish

0 – prosciutto ham, ham

0 – cheeses (choose those with less fat)

0 – cottage cheese – low-fat

0 – wine – dry white or red (one glass with a meal)***

0 – water

0 – herb tea

*As there is no data about the glycaemic index of fruit tea, it is listed here under medium GI, like dried fruit and sugar.

**Alcohol doesn't contain sugar and has a glycaemic index of 0. The problem arises when you drink spirits on an empty stomach, it makes you hungry and you reach for sweet snacks. You are allowed to drink a glass of dry white or red wine, or even fizzy wine. This does not make you hungry.

Alcohol appears with glucose fermentation. This is why it contains no carbohydrates, and its glycaemic index is thus zero. Vodka, rum, whisky, gin, tequila are obtained through fermentation of potatoes, cane sugar, malt (barley, rye, wheat and corn), juniper and agave. Even though alcoholic drinks are made from foods that have a high GI and contain a lot of carbohydrates, the distillation turns sugar into ethyl alcohol, which in the liver changes into acetate, which in turn changes into carbon dioxide and water and not into sugar. This is why the glycaemic index of these alcoholic drinks is zero and does not cause a rise in insulin.

Does this mean it is okay to drink spirits when you are trying to reshape your body?

The answer is no. Alcohol washes away metabolic vitamins and minerals, such as vitamins B and magnesium. But there are exceptions. You can have up to four glasses (100 ml) of wine or champagne a day but never drink on an empty stomach. The quantity of alcohol contained in a glass of spirits is approximately the same as the quantity of alcohol in three or four glasses or red wine or champagne. Choose from among the following wines:

- champagne,
- dry red wine – it contains antioxidants, which help to protect the body from harmful influences from the environment,
- dry white wine – contains no beneficial antioxidants.

Finally you can eat – the principle of the medium GI

Carbohydrates with a GI over 30 should always be combined with protein as this will balance the blood sugar and prevent a hunger attack.

Carbohydrates with a high GI cause tiredness and stifle brain activity. If you consume protein in the same meal, you prevent tiredness due to a sugar rush since protein contains the amino acid tyrosine. This is used by the body to produce the chemical substance dopamine, which enlivens you, makes you feel good and increases your strength. In addition, you are able to think more quickly and concentrate, you will be motivated and mentally and even sexually more lively. Tyrosine also reduces hunger. It appears in avocado, almonds, peanuts, eggs, beans, pumpkin and sesame seeds and all dairy, such as cottage cheese, yogurt, kefir and whey.

Losing weight and the medium GI principle

Don't think of calm seas! What thought comes to you? Of a sea that is almost without waves, doesn't it?

Don't think of beautiful, white mountains. What do you see? Beautiful white mountains, don't you?

Now, don't think about a meadow, full of blossoming flowers. What is there? A beautiful meadow, full of flowers, isn't it?

Don't think about your fridge! What are you thinking about? You see your fridge, don't you?

Now, don't thing about ice-cream! In front of your eyes appears an image of a delicious ice-cream that you are licking with great pleasure.

When you tell yourself: "I must not eat," your consciousness does not hear the word NOT, only the word EAT. The more you think about not eating because you are on a diet, the more your body wants to eat!

We think in images. With each thought, our brain paints a picture and doesn't hear the word NOT.

When you decide to lose weight, you tell yourself:

- **"I won't eat bread now."** Your brain gets the following order: **"Bread!"** And when bread appears in front of you, you cannot resist.

- **"I'm going to resist all sweet things."** Your brain gets an order: **"Sweets!"** And as soon as there is an opportunity, you stuff your mouth. This is why some people cannot leave a shop without buying chocolate or ice-cream.

Give your brain a different order: **"What healthy food can I eat to make my blood sugar stay level?"**

An example: The GI of white bread is 70.

If you eat white bread alone, your blood sugar will surge and then half an hour later, you will be desperately hungry. You are gaining weight now and in a short while you have a "hole" in your stomach, your body is demanding food again.

Add a slice of prosciutto ham to your white bread.

Protein doesn't raise your blood sugar, so you should eat it with every meal. Protein includes plain yogurt, kefir, prosciutto, cottage cheese, etc.

70 + 0 = 70: two types of food = 35.5

Now, you are neither putting on weight nor losing it.

With it, have a vegetable, for example preserved olives (GI 15).

Vegetables are excellent for slimming. They not only keep you full for a while, but contain a lot of fibre, vitamins and minerals; however, they have very little impact on your blood sugar.

70 + 0 + 15 = 85: 3 different foods = 28.33

Now you are losing weight!

Replace white bread with wholemeal bread with bran, which has a GI of 45.

Your blood sugar remains level.

Add a slice of prosciutto and a few olives.

45 + 0 + 15 = 60: 3 foods = 20

Although you have eaten a meal without denying yourself, your cells receive the order: "Use the stored fat!"

This is one example of a healthy mini-meal that your body needs between main meals so that you do not become desperately hungry.

Pizza and the principle of the medium glycaemic index

Pizza – because the base contains white flour (GI 75) and ketchup (GI 55) is added, which is full of sugar and flavour enhancers, your blood sugar rises very quickly. Just think – when you eat a whole pizza, you become very tired after half an hour; and an hour later, you want something sweet. Pizza's glycaemic index is 60.

Pizza and salad – you eat half a pizza and a green salad with it.

Let us calculate the glycaemic index: pizza 60 + salad 15 = 75: 2 foods = 37.5. You've eaten more, but your sugar remains level – in spite of the fact that you have just eaten pizza, you will not put on weight.

If you are very sensitive to sugar in food, then you should have a plain yogurt (GI 15) after this meal. This will further reduce your blood sugar.

Try it - you will see that your energy will not drop, and you will feel great, in addition, the fat cells will remain open and you will lose weight.

A piece of advice: if you are making a pizza at home, make dough using wholemeal flour (GI 45). This will reduce the glycaemic index by a half. In practice this means long-lasting energy, you will feel good, and you will be using energy from your fat cells – i.e. slimming.

Does fruit make you put on weight?

Throughout the year, there is an abundance of fruit and vegetables.

Recently, smoothies have been in fashion. They are, of course, healthy but you may get caught in the trap of unstoppable hunger and a desire for more sugar.

What happens in your body when you eat a banana, kiwi, orange, etc. for breakfast?

Or even worse – you drink a smoothie made with a banana, a kiwi and an orange? I can tell you what – a shock. Your body gets so much sugar at once that after this kind of breakfast you would have to run a marathon, or work really hard for two hours in a field, or spring clean your home, etc. These days, we usually don't do this – after breakfast, we sit in the car and drive to work, where we sit again. And after an hour and a half, we are already thinking where to find something substantial to eat because our stomach is saying or even shouting: "HUNGRY!"

With a banana (GI 60), have a plain yogurt (GI 15) – this will reduce the total glycaemic index to 37.5. But you may still find yourself hungry. If you replace the banana with a few apricots and eat a piece of cheese (GI 0), the sugar will remain balanced, your fat cells will be releasing stored energy and you will feel wonderful.

If you are sensitive to sugar in foods (sugar in fruit is still sugar), even an apple can make you hungry. How to avoid this? Eat a few walnuts and a piece of lower fat cheese with your apple. The result? You will be energised and, best of all – in half an hour you will not be hungry again!

Why it is not sensible to eat fruit in the evening

Fruit contains fructose – fruit sugar, which can result in blood sugar swings.

What happens in your body when you eat fruit (an apple, a peach, etc.)?

- If you are sensitive to sugar, your blood sugar will rise.
- Insulin steps in to help – the hormone that puts the excessive sugar into fat cells.
- The fat cells get "locked" for 5 hours.
- Because too much insulin has been released, there is a fall in the blood sugar.
- After a good hour, saliva collects in your mouth. Your body demands another "dose" of sugar.
- If you eat sugar in the evening, your evening meal will be full of sugar, but you will not consume the building blocks – proteins, which means there will be no regeneration in your sleep. More on the growth hormone on page 199.

Let me put it simply – if you eat carbohydrates in the evening, your body will not regenerate itself, but store weight instead.

Fruit – a table according to the glycaemic index

75 – watermelon	55 – pineapple (fresh)
70 – dates (dried)	55 – strawberry jam
65 – apricots (tinned, with syrup)	50 – kaki
65 – grape juice	50 – kiwi
65 – jam (sweetened)	50 – mango
65 – maple syrup	50 – soya yogurt, fruit flavoured
65 – marmalade (sweetened)	48 – grapefruit juice
65 – orange juice (industrially produced)	45 – banana (less ripe)
65 – pineapple (tinned)	45 – cranberries (dry)
65 – quince jam	45 – cranberry juice
65 – raisins*	45 – grapes (all kinds)*
60 – banana (ripe)	45 – jam (no sugar)
60 – melon	45 – orange juice (freshly squeezed)
60 – pineapple juice	45 – redcurrants (dry)
55 – apricot jam	
55 – fruit salad	
55 – papaya	
55 – peach (tinned, with syrup)	

40 – apple juice (100 %, fresh)	30 – nectarines (fresh)
40 – apricots (dried)	30 – plums
40 – figs (dried)	25 – blackberries
40 – prunes	25 – blueberries
40 – William pears	25 – cherries
35 – apricots (fresh)*	25 – gooseberries
35 – cooked apple (no sugar)	25 – grapefruit
35 – cranberries (fresh)	25 – raspberries
35 – dried apple slices	25 – redcurrants
35 – figs (fresh, ripe)	25 – strawberries (fresh)
35 – orange (fresh)	20 – acerola
35 – peaches (fresh)*	20 – lemon
35 – pears	20 – lime
35 – pomegranate	15 – blackcurrants
35 – quince	15 – lemon juice
30 – apples	
30 – mandarins	

*All dried or tinned fruits become a sugar concentrate. Use fresh or frozen fruit.

An example: A woman eats healthily. She avoids white flour and white sugar, eats every 3 hours. In the evening, in front of the television, she likes to eat an apple. She is aware of the saying "An apple a day keeps the doctor away." After an hour, her stomach begins to rumble. She is struggling internally, but in the end her stomach wins. The hunger is so strong that she looks in the fridge for something suitable to eat. And of course she finds something, but then she feels guilty because yet again she has eaten something before bed.

This woman has perhaps not heard of another old piece of wisdom: "An apple in the morning is gold, at midday silver, and in the evening a stone." If she wants to encourage the regeneration of her body and weight loss in her sleep, she should eat only vegetables and protein. Among the good proteins to be eaten in the evening are cottage cheese, plain yogurt, kefir, cheese, mozzarella, prosciutto, boiled eggs and vegetables – carrots, gherkins, pickled mushrooms, etc.

But not all vegetables are good, at least not in the evening. Cooked carrots have a high glycaemic index, as much as 85. This means that they contain as many carbohydrates as a white bread roll.

The ratio between vegetables and fruit should be 4:1

This means you should include vegetables in your breakfast; at lunch, you should consume cooked and fresh vegetables; for the afternoon snack, again add vegetables; and at dinner also. Always eat protein with vegetables. If you eat only salads, you will waste away and when you start eating normally, the "yoyo" effect will begin, and you will probably put on more weight than you lost.

Vegetables – a table according to the GI:

95 – potatoes (fried or oven roasted)	37 – tomato soup
95 – potato starch	35 – brown beans (boiled)
90 – mashed potato (instant)	35 – peas (dried or fresh, cooked)
85 – carrots (cooked)*	35 – tomato juice
85 – popcorn	35 – tomato sauce (no sugar)
85 – potatoes (microwaved)	35 – white beans
85 – potatoes (roasted)	30 – beetroot (raw)
85 – turnip (cooked)*	30 – carrots (raw)*
80 – mashed potato (freshly prepared)	30 – garlic
75 – pumpkin, watermelon	30 – string beans (dressed, with seeds)
70 – corn pudding	30 – tomato
70 – potatoes (peeled, boiled)	30 – turnip (raw or sour)*
70 – swede (cooked)*	
65 – beetroot (freshly cooked)	
65 – corn (fresh, steamed)	
65 – corn (tinned)	
65 – mushroom soup	
65 – potatoes (boiled in their skins)	
60 – melon	
55 – corn	
50 – sweet potatoes – Jerusalem artichoke	
45 – peas (tinned)	
40 – carrot juice (unsweetened)	
40 – beans – red (tinned)	
40 – beans (baked)	

20 – aubergine/eggplant	15 – spinach
20 – swede (raw)*	15 – sprouts
15 – artichokes	15 – string beans (young, no seeds)
15 – asparagus	10 – avocado
15 – broccoli	5 – parsley
15 – Brussel sprouts	
15 – button mushrooms	
15 – cabbage (raw or sour)	
15 – cauliflower	
15 – celery and celeriac	
15 – chicory, endive	
15 – chilli	
15 – kale	
15 – courgettes/zucchini	
15 – cucumbers	
15 – green salad	
15 – horseradish	
15 – leeks	
15 – mushrooms	
15 – olives	
15 – onions	
15 – peppers	
15 – radish	
15 – radicchio	
15 – shallots	

*Tubers like turnip, carrots, swede and radishes have a very low GI when raw, but when they are heated, their GI rises considerably.

Vegetables that contain a lot of starch very quickly turn to sugar.

• Pumpkins have a very high GI – 75. If you cook them in a sauce it increases the carbohydrate content even further. Pumpkins in a sauce have a GI of 85.

• Potatoes cooked in their skins have a GI of 65, but if you roast them the GI rises to 95 and as a result you get a desire for something sweet.

Advice: Cook vegetables that contain a lot of starch in advance and let them get completely cold. An example is a cold potato salad. The starch in the potatoes becomes partially indigestible and will therefore not result in a fall in energy and an attack of hunger.

The same applies to spaghetti, macaroni and all other pasta: if you cook it in advance, cool it and then reheat it, the starch becomes partly indigestible and does not cause a rise in blood sugar and severe hunger attacks. Cold pasta salads with vegetables are thus an excellent accompaniment to meat on hot summer days.

A better choice is vegetables that don't contain a lot of starch. These include courgettes and mushrooms. Courgettes have a GI of 15, even a sauce made with courgettes is not a problem, the GI rises only slightly, perhaps to 20.

If you make a cucumber and potato salad, you reduce the sugar level in the potatoes. In this case, the GI of the cooked potatoes 65 + the GI of cucumbers 15:2 foods = a total GI of 40.

Suggestion: Have some protein with the potato and cucumber salad, (e.g. a chicken fillet, a few almonds, a boiled egg or a fish fillet). This creates a perfectly healthy meal, which is nutritiously rich and tasty. But the GI of the whole meal is only 26.6.

Your body needs 5 meals

I know what your first thought was: "Do I have time to eat 5 times a day?!"

Cells "lock up" when they feel a lack of food. The biggest mistake you can make is to eat once or twice a day. Another "deadly sin" of healthy eating is trying to lose weight following the principle of "just eat less". This leads to it being more difficult for you to lose weight with each year, and when you reach the age of 50 you will not lose weight even if you consume nothing but water. In this way you gain 5 kilograms every 10 years and fall into the "yoyo" trap. One day you are losing, the next gaining.

In their book *The Carbohydrate Addict's Lifespan Program: A Personalized Plan for Becoming Slim, Fit, and Healthy in Your 40s, 50s, 60s, and Beyond,* Dr Richard F. Heller and Dr Rachael F. Heller say that you should not rejoice in your success in losing weight unless you are certain that you will never put the weight back on again.

Enjoy several meals a day:

- breakfast,
- morning mini meal,
- lunch,
- afternoon mini meal,
- dinner.

When your body gets food every few hours, which contains few carbohydrates – foods with a glycaemic index below 30 – and a sufficient amount of protein and fibre, the process of losing weight is set in motion. The body starts to use the stored fat on its own.

The process of losing weight has begun. Congratulations!

Breakfast and losing weight

If you have missed breakfast, you often find that around 11 o'clock in the morning you run out of motivation for work, you feel bad, you cannot concentrate and you get an unstoppable desire for chocolate. And what do you do? You have just one bite of chocolate or a coffee from the vending machine. And you feel better. But have you thought that this is precisely what is keeping you in the surplus weight trap?

Breakfast is very important for steady energy all day. But you can enter a trap first thing in the morning. If your breakfast consists of sweet, white coffee and white bread, it is only your fat cells that will be happy and they will be able to demand more sugar all day long.

A healthy breakfast with a low glycaemic index:

- rye bread, cheese with reduced-fat, pickled mushrooms,
- rye bread, yogurt, egg, tomato,
- rye bread, ham, olives,
- rye bread, egg, gherkins,
- rye bread, cottage cheese, tuna, pepper
- melon, prosciutto ham, handful of almonds,
- banana, 300 ml of plain yogurt,
- pineapple, handful of hazelnuts, cottage cheese,
- cottage cheese, avocado, handful of walnuts,
- handful of almonds, plain yogurt, a piece of reduced-fat cheese, raw carrot,
- boiled egg, spelt bread, tomato,
- fried egg, buckwheat bread and half of a raw pepper,
- boiled egg, tomato and a few soaked almonds,
- boiled egg, 5 walnuts, a few gherkins,
- prosciutto, reduced-fat cheese, slice of rye bread, cupful of olives,
- yogurt and plain oat flakes,
- turkey breast, fresh salami, slice of rye bread, 300 ml plain yogurt, pickled mushrooms,
- cottage cheese with avocado, pickled pepper,
- boiled egg, slice of rye bread, 2 gherkins,
- cottage cheese with avocado, slice of rye bread, pickled pepper.

Eggs

Start the day with a fried egg or, even better, a boiled egg which doesn't contain any added fat. An egg contains 6 grams of high-quality protein and 14 important nutrients, such as zinc, iron, vitamins A, D, E and B12. And egg has a GI of 0. Because it is rich in protein, it makes you feel full.

Volunteers who participated in a study in Missouri ate two eggs with toast every morning. Another group was offered a bread roll with cream cheese and a little yogurt. Both breakfasts contained the same number of calories, but the one with eggs included more protein and less carbohydrate. The glycaemic index of the first breakfast was 15 and of the second 33. The women who ate eggs, did not feel hungry until lunchtime, ate less at lunch and felt less hungry even in the afternoon.*

*Summarised from: *Reader's Digest: Food Heals.*

Advice: If after breakfast your energy still falls, you have probably eaten too much protein and carbohydrate and not enough vegetables. This happens to me if I eat two fried eggs, a slice of rye bread and no vegetables. This is why you should have a few preserved olives or half a raw pepper with your breakfast.

Advice: If you have a sedentary job, you can replace bread with soaked nuts – in the evening, soak almonds in a glass of water and pour the water away in the morning. The almonds become soft and easier to digest. Their glycaemic index is only 15.

You don't have the time, or you are not used to eating breakfast? Have a tasty protein smoothie instead and add to it sour fruit or vegetables. Mix 200 ml of yogurt, add fresh parsley or cucumber, a pinch of salt and drink it down – a refreshing start of the day. You can replace the smoothie with a protein shake.

The morning and afternoon mini meal

Small meals in between the main meals are of key importance for the body not to feel a shortage and starvation. If you miss meals, the next meal will be preserved by your body for "hard times". But don't think big meals! In the past, when people worked physically in the fields, they could afford to have a big meal mid-morning. But times have changed, these days we sit most of the time and need mini meals.

In the morning, eat fruit and protein and in the afternoon vegetables and protein.

Fruit has a lot of sugar and that is why sometimes people who are very sensitive to carbohydrates feel hungry after only half an hour. See: Why it is not sensible to eat fruit in the evening on page 104.

A few suggestions for the morning mini meal:

- a pear with a slice (30 g) of young cheese,**
- 200 g fat free yogurt (no sweeteners) with fruits of the forest (strawberries, raspberries or blackberries),**
- a skewer of fresh fruit (grapes, pineapple, strawberries, mandarin, etc.) and a glass of skimmed milk,
- cherries and almonds – a handful of each,
- a nectarine (or a similar seasonal fruit) and 15 g (two tablespoons) of ground hazelnuts,**
- a handful of nuts (around 10 almonds, pistachios or peanuts) and a half of a smallish avocado with lemon juice,**
- half an apple, a piece of low-fat cheese,
- a handful of soaked almonds, plain yogurt,
- half a banana* and 300 ml of plain yogurt,
- a handful of walnuts and 100 g of low-fat cheese,
- a pineapple, reduced-fat cheese – up to 100 g.

*A banana has a GI of 60, and yogurt only 15. 60 + 15 = 75: 2 foods = 37.5 – you will still get hungry soon; add a few almonds: 60 + 15 + 15 = 90: 3 foods = 30 – and now your blood sugar stays level and you feel wonderful.

A few suggestions for the afternoon mini meal:

- cheese spread with chilli on two celery sticks,
- 1 slice of prosciutto ham with 200 g of melon (or 200 g of melon with 2 slices of lean ham or 1 slice of turkey breast with 1 slice of low-fat cheese),**
- 100 g low-fat cottage cheese (1 % fat) with fruits of the forest (strawberries, blackberries, raspberries), 1 hard-boiled egg and fried wholemeal wheat bread,**
- 1 slice of toasted wholemeal bread with a green salad leaf, a slice of feta cheese, a slice of tomato, a slice or red onion, salt and pepper,**
- steak tartare on rye bread, pepper,
- 100 g tomato with 100 low-fat mozzarella, basil and lemon juice,**
- 200 g fresh vegetables, dressed with a low-calorie spicy sauce,**
- 100 g grapes and 2 slices of lean ham,**
- 100 g tomato and 30 g reduced-fat cheese (up to 25% fat),**
- a handful of hazelnuts, a piece of reduced-fat cheese,
- a handful of almonds, a piece of mozzarella,
- cheese wrapped in prosciutto, a cup of olives,
- cottage cheese with avocado – thin it out with yogurt (add herbs and salt) and pickled pepper,
- cottage cheese with tuna (no more than once a week), gherkins.

** *NeoLife: Success guide – the science of successful weight loss.*

Advice: During the afternoon, you can eat acidic fruit (fruit with a GI under 30) and protein, e.g. blueberries and yogurt. The yogurt annuls the sugar in the blueberries. In the afternoon avoid watermelon, grapes and all other fruit with a GI over 30. See also: The glycaemic index of fruit on page 105.

Coffee, cappuccino and ice-coffee

Coffee has a GI of 0. It can stimulate cell metabolism, and this is why we feel good after having a coffee. One or two coffees a day can benefit you. Drink coffee without sugar and avoid coffee replacements.

Is there a coffee vending machine within reach?

Two colleagues, both young mothers and friends, are trying to lose weight together. They are encouraging each other on their way to an ideal figure. They don't eat anything at work, just have a few coffees, mochaccinos and cappuccinos. But in spite of the fact that they are eating practically nothing, the kilograms refuse to budge.

This also happens to a lady who only has a cappuccino for dinner – the one you buy in sachets. Nothing to eat, only a few sips of cappuccino, but the kilograms refuse to go, in spite of the fact that she hardly eats and watches what she eats. Where lies the problem?

Cappuccino is a dessert and ice-coffee is also a dessert!

The same applies to everything that comes out of a drink vending machine. We are living in an "instant" era. Everything has become semi-prepared. You press a button and hey presto, there it is. All things instant are filled with various forms of sugar (on the label it says carbohydrates) which all cause an attack of severe hunger and inability to lose weight.

What happens in our body when we have a drink from a vending machine?

Suddenly, a lot of sugar enters our blood and needs to be "removed" from the bloodstream. Our body releases insulin, which controls the blood sugar level, but because we are not doing physical work, we are not using this sugar and the insulin "stashes" it into our fat cells for later, when we need the energy. Sadly, insulin also causes hunger attacks. As soon as the sugar has been stored in fat cells, we again get the message: "Eat something – something sweet!"

Are you familiar with the feeling of saliva building up in your mouth?

We never crave a carrot, always something sweet. But this desire for something sweet can be successfully controlled, you just need to know how. See also: The principle of the medium glycaemic index on page 101.

Advice: If you don't have the time to eat in-between meals, you can consume protein bars.

Pay attention to the content of protein, vitamins, minerals and fibre. Fruit bars are not suitable as an in-between meal because they are an energy bomb!

If a protein bar contains linseed, brown rice and oats, you will consume fibre. Fibre swells up in your stomach and ensures that you feel full for a long time; in addition, it helps with detoxification and the removal of waste from your body.

Good sources of fibre:

- Oats encourage the detoxification of liver and act against cholesterol.
- Besides fibre, linseed also contains lignans and ALA omega-3 fatty acid. These are omega-3s, which have a beneficial effect on cell metabolism. Lignans act as a strong antioxidant and help strengthen the immune system. Research has shown that linseed also has a preventative effect on certain cancers, such as cancer of the large intestine, prostate cancer, breast cancer and cervical cancer. Lignans are plant nutrients (phytonutrients) which can help in the balancing of hormones. They compete with oestrogen and help ease menopausal symptoms, such as hot flushes. Lignans can also help with lowering the release of cortisol and alleviating diabetes, as well as preventing its development. In addition, lignans can prevent hair loss and even help in hair restoration.

How to put together the main meal so that you don't get an attack of hunger in the afternoon

It doesn't matter when your main meal is, what is important is to eat it within one hour (because of the release of insulin, the hunger hormone).

Clear soups, that are very popular in some parts of the world, can be enriched with dumplings or noodles made by mixing wholemeal flour and eggs (GI 23), pouring the mixture into the soup into the desired shape and letting them cook; white noodles, on the other hand, have a GI of 55. You can eat as much salad as you wish – either as a starter or at the end of the meal, it doesn't matter. You can dress the salad with olive or pumpkin oil.

Divide your plate into three equal parts – like the Mercedes symbol – and put in the individual parts the same quantity of protein, carbohydrates and cooked vegetables:

- 1/3 of vegetables,
- 1/3 of pasta or rice,
- 1/3 meat.

*Summarised from: Dr Richard F. Heller and Dr Rachael F. Heller, *The Carbohydrate Addict's Lifespan Program: A Personalized Plan for Becoming Slim, Fit, and Healthy in Your 40s, 50s, 60s, and Beyond.*

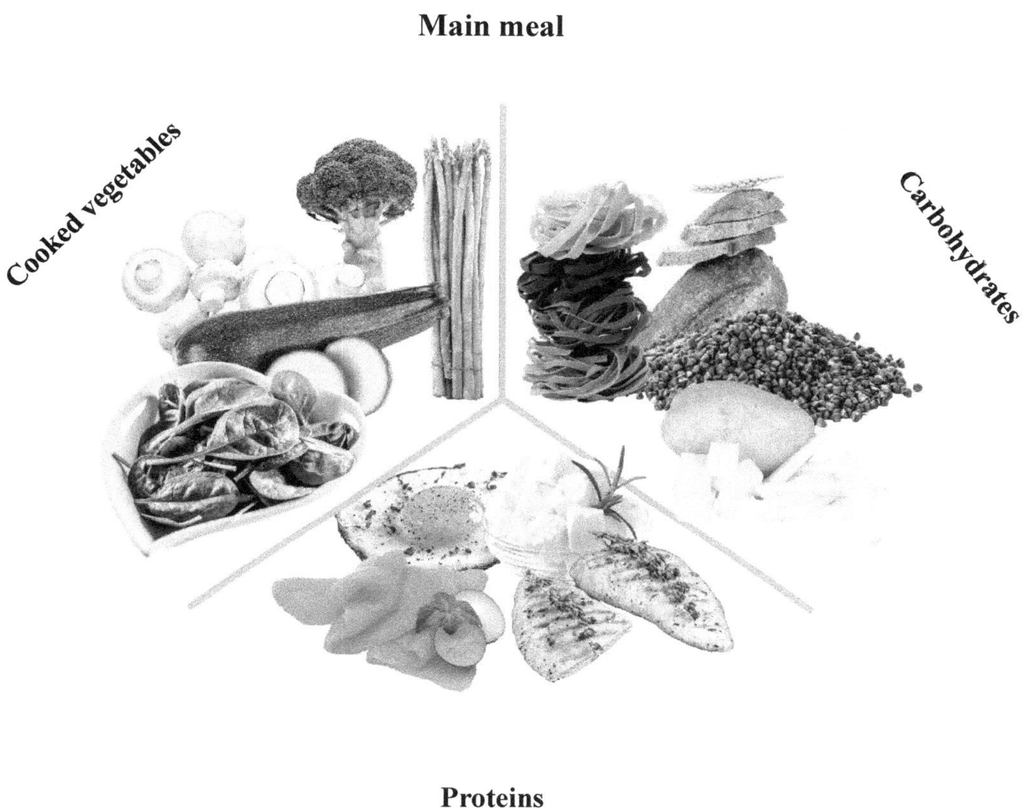

The cooked vegetables are necessary because of the fibre. Cooked vegetables include string beans, broccoli, cauliflower, fried courgettes and mushrooms.

Carbohydrates (the food that causes hunger) include potatoes, pasta, rice. You speed up weight loss if you limit this group to a minimum or, even better, consume wholemeal pasta and unrefined rice, which both have a low glycaemic index. When your family has a celebration, you can have the cake, but don't have pasta and potatoes. As far as potatoes are concerned, it is actually better to exclude them while you are trying to lose weight.

Proteins include meat, fish, milk, yogurt, etc. If you are still hungry after the first helping, you can fill your plate again, but in the same proportions: 1/3 vegetables, 1/3 pasta and 1/3 meat.

If you stick to this rule, you will not get hungry an hour after lunch and you will not feel you need something sweet. After a few days, your body will become balanced and will no longer demand sweet things, so keep going those two or three days and then the kilograms will start melting away.*

*Summarised from: Dr Richard F. Heller and Dr Rachael F. Heller, *The Carbohydrate Addict's Lifespan Program: A Personalized Plan for Becoming Slim, Fit, and Healthy in Your 40s, 50s, 60s, and Beyond.*

Advice: When you don't have enough protein at lunch, e.g. when you are eating a stew, drink 200 ml of plain yogurt as a starter or have a handful of almonds. Protein is the key to feeling full.

A few ideas for lunches that will help you feel full:

- wholemeal spaghetti, cooked "al dente", broccoli, a sauce made with chicken + salad,
- roast chicken, string beans, boiled rice + salad,
- goulash, polenta, fried sauerkraut + salad,
- sausage, potatoes cooked in their skin, boiled broccoli + salad,
- risotto with meat and peas, fried mushrooms + salad,
- fish, kale, potatoes + salad,
- courgettes and mushrooms fried with onion, roast meat (any meat), buckwheat kasha cooked in salty water + salad,
- risotto (oat rice or wholemeal rice or basmati) with prawns, kale or some other cooked vegetable + salad,
- mushrooms fried with onions, add some grated courgettes and at the end of cooking two eggs + salad,
- fry a fish fillet in butter; to get crispy skin, dip it in wholemeal flour before cooking; cooked kale + tomato salad with onions,
- chicken fillet fried in butter, add 3 courgette slices + salad,
- fry some onion in butter, add tomato and pepper; let it cook a little; break 2 eggs into the pan + salad,
- spinach omelette (two eggs, steamed spinach) + salad,
- roast chicken thigh, boiled brown rice, broccoli + salad,
- omelette with mozzarella and chives (one egg, low-fat mozzarella and chives) + salad,
- grilled fillet of sole with lemon slices, string beans + salad,
- chicken meat, rice with peas, fried mushrooms + salad,
- fish fillet, rice with peas, kale + salad,
- fish fillet, rice with peas, fried courgettes + salad.

Advice: As you can see, there is no dessert. But let me give you some comfort – you don't have to give up desserts completely. On page 146 you can find desserts for slimming, which can be enjoyed as part of lunch without feeling guilty. This means that the whole meal must be eaten within an hour. Even though you will be having a dessert, you will not get hungry in the afternoon. But if you still have a craving for sugar, this means that you have had too many carbohydrates at lunch (rice, pasta, etc.) and not enough protein. If this happens, have 200 ml of yogurt or a few soaked almonds.

The most important meal of the day is the evening meal

After two hours of solid sleep, the growth hormone starts to be released, which reshapes us while we sleep. The growth hormone uses stored fat and transforms it into energy. More about the growth hormone on page 199.

I recommend you eat protein and vegetables for the evening meal: prosciutto, yogurt, cottage cheese, almonds and cucumbers, salad, kohlrabi, etc., as in this way your body will have the building blocks for making new cells, and the process of burning fat will also begin.

People who insist on only salad in the evening, begin to sag with time. The skin on their faces sags, as does their chest, backside, etc. And who wants everything to sag? This is why your evening meal should consist of proteins and vegetables. There have to be vegetables, otherwise the protein will acidify your body.

A few ideas for a tasty evening meal:

- prosciutto ham, piece of cheese, handful of almonds, olives,
- boiled egg, gherkins,
- reduced-fat yogurt, almonds, reduced-fat cheese,
- cottage cheese, add some salt with herbs and a yogurt, pepper,
- almonds and yogurt,
- asparagus with an egg,
- egg, 5 pistachios, 1 small carrot, 200 ml yogurt,
- fish – e.g. trout, spinach, 5 walnuts
- cottage cheese, avocado, handful of almonds, 5 strawberries
- cottage cheese, blueberries, 10 peanuts,
- egg, pepper, cup of fruits of the forest,
- prosciutto ham, mozzarella, olives, 5 walnuts.

Advice: The last meal of the day should ideally be eaten 2 or 3 hours before bed. If there is a long gap between meals – particularly between the evening meal and breakfast – the first meal you eat will be fully stored for the "bad times". The body will start storing. If nothing else, have 300 ml of plain yogurt or 3 spoonfuls of cottage cheese thinned with plain yogurt in the evening.

Slimming menus

DAY ONE:

• breakfast: handful of soaked almonds, cheese, cucumbers,

• mini meal: yogurt 1.3 % fat and a nectarine,

• lunch: wholemeal pasta with chicken sauce, broccoli, salad,

• mini meal: handful of almonds and a yogurt,

• evening meal: cottage cheese, avocado, handful of almonds, 5 strawberries.

SECOND DAY:

• breakfast: rye bread, yogurt, egg, tomato,

• mini meal: prosciutto ham on rye bread and a slice of melon,

• lunch: risotto (oat rice or wholemeal rice) with prawns, kale, salad,

• mini meal: handful of walnuts and 100 g of reduced-fat cheese,

• evening meal: cottage cheese, add some salt with dried herbs mixed in and yogurt, pepper.

THIRD DAY:

• breakfast: ham with a piece of cheese, olives,

• mini meal: mozzarella, tomato,

• lunch: roast chicken, one potato (can be replaced with rye bread), cauliflower with pumpkin oil drizzled over, salad,

• mini meal: ham, pepper,

• evening meal: prosciutto, piece of cheese, handful of almonds, olives.

The interval between meals should be around 3 hours.

Begin the day with 650 ml of water and the Fountain of Youth exercise. More about the Fountain of Youth on page 224.

FIRST DAY

Breakfast:

• 2 tablespoons cottage cheese with 200 ml plain yoghurt mixed in

• 10 preserved olives, stuffed with almonds

Coffee without sugar

GI: 0 + 15 + 15 + 15 = 45: 4 = 11.25

Mini meal:

• lean cottage cheese – 4 spoonfuls

• 10 gherkins

GI: 0 + 15 = 15: 2 = 7.5

Lunch:

• wholemeal macaroni "al dente"

• tinned tuna

• peas

• cucumber salad

Coffee without sugar

GI: 45 + 0 + 30 + 15 = 90: 4 = 22.5

Mini meal:

• 10 almonds

• coffee with a little ice-cream

GI: 15 + 0 + 60 = 75: 3 = 25

Evening meal:

• reduced-fat cheese

• 10 olives, stuffed with almonds

GI: 0 + 15 + 15 = 30: 3 = 10

SECOND DAY

Breakfast:

• 1 pepper

• 3 tablespoons of cottage cheese mixed with plain yogurt

• 15 almonds

Coffee without sugar

GI: 15 + 0 + 15 + 15 = 45: 4 = 11.25

Lunch:

At the children's request, we made cream sauce with chicken and wide white noodles – very unhealthy – GI at least 65, but combining them with vegetables can reduce the sugar considerably:

• wide noodles made with white flour

• chicken in a cream sauce

• chicken bits cooked in butter

• fried courgettes

• green salad

Coffee without sugar

GI: 70 + 50 + 0 + 15 + 15 = 150: 5 = 30

Evening meal:

• low-fat cottage cheese

• 5 olives stuffed with almonds

• green salad and tomato

GI: 0 + 15 + 15+ 15 + 30 = 75: 5 = 15

Mini meal:

• 1 nectarine

• 200 ml yogurt

GI: 30 + 15 = 45: 2 = 22.5

Mini meal:

• low-fat cottage cheese

• 15 soaked almonds

GI: 0 + 15 = 15: 23 = 7.5

THIRD DAY

Breakfast:

• 2 tablespoons of cottage cheese mixed with 200 ml of plain yogurt

• 10 peanuts

• 5 preserved olives

• 2 small tomatoes

Coffee without sugar

GI: 0 + 15 + 15 + 15 + 30 = 75: 5 = 15

Mini meal:

• coffee with milk and a little ice-cream (less than a scoop)

• 10 almonds

GI = 0 + 65 + 15 = 80: 3 = 26.7

Lunch:

wholemeal spaghetti “al dente”

chicken cooked in a sauce

fried courgettes

2 pieces of chicken cooked in butter

tomato salad

Coffee without sugar

GI: 45 + 20 + 15 + 0 + 30 = 110: 5 = 22

Mini meal:

2 spoonfuls of cottage cheese with yogurt

10 olives stuffed with almonds

GI: 0 + 15 = 15: 2 = 7.5

Evening meal:

• cottage cheese with yogurt

• 10 olives stuffed with almonds

GI: 0 + 15 + 15 = 30: 3 = 10

FOURTH DAY

Breakfast:

- 2 tablespoons of cottage cheese mixed with 200 ml of plain yogurt
- 15 soaked almonds
- 10 gherkins
- Coffee without sugar

GI: 0 + 15 + 15 + 0 = 30: 4 = 7.5

Lunch:

As I was very hungry, I ate 5 almonds and drank at least 300 ml of water before I began cooking. I had no problems cooking and ate my lunch normally (instead of gulping it down).

I made risotto:

- rice – white (you must be careful not to overcook it), peas, a few mushrooms, a chicken fillet
- courgettes with mushrooms as an accompaniment
- tomato salad with a lot of pumpkin oil
- Coffee without sugar and a scoop of ice-cream

GI: 70 + 30 + 15 + 0 + 15 + 15 + 15 + 0 + 60 = 220: 9 = 24.44

Evening meal:

- boiled egg
- gherkins

GI: 0 + 15 = 15: 2 = 7.5

Mini meal:

Because I had no time to eat, I had:

- a cupful of blueberries
- 300 ml yogurt

GI: 25 + 15 = 40: 2 = 20

Mini meal:

- a very large piece of reduced-fat cheese
- 3 small tomatoes
- 300 ml yogurt

GI: 0 + 30 + 15 = 45: 3 = 15

FIFTH DAY

Breakfast:

• tinned mackerel with vegetables – I don't really like this, but I ate it

• 15 soaked almonds

• 5 gherkins

• 200 ml milk

• Coffee without sugar

GI: 25 + 15 + 15 + 30 = 85: 4 = 21.25

Mini meal:

• 1 nectarine

• 10 soaked almonds

GI = 35 + 15 = 50: 2 = 25

Lunch:

• trout in batter made from wholemeal flour and an egg (delicious)

• string beans

• tomato salad

You can have a potato in its skin, but this will raise your blood sugar. If possible, have a slice of rye bread instead.

Coffee without sugar

GI: 0 + 0 + 45 + 15 + 30 = 90: 5 = 18

Mini meal:

• 2 spoonfuls of low-fat cottage cheese

• 10 almonds

GI: 0 + 15 = 15: 2 = 7.5

Evening meal:

• 2 pieces of cheese (the size of a wafer)

• 15 olives

• 0.5 l plain yogurt

GI: 0 + 15 + 15 = 30: 3 = 10

SIXTH DAY

Breakfast:

- low-fat cottage cheese – 3 spoonfuls
- 10 gherkins
- 10 soaked almonds
- Coffee without sugar

GI: 0 + 15 + 15 = 30: 3 = 10

Mini meal:

- 15 raw peanuts
- 300 ml milk

GI: 15 + 30 = 45: 2 = 22.5

Lunch:

- fish – freshwater sheatfish (the size of a palm of a hand) fried in butter
- rice and peas – 1 spoonful of rice and 3 spoonfuls of peas
- 4 slices of courgette
- tomato salad with onion and pumpkin oil
- Coffee without sugar

GI: 0 + 15 + 70 + 15 + 30 + 15 = 145: 6 = 24.17

Mini meal:

- 10 soaked almonds
- 0.5 l yogurt

GI: 15 + 15 = 30: 2 = 15

Evening meal:

- 1 tablespoon of low-fat cottage cheese
- 3 gherkins
- 1 tomato
- piece of reduced-fat cheese the size of a large wafer
- 300 ml plain yogurt

GI: 0 + 15 + 30 + 0 + 15 = 60: 5 = 12

Advice 1: I recommend you take some vitamin C supplement every day because it activates the melting of old fat, omega-3 fatty acid because it influences the hormonal balance and a multivitamin and mineral supplement. Pay special attention to B vitamins, chromium, calcium, magnesium and iron.*

Take the glycaemic index into account and prepare tasty meals. The meals on the following pages will help you to keep your blood sugar level and consequently you will feel full.

Advice 2: Vinegar reduces the desire for food. It contains acetic acid, which slows the metabolism of starchy foods. This reduces the GI of foods by as much as 20 percent. As a result, your feeling of fullness lasts longer. You don't need to drink vinegar before meals, it is enough to consume a salad as part of your meals, dressed with salt, oil and vinegar or consume pickled vegetables.

Recipes for losing weight

Chicken, broccoli, potatoes, salad

The overall glycaemic index of the meal: 31.25

If you want to accelerate weight loss, eat only vegetables and meat and a slice of rye bread instead of potatoes. This way the overall GI will be only 18.75.

GI: 0 + 15 + 95 + 15 = 125: 5 = 31.25

Cooking time: 30 minutes

Ingredients:

- chicken breast
- dandelion as a salad
- potato
- broccoli
- onion
- garlic
- cumin

Preparation:

Fry the **chicken** in a bit of butter, add 1 chopped onion and a few garlic cloves. Add nothing but salt. If needed, add some water to prevent it from burning.

Chop the potatoes into small pieces and fry in some butter. Add salt and cumin. Cook until soft and if needed, add a small quantity of water.

Cook the **broccoli** in a small quantity of salted water. Make sure you do not overcook it, because starch is released from it during cooking. Boil for only a few minutes.

A hint: If you want to lose weight faster, eat a slice of rye bread instead of the potatoes. This will reduce the overall GI of the meal. Instead of 31.25 (with the potatoes), the GI will be only 18.75. That really will be a slimming meal.

Wide noodles, sauce, chicken, mushrooms and a cabbage salad

Overall glycaemic index of the meal: 22.88

GI: 70 + 15 + 0 + 15 + 15 + 5 + 45 = 160: 7 = 22.88

Preparation: 10 minutes

Cooking time: 20 minutes

Ingredients:

- wide noodles
- mushrooms
- chicken
- cabbage as salad
- onion
- seasoning, herbs and spices
- flour for the sauce

Preparation:

First, fry the onion in a bit of butter, chop the meat into small pieces and fry it. Boil some water for the noodles. In another pan, fry another onion. Add the mushrooms, which can be fresh or frozen. Salt the mushrooms just before serving.

When the meat is cooked, mix 2 tablespoons of wholemeal flour with water; you can add a spoonful of cream or cream cheese with herbs to enhance the flavour; add the condiments – salt with dried herbs, oregano, a little sweet paprika.

When the water for the noodles is boiling, cook the pasta according to the instructions – make sure you do not overcook it because this releases additional starch.

Grate the raw cabbage and serve. This lunch is healthy, tasty and will keep you full for quite a few hours. Enjoy!

A hint: When making sauces, do not overdo the cream. One spoonful a day is allowed; anything more will block your metabolism and result in either the end of weight loss or even weight gain.

Wholemeal spaghetti with chicken sauce and broccoli

Overall glycaemic index of the meal: 20

GI: 45 + 15 + 0+ 15 +15 + 5 + 45 = 140: 7 = 20

Preparation: 10 minutes

Cooking time: 20 minutes

Ingredients:

- wholemeal spaghetti
- broccoli
- chicken
- salad
- onion
- seasoning, spices and herbs
- flour and cheese spread for the sauce

Preparation:

First, fry the onion in a little butter, chop the meat into small pieces and fry it. Boil some water for the spaghetti. Put a little water in another pan for the broccoli.

When the meat is cooked, mix 2 spoonfuls of wholemeal flour with water – you can add 1 spoonful of cream or cream cheese – add salt with dried herbs, oregano, a little sweet paprika.

When the water boils, add the spaghetti and cook according to the instructions on the packet – make sure not to overcook, because this releases additional starch.

This lunch is healthy, tasty and will keep you full for a few hours. Enjoy!

A hint: If you are still hungry and want more, then take just a little of everything – a little bit of the sauce with the meat, a small quantity of spaghetti and a little broccoli. The same quantity of each. You can have as much salad as you want.

Fried sauerkraut, meat and cabbage

Overall glycaemic index of the meal: 14.5

GI: 0 + 42.5 + 15 + 15 + 0 = 72.5: 3 = 14.5

Preparation: 10 minutes

Cooking time: 20 minutes

Ingredients:

- beef, onion, garlic and salt

For cabbage (due to the potatoes, the cabbage has a GI of 42):

- 5 potatoes
- 2 handfuls of sliced cabbage
- salt
- a little butter for flavour

For the fried sauerkraut:

- 0.5 kg sauerkraut
- 2 onions
- a little butter
- salt with dried vegetables, sweet paprika, cumin

Preparation:

Meat: First fry the meat. Add a lot of garlic, onion and salt.

Cabbage: Peel the potatoes – one potato per person. Cut it into thin slices. Cook it in salted water, add 2 handfuls of sliced cabbage, salt and salt with dried vegetables. Cook for 20 minutes. When cooked, pour the excess water into a cup, and mash the potato and cabbage. If needed, add some water. Add a small cube of butter for flavour.

Fried sauerkraut: Fry the onions in butter. Add the sauerkraut, cumin, salt and paprika and fry on a moderate heat. If necessary, add some water. Cook for 15 minutes.

A hint: If you want to avoid getting hungry in the afternoon, have only a little of the cabbage and potato mix and concentrate on the fried sauerkraut and meat.

Macaroni with tuna and peas

Overall glycaemic index of the meal: 19

GI: 45 + 35 + 0 + 15 + 0 = 95: 5 = 19

Preparation: 5 minutes

Cooking time: 10 minutes

Ingredients:

- wholemeal pasta
- peas
- 4 tins of tuna
- garlic
- reduced-fat cheese

Preparation:

Cook the pasta in boiling salted water. Make sure not to overcook it. Add peas to the same water. As peas are a protein, use a sufficient amount of water. Meanwhile, heat the tuna and add some chopped garlic and when the pasta is cooked, mix the pasta into the tuna.

Serve with a salad. Grate some reduced-fat cheese over the dish.

A hint: Avoid full-fat parmesan as it contains too much saturated fat.

Gnocchi Bolognese, broccoli, salad and fried chicken pieces

Overall glycaemic index of the meal: 35

GI: 70 + 45 + 0 + 15 + 15 = 145: 5 = 35

Preparation: 10 minutes

Cooking time: 10 minutes

Ingredients for 4 persons:

- 2 packets of gnocchi
- Bolognese sauce
- 1 chicken fillet
- 1 broccoli
- salad

Preparation:

Get two pans, one for the gnocchi and the other one for the broccoli. Boil some water in them. Add a spoonful of salt to the pan for broccoli. You do not need to salt the water for the gnocchi.

While waiting for the water to boil, chop the meat, beat it lightly and rub with a bit of salt. Heat some butter in a frying pan. Dip the meat in wholemeal flour and fry it – a few minutes on each size.

Heat the ready-made Bolognese sauce.

As soon as the water boils, add the chopped broccoli. Cook 4 to 5 minutes. Do not overcook it, because this will increase its GI.

When the water for the gnocchi is boiling, add the gnocchi. They are cooked within a few moments – as soon as they float, they need to be taken out of the water. Add them to the Bolognese sauce and gently mix them in.

Make the salad.

A hint: If you want your blood sugar to remain level, eat just 6 gnocchi, the rest of your meal should consist of the vegetables and meat. If you eat a plateful of gnocchi and use the vegetables as an accompaniment, omitting the meat, your blood sugar will rise dramatically; and later, you will get very hungry.

Cottage cheese dumplings

Overall glycaemic index of the meal: 15

GI: 45 + 0 + 0 + 0 + 30 =75: 5 = 15

Preparation: 10 minutes

Cooking time: 20 minutes

Ingredients for 5 people:

- wholemeal flour
- 150 g butter
- 5 eggs
- 0.5 kg cottage cheese
- 10 plums

Preparation:

Mix together the cottage cheese, melted butter, eggs and salt. Add flour to make a dough. Divide it into equal parts and place one plum on each – can be frozen plums. Make the dumplings. Cook them in salted water for 20 minutes.

A hint: Eat some vegetables as a starter, it will make you full for longer. It can be a bit of cabbage or fresh salad.

Sunday lunch with buckwheat kasha

Overall glycaemic index of the meal: 19

GI: 0 + 15 + 15 + 50 + 15 = 95: 5 = 19

Cooking time:

- roast meat – 2 hours in the oven
- accompaniment, salad, broccoli – 25 minutes

Ingredients for 5 people:

- veal – 700 g
- broccoli – 1
- salad – 1 head
- rice – 5 handfuls

Preparation:

Place the meat in a roasting tin, rub with salt, add some butter and garlic and roast at 200°C for two hours.

Fry the onion in butter, add 5 handfuls or rice and fry for a few minutes, add a few mushrooms for flavour (either frozen or dried). Pour some water over and add oregano, salt, half a teaspoonful of paprika and salt with dried vegetables. Cook for 18 minutes. While the rice is cooking, boil some water in another pan and add a spoonful of salt; when it boils, put in the broccoli and cook for 5 minutes. The broccoli has to be "al dente", otherwise it will release starch which will soon make you hungry.

A hint: Make the quantities of the meat, rice and broccoli on your plate the same. You can have as much salad as you wish.

Stuffed courgettes (an excellent vegetarian meal)

Overall glycaemic index of the meal: 15

GI: 15 + 15 + 15 + 0 + 30 = 75: 5 = 15

Preparation: 20 minutes

Cooking time: 20 minutes

Ingredients:

- 4 smallish courgettes
- onion
- butter
- mushrooms (4 fresh mushrooms or half a kg of frozen porcini mushrooms)
- cheese
- tomato salad

Preparation:

Fry the onion in butter. Add thinly sliced mushrooms and fry. Meanwhile, cut the courgettes in half lengthwise. Spoon out the soft centre so that you get a little boat. Add the courgette flesh to the mushrooms and fry until the water evaporates. Add salt, oregano and parsley.

Put the courgette boats into a greased narrow roasting dish. Stuff the boats with the fried mushrooms. Grate over some cheese and place in an oven, heated to 180 °C, for 20 minutes.

To make the meal a bit more colourful, serve it with a tomato salad.

Advice: Stuffed courgettes can be eaten as a main vegetarian meal or served as a vegetable accompaniment to roast turkey or veal.

Cottage cheese spread with avocado

Ingredients:

- cottage cheese – the best is lumpy, low-fat cottage cheese – 1 pot
- avocado – if it is not soft, place it on the windowsill for a few days
- salt
- plain yogurt – 100 ml for 500 g of cottage cheese
- to add some colour – a little parsley or chives (if you don't have any, don't worry)

Preparation:

Put the cottage cheese into a mixer, add the peeled avocado without the stone and some salt, then mix them together. Add some yogurt, as much as needed to get the right consistency. So simple and yet so tasty!

This spread can be served on wholemeal bread or in a separate dish as an accompaniment to some cold cuts. I often make it for my evening meal and eat it together with vegetables – a red pepper or gherkins.

When the avocado is mixed with the cottage cheese – an animal protein source – the spread becomes an excellent treasure house for the regeneration of the body and helps with the production of the growth hormone.

Egg baked in avocado

Ingredients for 4 people:

- 2 ripe avocados
- 4 fresh eggs
- pinch of pepper and salt
- 1 spoonful of chopped chives or parsley

Preparation:

Turn the oven to the highest temperature.

Cut the avocados in half and remove the stones. Scoop out approximately two spoonfuls of flesh from the middle, so that the egg fits in the space available.

Place the avocado halves into a small baking dish – they should fit snugly.

Break an egg into each avocado half.

Place the baking dish in the oven and bake for 15 to 20 minutes. The time depends on the size of the avocado and eggs.

Remove from the oven, season with salt and pepper, add the chives or parsley and enjoy!

Serve with rye bread and a glass of plain yogurt.

The overall glycaemic index of this meal is 15.8.

10 + 0 + 5 + 40 + 24 = 79: 5 = 15.8 – a very good meal for losing weight. An even better option is to replace the rye bread with some vegetables – it can be either fresh or pickled cucumbers.

Avocado's glycaemic index is only 10. This is an excellent food that will help to quickly melt fat. Avocado has a wonderful taste if you mix it with cottage cheese or yogurt. Add a little salt and perhaps some paprika. Avocado contains good fats and lots of vitamins B, which calm the body.

Avocado contains:

- all 18 essential amino acids,
- vitamins from the B group – necessary for more energy,
- vitamin E – good for skin and circulation,
- vitamin C – prevents ageing,
- vitamin K – necessary for normal blood clotting – people who often have nose bleeds may have a deficiency of this vitamin,
- magnesium – influences energy production,
- potassium – prevents depression,
- zinc and selenium – help with detoxification,
- carotenoids, which improve the immune system and also act against cancer,
- copper – improves the blood,
- good fats that protect the heart.

Desserts with a low glycaemic index – desserts for losing weight

A HEALTHY CAKE RECIPE*

*Taken from: Michel Montignac: *The Montignac Method.*

Overall glycaemic index: 20

- For 6-8 people.
- Preparation time: 30 minutes, plus cooling time.
- Cooking time: 8 minutes.

Ingredients:

- 310 g dark chocolate (70 % cocoa), broken into pieces, plus another 185 g for the icing
- 10 large eggs, the whites separated from the yolks

Preparation instructions:

Line a round cake tin with a diameter of 20 cm with parchment paper, which should be slightly higher than the edge of the tin. Heat the oven to 250°C (the oven must be really hot).

Melt the broken-up chocolate over steam (approximately 15 to 20 minutes). The dish in which you are melting the chocolate must be dry and should not be in contact with the boiling water.

Whip the egg whites into stiff peaks.

Beat the egg yolks and gently fold them into the melted chocolate. Slowly add the egg whites (2 teaspoons at a time) and fold them in. Quickly but gently stir in the rest of the whites so that you get a light, fluffy mixture. Do not over mix or the cake batter will collapse.

Pour the mixture into the tin, put in the oven and bake for exactly 8 minutes.

Take the cake from the oven and cool it for 30 minutes and then put it in the fridge for at least 12 hours or overnight.

Before serving the cake, tip it onto a large plate. Make the chocolate icing and thinly spread it over the cake. For the icing, simply melt the chocolate over boiling water.

Place the cake in the fridge for 5 minutes. Cut it with a sharp knife, dipped each time in hot water, and serve.

VEGAN CAKE

Overall glycaemic index: 20

Ingredients:

For the base:

- 200 g almonds (GI 15)
- 200 g dates (GI 65)
- pinch of salt (GI 0)

Cream:

- 400 g cashew nuts (GI 45)
- juice of 2 lemons (GI 15)
- 1/2 tsp vanilla (GI 0)
- 100 ml coconut oil (GI 0)
- 100 ml agave syrup (GI 15)
- 250 g blueberries (fresh; if frozen, they have to be defrosted first) (GI 25)

Preparation instructions:

Soak the cashew nuts overnight. For the base, mix all the ingredients into a smooth mixture, but so that it is still nicely crunchy. Test it with your fingers – it is just right when it becomes sticky.

Put the mixture into a cake tin and push it down with your hands.

Strain the cashew nuts and blend them together with the lemon juice, vanilla, coconut oil and agave syrup into a smooth mixture. Put two thirds on top of the base in the tin, then add the blueberries to the remaining third and blend a little again. Add this mixture to the rest of the cake and place it in the freezer for 30 minutes. Serve immediately.

A hint: You can play around and use another type of fruit/nuts, you can also pour melted dark chocolate over the cake; the agave syrup can be replaced with maple syrup, but the GI of maple syrup is 64. Use your imagination!

The cake is very good, and it is a healthy dessert that is almost a full meal. As the overall glycaemic index of the cake is only 20 (add up all the ingredients and divide them with the number of ingredients – 180: 9 = 20), this is an excellent food even for slimming. In order to keep the blood sugar even more stable, have 100 ml of plain yogurt with the cake.

TYROLIAN CHOCOLATE CAKE

*Taken from: Annette Wolter: *Pastries and Cakes*.

Overall glycaemic index: around 20 – depending on the sugar

Ingredients for an elongated cake tin, measuring 30 cm in length:

- 200 g almonds
- 150 g bitter chocolate – 70 % dark chocolate
- 200 g softened butter
- 200 g agave syrup (can be less)
- 6 eggs
- 125 g wholemeal flour
- 1 tsp baking powder (cream of tartar is even better)
- 2 tablespoons of rum
- 200 g chocolate icing – 70 % dark chocolate

Preparation instructions:

Beat the butter until fluffy and slowly add the sugar. Separate egg whites from the egg yolks. Mix the yolks one by one into the butter and sugar mixture. Mix the flour with the baking powder, sieve it into the butter and egg mixture and add the ground almonds and roughly grated chocolate. Mix everything together.

Whip the egg whites until stiff and slowly fold them, together with the rum, into the cake batter.

Heat the oven to 180°C. Grease the tin with butter and sprinkle with breadcrumbs. Pour the batter into the tin, smooth it on top and bake on the middle shelf for 1 hour. Test the cake with a skewer to see if it is done. The cake should rest in the turned-off oven for 10 minutes.

Tip the cake onto a rack. Melt the chocolate for icing in a bain marie and use it to ice the cake.

CHOCOLATE COATED NUTS

*Taken and adapted from: Reinhardt Hess: *Chocolate.*

Overall glycaemic index: 17.5

Ingredients:

- 50 g hazelnuts (GI 15)
- 25 g peeled almonds (GI 15)
- 25 g walnuts (GI 15)
- 200 g dark chocolate with at least 70 % cocoa (GI 25)

Preparation instructions:

Toast the hazelnuts in a frying pan on moderate heat so that the skins come loose. Shake the nuts out of the pan. Lightly toast the almonds and walnuts so that they give off an aroma. Rub the skins off the still warm hazelnuts. Cool all the nuts.

Break the dark chocolate into pieces and melt in a bain marie. Pour some of the melted chocolate into a shallow baking tin (or another rectangular dish). Put the nuts in and then pour the rest of the melted chocolate over them. Let it cool. When the chocolate hardens, break it into pieces.

A hint: This desert is excellent for after lunch. If you have it with a bitter coffee, your taste buds will have a party.

CHOCOLATE MOUSSE

*Taken and adapted from: *Cookery Book for Girls.*

Overall glycaemic index: 12.5

- For 4 people.
- Preparation time: 20 minutes.
- Cooling time: 1 hour or longer.

Ingredients:

- 175 g dark chocolate with at least 70 % cocoa (GI 25)
- 4 eggs (GI 0)

Preparation instructions:

Break the chocolate into pieces and melt it in a bain marie. Stir it frequently. Meanwhile, separate the eggs. Beat the egg yolks until fluffy. Whip the egg whites until stiff (when you turn the bowl, the whites should not run out).

Mix the egg yolks with the melted chocolate. Then carefully fold in the egg whites until the mixture is smooth. Dived into cups and place in the fridge or freezer for at least an hour. The mousse can be served with dark chocolate or a scoop of ice-cream.

CHOCOLATE MOUSSE WITH RASPBERRIES

*Taken from: Michel Montignac: *The Montignac Method.*

Overall glycaemic index: 12.5

Chocolate and raspberries go well together. This simple dessert wonderfully emphasises the flavour and aroma of the raspberries. Like with all mousses, the beaten egg whites must be carefully folded into the rest of the mixture so that the air beaten into them does not escape and the dessert is light and airy.

- For 4 people.
- Preparation time: 20 minutes.
- Cooling time: 4 hours or more.

Ingredients:

- 150 g dark chocolate with at least 70 % cocoa (GI 25)
- 1 tablespoon of cream, heated to room temperature (GI 0)
- 4 eggs – separate the whites from the yolks (GI 0)
- 250 g mashed raspberries (GI 25)

Preparation instructions:

Melt the broken-up chocolate in a bain marie. When it is melted, cool a little and mix in the cream.

Beat the egg yolks until fluffy and mix them into the chocolate mixture. Then fold in the mashed raspberries.

Whip the egg whites into stiff peaks and gradually, a third at a time, gently fold them into the mixture. Make sure not to overmix otherwise the mousse will not be light and airy.

Divide the mousse into 4 suitable dishes. Before serving, put it in the fridge for at least 4 hours so that it cools thoroughly.

BALLS – an excellent sweet with a very low glycaemic index

WALNUT BALLS WITH COCONUT

Overall glycaemic index: 17

Ingredients:

- 180 g ground walnuts (GI 15)
- 180 g dark chocolate (GI 25)
- 50 g desiccated coconut (GI 45)
- 1 egg white (GI 0)
- 2 tablespoons rum (GI 0)*

Mix the walnuts and the chocolate over a very gentle heat until you get a smooth mixture. Add the egg white and rum. Make small balls out of the mixture and roll them in desiccated coconut.

CHOCOLATE BALLS

Overall glycaemic index: 16

Ingredients:

- 3 tablespoons milk (GI 30)
- 125 g dark chocolate (GI 25)
- 50 g butter (GI 0)
- 1 egg yolk (GI 0)
- grated dark chocolate and dark cocoa powder (GI 20)

While mixing chocolate and milk, slowly heat them until the chocolate melts completely. Mix in butter, cool a little and add the egg yolk. Let the mixture rest for a few hours, then make the balls and roll them in the grated chocolate with a little coconut.

ALMOND BALLS

Overall glycaemic index: 11.7

Ingredients:

- 150 g ground almonds (GI 15)
- 150 g grated dark chocolate (GI 25)
- 100 g agave syrup (GI 15)
- 1 egg white (GI 0)
- 3 tablespoons rum (GI 0)
- almond slivers (GI 15)

Grate the chocolate and add the egg white. Mix until smooth, add the almonds, agave syrup and rum. Let the mixture rest for a few hours. Make balls and roll them in crushed almond slivers.

HAZELNUT BALLS

Overall glycaemic index: 13.3

Ingredients:

- 180 g ground hazelnuts (GI 15)
- 100 g agave syrup (GI 15)
- 180 g dark chocolate with at least 70 % cocoa (GI 25)
- 3 tablespoons rum (GI 0)
- 2 egg yolks (GI 0)
- 75 g dark cocoa powder (GI 25)

Grate the chocolate, add the hazelnuts and agave syrup and mix it all until smooth. Add rum and egg yolks and knead thoroughly. Shape into balls and roll them in cocoa. Keep in a cool place.

*10 simple steps to accelerate weight loss **

*Summarised from: Dr Richard F Heller and Dr Rachael F Heller: *The Carbohydrate Addict's Lifespan Program: A Personalized Plan for Becoming Slim, Fit, and Healthy in Your 40s, 50s, 60s, and Beyond.*

1. Drink more water.

2. Exercise more.

3. Avoid food additives and semi-prepared foods.

4. Avoid over the counter medicines.

5. Reduce stress.

6. Sleep at least 7 hours a night.

7. Give up all sweeteners – even the natural ones cause an insulin reaction.

8. Chewing gum and drinking diet drinks without sugar stimulate the release of insulin and the appearance of hunger. Because a lot of saliva is produced, your stomach gets a message that there is a large amount of food coming.

9. Avoid alcohol consumption.

10. Supplement your diet with vitamins, minerals and good oils:

• For metabolising carbohydrates, you need B vitamins (contraceptive tablets use B vitamins in order to be flushed out of the body and as a result of this, the metabolism worsens and cellulite appears).

• Sometimes, the reason for a plateau in weight loss is lack of iron, which helps in the transfer of fat stores to the cells that burn the fat.

• Chromium prevents attacks of unstoppable desire for food.

• Activate the melting of old fat by adding vitamin C.

• Magnesium is the activator of cell metabolism. If you are having muscle cramps, this can be an indicator that you don't have a "match" that would trigger the burning of surplus fat.

• The fats you consume are bound to fibre, which is why you need a sufficient amount of fibre in your diet. At each meal, have some vegetables and fruit.

• The red pigments in peppers, tomatoes, berries – the carotenoids – influence the protection of the thyroid hormone, which is responsible for the good functioning of the thyroid. People who have problems with their thyroid find it a lot harder to lose weight than those whose thyroid is functioning properly.

• Omega-3 fatty acids help with weight loss by accelerating metabolism, prevent the loss of muscle mass and increase the sensitivity of insulin receptors. Omega-3 keeps the muscle tissues firm and flexible and has a positive influence on gaining muscle mass and increasing muscle strength (at least 3 times a week, eat fish and supplement your diet with a high-quality omega-3 supplement).

Chapter 4. The Thyroid Hormone

I freely express and speak the truth

The thyroid gland is connected to the windpipe, which plays a crucial role in respiration. Breathing is essential for life, starting from a baby's first breath at birth until their final one. It is often expressed that someone breathes out their soul.

Our feelings, such as happiness and sadness, laughter and crying, are also expressed through the throat.

When we are happy, we sing. When we are happy, we speak gently, sweetly. When we are happy, we express our joy via our vocal cords.

When we are unhappy, it is our throat area that feels “tight”. Feelings get stuck in the throat particularly when we cannot say what we feel. We swallow our feelings, our pride, our tears. Especially the tears we swallow get trapped in the throat and we feel as if we are suffocating. And this results in a blockage in the throat chakra area. Unexpressed feelings cause anger and disappointment. Anger is a fire that dries out moisture; the moisture we should have cried out is dried out by fire. And the more this fire grows, the more something makes us angry, the more our tissue and thyroid energy also dry out.

And that is when we get a problem. It starts with recurring colds, continues with occasional loss of voice, hoarseness, a lump in the throat and then, in the long term, we “produce” thyroid problems. When this happens, we comfort ourselves with excuses: “I work with people, I talk a lot, I’ve caught a virus again, the virus came back, I have a chronic inflammation of my glands, I am prone to hoarseness …”

These are a million excuses, but the truth lies elsewhere. We don’t want to see it and we tell ourselves the problem will get better.

But your body has started rebelling, it has had enough of you denying your feelings; enough of you swallowing your tears; enough of you being consumed by anger; enough of you not standing up for yourself and raising your voice.

In her book *You Can Heal Your Life*, Louise L. Hay says that:

• The **throat** represents our ability to "speak up" for ourselves, to "ask for what we want," to say "I am," etc. Throat problems usually mean we don't feel we have the right to do these things. We feel inadequate to stand up for ourselves.

• A sore throat always represents anger. If we also have a cold, our mind is confused. A **sore throat** usually means we are so angry we cannot speak.

• The throat also represents the creative flow in the body. Through the throat, we express creativity. When our creativity is stifled and disabled, we often have problems with our throat. Everyone knows people who spend all their life living for others. They never do what they want to do. They are always trying to please their mother/father/husband/lover/boss/children. If a person has tonsillitis or thyroid problems, it means her creativity is suppressed she cannot do what she would like to do.

• The throat energy centre – the fifth chakra – is the place in the body where changes occur. When we resist change or we are in the middle of a change or we are trying to change ourselves, there is often a lot going on in our throat.

In his book *Ancient Secret of the Fountain of Youth,* Peter Kelder also talks about the voice, which expresses our strength. He says we have all heard the shrill and weak voice of an old man. When our voice gets like that, this is sadly a certain sign of our physical decay. The fifth chakra controls our vocal cords and is directly connected with the first chakra in our sexual centre. All the chakras are connected among themselves, but these two are "yoked" together. That which influences one, influences the other. So, if a man's voice is shrill and weak, it means his sexual strength is weak. All that is necessary to accelerate the first and fifth chakra, as well as all the others, is to regularly perform the five rites of rejuvenation – the Fountain of Youth. More about the Fountain of Youth on page 224.

When we are most resisting change, when we are afraid and our fear may be connected to our physical survival, or when we are under stress and if stress originates in our relationship with our partner, this energy is reflected in our voice and often we also have problems with passing stools – it is as if we want to keep our life's waste inside.

What burdens you the most?

Why do you cry? Which relationship is making you act like you are happy, but inside you know that you deserve more, that you deserve love, acceptance and open discussion? Which relationship has upset you so much that you cannot go on? And there is no one you can tell because everything looks different to how it is. Your thyroid, your throat, your tonsils, your vocal cords and your throat chakra know – you cannot lie to them. They know the truth.

The truth is painful. Risk, fear and uncertainty hide behind the truth. *How will I manage on my own? Will I be able to live on my own, without a job that is stifling me, but still represents my means of survival? How will my parents receive the truth? Will they judge me? Will they hate me? Will they abandon me if I stand up for my happiness?*

All of these are possible. They may all happen. Particularly if you think about what can go wrong, it may happen that you will get stuck and not achieve anything. When you are stuck, the accumulated anger, the unexpressed disappointment and lack of acceptance may express themselves as polyps on your vocal cords, cysts in your throat or thyroid problems; you may even get cancer.

But the pain remains. Unexpressed truth hurts.

Feelings must be expressed

If countless times you have tried to talk about your feelings and you were always met with resistance, emotional aggression and lack of understanding, you have to take a different path. First take care of your inner harmony.

• **Nature heals.** Go into the woods and express your pain to a tree that you can hug. Nature will be able to process your feelings. Sense that you are part of the whole.

• **Go near water.** The fire inside you is drying up the moisture in the tissues in your body. Listen to the healing sound of water. Throw a leaf or a flower into the water and watch the water take it away, take the pain away. Imagine that you have put on this leaf or into this flower your pain and the water is now carrying it away. Throw into the water a leaf onto which you have written everything that is weighing down your soul. And let the water carry away your pain. Let it cleanse the pain and erase it.

• **Look at a flower** – and just observe its perfection. Let peace fill your soul.

• **Take deep, conscious breaths**. With each breath in, you are inhaling strength and with each breath out, you are exhaling pain. Exhale everything that is weighing you down and inhale new energy so that you have the strength to stand up for yourself.

• **As the throat chakra is blue, dress in blue**. Wear a turquoise top or jumper; put on a turquoise necklace or wrap a blue scarf around your neck; a scarf that decorates your neck will give you additional help in the energy healing of your throat and thyroid. Never wear turtleneck tops that squeeze your neck. Is it not enough that you are being squeezed and suffocated from inside? There is no need for it happening on the outside as well.

Healing sounds

You have seen above that the sound of a stream or other moving water heals. However, if you have thyroid problems, if you are completely blocked in the throat area, you need more, a stronger "medicine".

This medicine is the sound of gongs, or of Aboriginal instruments, or the vowels A, E, I, O, U.

The healing sound of a gong or another percussion instrument is a natural medicine. Ancient peoples knew this. All ancient peoples used drumming in order to increase energy. Tibetan singing bowls, the drums of the Native Americans, the Aborigines' didgeridoo, the ocarina and pentatonic flute, the gong that originates in Mesopotamia, etc. Ancient peoples knew. The Incas, Mayas, Aztecs, Ancient Greeks, Egyptians, Tibetans, Indians, Chinese, Old Slavs and all the other ancient peoples used sound for healing and to relax the mind. The sound of these instruments is communication with God. Sound harmonically influences energies in the body, contributing to a balance, which is a prerequisite for self-healing.

When I was a child, I had a chronic inflammation of my glands; I constantly had a cold and often an earache. Now I know this was not the result of a low resistance, but a sensitivity to the frequency and energy of my family.

If we often hear that we should be quiet, that we should be patient and that it is not worth arguing, the message stored in our subconscious is that we have to swallow and deny our feelings in order to keep peace in the family.

When I had happier periods in my life, the throat problems faded away completely. No colds, no vocal cords problems. But when my life hit the rapids again, when I swallowed my tears and my feelings, my emotional state was reflected in my voice.

The last period when my life went over rapids had a profound effect on my voice. When I wanted to sing, all I could do was croak, all the time I had a lump in my throat that I could not cough up. My throat was beginning to get constricted, I even felt like I was suffocating.

I believe that we are led. Some time before this, my friend Aleš sent me a link to the healing gongs, but at that time I didn't feel a need for the healing energy of sound. But then, suddenly a thought came to me – look for information about healing gongs. Unbelievable! That night I had a sound bath – a bath with gongs. As this was something new for me, my ego, my conscious mind, said: "Oh, I don't know where to go, who is going to be there, I don't know anyone, I don't know what to wear …" You know that negative voice inside that is keeping you in the drama, dissatisfaction and suffering. Forty-five minutes before the session I made the decision. I called, got dressed and went. Great! An hour and a half of unbelievable sounds that reverberated through every cell of my body. I observed the pain that first appeared around the heart, then moved to the throat, then to the top of the head, then to the middle of my left foot and then to my left shoulder. And then the pain gradually disappeared.

I knew my energy points were healing, I could feel my chakras resonating with the healing sound that was flowing through my body. I felt the presence of God, of the one energy that connects everything; I felt love.

But what really amazed me was the feeling of the flow through my throat; the lump began to peel off. On my way home I coughed. The sound had freed the blocked energy in my throat area.

The healing power of the vowels A, E, I, O, U.

In his book The Alchemy of Voice, Stewart Pearce observes that the five vowel sounds A, E, I, O, U have for a long time been linked to mysticism and spirituality. In numerology, the number five is a vibration that is beyond communication. In ancient societies, there was a belief that these vowel sounds were a master code that facilitated contact with certain higher states of consciousness and with this, access to the Divine. They can even stimulate certain DNA processes as they act as cell spells. These vowel sounds are certainly the "original elements" of the sounds of numerous languages.

Pearce also says that it is a well-known fact that many Native American shamans use these five vowels as sound energy for transformational purposes, which helps to achieve a better connection with the spiritual world and through this, the healing of the mind and the body. In addition, many original tribes use the master code for strong healing effects. With a combination of sounds they influence a specific part of the body in such a way that harmony and balance is achieved in the affected organs. The Native Americans are said to use the master code of vowels in the following way:

A *connection with the heart and chest area*

E *connection with the throat area*

I *connection with the head*

O *connection with the abdomen*

U *connection with the lower abdomen*

The vowel forms produce sounds that create harmonic patterns known as overtones. These tones give colour to our voice, with all its different hues. If we sing a vowel, it is easier to recognise the tonal pattern and colour. Say, for example, the word "Alleluia" and then prolong every vowel so that the whole spectre of the vowels A, E and U is heard. Now repeat this, but this time with an easily sung note from the heart chakra, so that each vowel is clearly supported and shaped with a long, easy breath. You will feel and hear how the basic tones are combined into overtones. You will feel it particularly strongly on your lips, while a part of the tone will slide along your tongue.

Pearce goes on to say that the resonance of every tone is based on the following principle: the smaller the opening – your lips and throat – the lower the tone; the smaller the resonator – your mouth – the higher the tone. These tones appear in your mouth and disappear in your throat.

The word Alleluia means "Glory to God" and includes a spectre of vowels that people produce. It is an Abramic chant that goes back to the history of the Hebrew people. It originates in the esoteric practice of the Kabbala, an ancient discipline that lies at the very centre of the Jewish rabbinical teachings. The Kabbala teaches that vowel sounds give spirit to words and to the person producing the sound, allowing a connection with powerful and magical forces.

The use of holy sounds helps us to simply be here, to release energy and, above all, to free the obstructions blocking our energy centres due to stress and sadness.

The healing power of positive affirmations that give you strength

With these affirmations, you will support your decision to stand up for yourself. Keep repeating the following:

- I'm learning to give and receive unconditional love.
- I'm worthy of love.
- I am love.
- Every night, I get more beautiful. God has a beauty salon. With every day, I accept myself more.
- I allow myself to be strong.
- I allow myself to speak the truth.
- I am made in God's image. My world is the world of love.
- My emotional state is always in balance.
- I express myself freely and joyfully. I can stand up for myself. I am prepared to grow.
- Today, I am creating order in my spirit, creating space for new, positive experiences.
- With every inbreath I become stronger; with every outbreath, I release everything that is weighing me down.
- I am ready to progress. God's love and light flow through me.
- I have the strength to decide and to stick to decisions.
- The Universe lovingly supports me in all my decisions.

When you are in balance, you will not cry for a relationship that has exhausted you psychologically, emotionally and often even financially. When you are in an emotional balance, you know and feel that you are destined for something better; even if you don't see it yet, you feel and know that there is something better on the horizon.

I was inspired by the story of Alen Kobilica. As a successful Slovene model and businessman, he became ill. He had to have an urgent operation to remove a tumour near his eyes. The operation was a success, but after two weeks, he lost his eyesight.

"Try writing an email or calling someone without seeing, or getting dressed to go out, or preparing something to eat." At this point, one could give up, but Alen went on: "I decided for the other option – I took blindness as a challenge." Since he went blind, he runs and swims faster, takes part in triathlons, etc.

And what is my inspiration? His project "I SEE THE GOAL", which unites children with any type of a physical handicap in a non-profit organisation. Children who are blind see a goal, Alen who is blind sees a goal. But we who can see, often don't see a goal.

Start repeating: "I see the goal, I see the goal, I see the goal ..." and suddenly you will see what you want, what you have to do, what is your path. Suddenly, you will be able to take a step because you can see the goal. And there, you are happy; there you glow; there you are content; and there at the goal you can speak. You don't have to pretend; there, you can be what you are; there, you can express your creativity; there, you will be financially supported because you will be doing that which you are passionate about.

This is the path of growth and freedom – the path to truth. It is the more difficult path – at least in the beginning; but in the long run, it is the only right solution – the path to complete joy, health, harmony and love.

Until now, we have been talking about the emotional background, but we also want to have a "technical" proof. Here follows a test of the functioning of your thyroid that you can do at home, and the meal plans that will help you achieve a more balanced functioning of your thyroid gland.

In the book by Dr David W Rowland, *Listen to Your Body*, you can find a thyroid test:

As soon as you wake up in the morning, even before getting up, put a mercury thermometer under your arm and keep it there for at least ten minutes. Repeat this for three consecutive mornings and then calculate the average temperature. Women who still menstruate should take their temperature on the second, third and fourth day of their cycle. Normal morning temperature should be ***between 36.5 and 36.8°C****. If your temperature is below 36.5, the functioning of your thyroid is reduced. If it is above 36.8, it is increased.*

A hyperactive **thyroid** can affect allergies, there can be skin problems (dry skin), dry hair, tiredness, irritability, digestive problems, sleeping problems, weight gain or loss, oedema, hoarseness, intolerance to cold; it can also influence various types of pain and autoimmune diseases.

If you don't treat thyroid problems, you can risk diabetes, high blood pressure, breathing problems, joint inflammation, depression, migraine and the carpal tunnel syndrome (numbness or burning sensation in your fingers: thumb, index finger, middle finger and the radial half of the ring finger).

The thyroid hormone is the main metabolism regulator. It has a strong influence on appetite control, the metabolism of carbohydrates and energy levels. It is no surprise that people whose thyroid is not functioning properly have problems with how they feel.

The stress hormone, cortisol, can affect the thyroid gland

Cortisol can prevent the transformation of the T4 thyroid hormone into T3, which results in the reduced functioning of the thyroid. Signs of the reduced functioning of the thyroid are:

- sudden weight gain,
- excessive weight or inability to lose weight,
- muscle weakness,
- skin problems,
- tiredness and chronic tiredness,
- nausea,
- low concentration and memory problems,
- loss of libido,
- loss of menstruation,
- impotence/infertility,
- breast pain,
- irritability and mood swings,
- cold hands and feet and intolerance to cold,
- palpitations,
- unhealthy hair that is falling out,
- weak nails and teeth.

Iodine stimulates the functioning of a lazy thyroid

The thyroid gland is an exceptionally important link in the metabolic system of humans. When it is functioning well, it prevents fat from collecting in the body. People whose thyroid is working too slowly, can suddenly put on 5 kg or more, with no changes in their diet. In addition to this, they are chronically tired, weepy and displaying psychological problems.

A lazy thyroid slows down metabolism, resulting in too few calories being used. The thyroid cannot function properly without iodine and if there is not enough iodine, hypothyroidism occurs (an inflammation of the thyroid), which slows down the metabolism and this, in turn, causes a sudden weight gain.

Iodine can be obtained from sea food and from vegetables grown in soil that is rich in iodine, or with a natural supplement that contains all the vitamins and minerals.

Taking iodine as part of a natural and balanced vitamin and mineral supplement is a very good idea as it means that you are not taking too much iodine, which can make your thyroid work excessively. It has to be consumed in small quantities that are just enough to normalise the functioning of the thyroid. The best absorption of iodine is achieved when it is taken together with B vitamins and minerals such as calcium, potassium, zinc and chromium. The supplement must be natural; add a pure source of omega-3 fatty acids as good fats help balance the hormones.

Although you can find a great deal of information about the thyroid (some sources talk about not consuming cabbage and broccoli), my advice is to eat as healthily as possible and to laugh a lot; if you cannot laugh, at least use the healing sound and music techniques. Thyroid problems originate in your emotional state and healthy food will help in balancing the functioning of your thyroid.

Advice: If you have thyroid problems, listen to your body with regard to food. If you crave broccoli, have some as part of a balanced lunch. Broccoli, like all the other cruciferous vegetables (cabbage, cauliflower, Brussel sprouts, turnip, kohlrabi), should always be cooked. I advise you not to eat raw cruciferous vegetables in smoothies, because you may consume too many sulphur glycosides, which reduce the absorption of iodine. Iodine is also not absorbed well when there is a shortage of vitamin A and the minerals copper, zinc, selenium and iron.

Your body needs the following to be able to produce the thyroid hormone and balance your thyroid functioning:

- **iodine**: onions and tarragon, all seafood, ionised sea salt;
- **omega-3 fatty acids**: fatty fish: salmon, mackerel, tuna, anchovies, sardines;
- **B vitamins** (B2, B3, B6, B8 and B12): eggs, milk, fish, mushrooms, cabbage, walnuts, peanuts, almonds, avocado;

• **vitamin C**: lemons, cherries, blueberries, rosehip, parsley, dandelion, cabbage;

• **selenium**: mushrooms, Brazil nuts, walnuts, onions, garlic, tomato, broccoli, seafood;

• **copper**: peanuts, mushrooms, peanuts, sunflower seeds, oysters, sardines;

• **manganese**: peas, mushrooms, beetroot, nuts: macadamia, hazelnuts, almonds;

• **zinc**: mushrooms, soya, lentils, pumpkin seeds, spinach, seafood: sardines, oysters, crabs;

• **amino acid tyrosine**: eggs, milk, cottage cheese, peas, spinach, almonds, peanuts, avocado, beans, pumpkin and sesame seeds, cow liver, beef, pork, rice, rye, tofu, low-fat cheese.

The amino acid tyrosine and iodine create thyroxine – the thyroid hormone

For fat molecules in cells to start burning, there has to be thyroxine. This hormone is produced in the thyroid and is responsible for switching on the cell "power stations" – mitochondria. When there is enough thyroxine, we have sufficient energy all day, but when we are short of thyroxine, we feel wiped out – the cell power stations stay cold. This is why people whose thyroid is not functioning properly are prone to being overweight and tired.

Klaus Oberbeil in his book *Fit durch Vitamine* (Fit With Vitamins) says that doctors often give the wrong diagnosis of a badly functioning thyroid. What is in fact happening is that often the thyroid is working quite well, but its hormones are destroyed in the blood (during their journey through the blood, the thyroid hormones are one of the first substances attacked by free radicals) and they never reach the cells of the body. And that is why in blood tests, the value of these hormones is so low. In many people, according to Oberbeil, only 20 percent of thyroxine molecules released by the thyroid reach the cells.

Protect hormones against oxidation with vitamins A, C and E

The strongest antioxidant found in food are the red pigments in fruit and vegetables – the carotenoids, from which vitamin A is produced and on which we cannot overdose. Research has shown that carotenoids are a 50 percent stronger antioxidant than vitamin C and 3 times as strong as vitamin E.*

The most powerful tools for the prevention of oxidation can be found in carrots, tomatoes, red peppers, spinach, avocado, peaches, apricots, etc., in all the fruit and vegetables that have a red, orange, yellow or dark green colour.

Vitamin E protects vitamin A against free radicals and oxidation. If there are too many free radicals, vitamin E can also oxidize, but is corrected by vitamin C.*

As you can see, these three vitamins are urgently needed for the protection of hormones. Problems appear when we are under stress, since only a 20-minute period of emotional stress "burns up" as much as 300 mg of vitamin C; perhaps during stress we also reach for unhealthy food and if you smoke as well, you are doing immense damage to yourself. Even the vitamins that are still in the body decay, the thyroid hormone oxidises, this means that there is no one there to turn on the energy and as a result we are chronically tired and feeling even worse. *More about antioxidants on page 209.

Here are a few meals to improve the functioning of the thyroid

Lunch:

- beef liver, fried with a lot of onions,*
- fried porcini mushrooms with courgettes,
- cabbage salad,
- slice of rye bread.

Lunch:

- roast veal,
- brown rice with peas and mushrooms,
- broccoli,
- cup of forest fruits.

Late lunch or evening meal:

- porcini with eggs and roasted onions,*
- slice of rye bread,
- cup of blueberries – you can mix them with cottage cheese and turn them into a delicious creamy dessert.

Evening meal:

- salmon, fried with butter, lemon and wine,
- side dish of cottage cheese, avocado, parsley and onions, *
- 10 previously soaked nuts.

Evening meal:

- sardines,
- salad made from tomatoes and onions*, dressed with pumpkin oil, vinegar and sea salt,
- fresh lemonade.

Evening meal:

- a spread made with cottage cheese, avocado, onions* and lemon,
- handful of nuts – macadamia, walnuts, almonds, Brazil nuts (10 nuts).

* **Note**: People with a lazy thyroid gland and consequently a slow metabolism, should not skimp on onions.

Mushrooms are a superfood, particularly beneficial for detoxification and for a better functioning of the hormone system

Mushrooms are rich in minerals. They contain 1 percent minerals, which is a lot in comparison with other foods. Among the minerals in mushrooms there is a high proportion of phosphorus and potassium, a considerable proportion of zinc, copper and iron, as well as some sodium, calcium, magnesium, manganese, cobalt, chlorine, fluoride and iodine. Mushrooms also contain vitamins, but different species contain different amounts. In yellow chanterelles and Caesar's mushrooms there is a lot of vitamin A, many species also contain vitamins E, D, K, B1, B2 and B3, shiitake even the otherwise rare B12.

Mushrooms contain practically everything you need for the regeneration of the thyroid hormone:

- **chromium** – prevents attacks of hunger and helps with slimming;
- they have a very **low glycaemic index** – only 15;
- **protein** – mushrooms are an excellent protein replacement for those who do not consume animal protein; they are even better when combined with meat since you get all the amino acids necessary for the regeneration of your body;
- **silicon** – a mineral that helps with the renewal of the connecting tissue: joints, cartilage, skin;
- **selenium** – a mineral that helps improve the immune system, even acts against cancer;
- **copper** – if you don't have enough of this mineral, you go grey quickly and have pigment marks on your skin;
- **phosphorus** – if you don't have enough, you are often tired;
- **potassium** – a shortage causes water retention in the body;
- **zinc** – helps with the detoxification and in the functioning of the immune system;
- **iron** – influences the blood;

• mushrooms also contain small amounts of **sodium, calcium, magnesium, manganese, cobalt, chlorine, fluoride and iodine** – your body needs these minerals for its proper chemical functioning – various reactions in your body – which result in you feeling good;

• **vitamin E** – acts on the blood supply and the regeneration of the body;

• **vitamin D** – helps with the binding of calcium and magnesium, and in the detoxification of the body;

• **vitamin K** – acts against intestinal problems;

• **B vitamins** – if you are short of these, you have problems with your skin, nerves, hair, etc. And with a lack of energy.

Hormone disruptors – when toxins stay in the body

Hormone disruptors are food substances that may mimic hormones, block or completely disrupt them. These substances are heavy metals, such as cadmium, mercury and aluminium. Even pesticides and herbicides can cause a hormonal disruption in the body.

Our environment is overburdened with chemical substances and heavy metals, such as:

• aluminium – can be found in all antiperspirants and aluminium foil,
• cadmium – contained in cigarettes,
• mercury – contained in fish (e.g. tinned tuna) and in amalgam tooth fillings
• pesticides,
• components of synthetic substances,
• industrial substances,
• pharmaceutical drugs.

In his book *100 % Health,* Patrick Holford says that these chemical substances disrupt hormone messages sent by the body, thus altering the sexual and reproductive development. They should really be called hormone disruptors that undermine the body's ability to react to the environment and adapt to it. An increasing number of chemical substances are disrupting the hormonal balance. The author goes on to say that these substances, with their ability to lock onto hormone receptor sites, destroy the body's biochemistry. This means that the communication of genes with the cells of the body, which is of crucial importance for the preservation of health, is hindered. Holford says that in some cases, these chemical substances actually block the hormone receptor, or they appear in the role of the hormone, while others distort the hormone messages. This introduces considerable confusion into the body's biochemistry. The body becomes more toxic, there is a series of unwanted effects and the likelihood of some illnesses becomes greater. These chemical substances could be called "anti-adaptogens". Or, to put it differently, they intervene in our innate ability to adapt to our environment and they spoil the neuro-endo-immune system's plan, which otherwise ensures that through the adaptation of the body systems we preserve good health (the nervous system, immune and digestive systems are connected into the neuro-endo-immune network). If at the same time not enough "adaptogens" are given to the body – vitamins, minerals, essential fatty acids and phytonutrients, which help detoxify the body, balance the hormones and increase the ability to adapt – these chemical substances lead directly to our decline as they slowly undermine our health.

Note: Adaptogens are nutrients which correct the genetic code. They include the good fats omega-3, vitamins A, C, E, B2, B3 and B6, and the minerals magnesium, zinc, copper and selenium. These nutrients help alleviate stress at the cell level and inflammation, they speed up detoxification and improve the body's immune system.

Adaptogens prevent oxidation, reduce inflammation, have a calming effect, clean the liver, balance the functioning of the hormone centres, protect the heart, increase the blood supply to small capillaries, balance blood sugar level and the desire for food with a high glycaemic index, balance the functioning of the sex organs, encourage sharpness of memory and increase concentration.

Adaptogens can also be found in plants such as ginseng, rhodiola rosea, sweet potato and milk thistle.

“If a man who lived fifty years ago was injected with as many toxins as the bodies of people today have to battle with every day, he wouldn’t survive even two days!” claims the Belgian biologist and scientist Gabriel Devriendt.

Check your detoxifying abilities*

*Summarised from: Patrick Holford: 100 % Health

Dr Jeffrey Bland created a questionnaire for checking an individual’s metabolism, in which he included the common symptoms that show a reduced ability to detoxify. Here is a shorter version.

Read the following problems. For every symptom you occasionally have, add one point and for those you often get, two points.

- **Head**: headache, faintness, dizziness, insomnia.
- **Eyes**: tearful or itchy eyes, swollen, red or sticky eyelids, bags or dark circles under the eyes, blurred eyesight.
- **Ears**: itching, pain, infection, discharge, ringing, loss of hearing.
- **Nose**: blocked nose, problems with sinuses, hay fever, sneezing attacks, copious mucus production.
- **Mouth**: chronic cough, choking, frequent need to clear the throat, hoarseness, loss of voice, swollen or pale gums, lips or tongue, mouth ulcers.
- **Skin**: acne, rash, spots, dry skin, hair loss, hot flushes, excessive sweating.
- **Heart**: irregular heartbeat or missing heartbeats, fast or strong heartbeat, chest pain.
- **Lungs**: catarrh in the chest, asthma, bronchitis, shortness of breath, breathing difficulties.
- **Digestion**: nausea, vomiting, diarrhoea, constipation, bloating, hiccupping, wind, heartburn, abdominal pains.
- **Muscles**, joints: pain in the muscles or joints, arthritis, stiffness or limitation of movements, weakness or tiredness.

- **Weight**: excessive consumption of food and/or drink, a desire for particular types of food, excessive weight, forced eating, water retention, low body weight.
- **Energy**: tiredness, laziness, apathy, lethargy, hyperactivity, restlessness.
- **Mind**: bad memory, confusion, reduced ability to understand, low concentration, bad ability to connect facts, difficulties in accepting decisions, stammering or having speech difficulties, swallowing syllables, learning difficulties.
- **Feelings**: mood swings, anxiety, fear, nervousness, anger, irritability, aggression, depression.

If you have collected over 25 points, you have the initial detoxification problems. Make some changes in your way of eating.

If you have collected over 50 points, your detoxification ability is below average.

If you have collected over 75 points, it will be best if you visit a doctor.

Some advice about how to consume as few hormone disruptors as possible:

- Eat organic food. If you cannot get organic food, soak fruit and vegetables in water with 2 tablespoons of vinegar and 1 tablespoon of bicarb of sodium added to it. This will partly remove the pesticides.
- Filter your drinking water. An even better solution is to find a spring and fill your bottles.
- Never heat food in plastic packaging.
- Use plastic packaging and eat food packaged in it as little as possible.
- Don't use pesticides in your own garden.

Detoxify your body

Cleanse the body of heavy metals – hormone disruptors.

Heavy metals bind to other minerals. Heavy metals, such as aluminium, mercury and lead bind to the following minerals:

- Mercury binds to zinc, iodine, magnesium, silicon and selenium.
- Aluminium binds to silicon, phosphorus and fluoride.
- Lead binds to silicon and calcium.

Perhaps this doesn't tell you much. Let me put it more simply: when there are too many toxins in the body and not enough vitamins and minerals that help with detoxification, this first appears as a hormonal imbalance. When you add varied and healthy food, the body begins to detoxify.

A key element in detoxification is calcium. Calcium binds acids, which it turns into salts, which are then excreted by the kidneys. We need at least 1000 mg of calcium a day; but for the calcium to bind, we also need magnesium, vitamin D3 and vitamin C. The needed dose of magnesium is 500 mg, or in the ratio 2:1 in favour of calcium.

I recommend you take a good supplement with 1000 mg calcium, 500 mg of magnesium, 10 micrograms of vitamin D3 and 1000 mg vitamin C.

In addition, I recommend you consume cow's or goat's milk. One cup of cow's milk contains as much as 3 mcg of vitamin D; a cup of goat's milk is even richer in vitamin D – 6 mcg. Cow's and goat's milk also contain calcium and magnesium, which are necessary for detoxification. You can easily discount the theory that "you should stay away from milk because it acidifies the body and causes the formation of mucus". But let us be clear here – we are talking about a cup of milk that is not boiled, not "industrially" processed and is organic. This means we are talking about cows and goats that have grazed in meadows!

In his book, Patrick Holford notes that many vitamins and minerals are involved in the maintenance of the hormonal balance and that is why he also recommends you take a good multivitamin and mineral supplement. He also says that there are another three nutrients which have been shown to alleviate hormonal problems. These are vitamin B6 (100 – 200 mg a day), magnesium

(200-400 mg a day) and zinc (20 mg a day). One of the new studies carried out by the Institute for Optimum Nutrition, which included 182 women, showed that adding vitamin B6 and magnesium is twice as effective as vitamin B6 alone. Vitamin B6 is ineffective without a suitable amount of zinc, which also performs many tasks in the process of hormone balancing, as well as being an important fertility factor. These nutrients and essential fatty acids are the "adaptogens" for our hormonal system.

Minerals that greatly help in detoxification:*

- Silicon is obtained from all vegetables with hard stems: cabbage, carrots, broccoli, asparagus.
- Magnesium – mostly in nuts and seeds: pumpkin seeds, linseed, almonds, hazelnuts.
- Selenium can be found in the following nuts: Brazil nuts, walnuts, sunflower seeds.
- Zinc can be obtained mainly from mushrooms, spinach, oat flakes, nuts such as almonds, peanuts, pine nuts, pumpkin and sunflower seeds, and all fish and seafood.
- Phosphorus can be obtained from parsley, cabbage, garlic and sprouts.
- Vitamin B6 is found in fish, cabbage, spinach, red pepper, oats and oat flakes, millet and buckwheat kasha, peanuts, walnuts and eggs.

Glutathione – a substance that detoxifies you

Produce glutathione and your body will detoxify itself. As a result, your hormones will also balance themselves.

Glutathione can be found in our bodies, it is a molecule produced by the body itself. You cannot take it in the form of a supplement, but it is necessary to provide the body with enough amino acids every day so that glutathione can be produced. Whey is one of the best sources of the amino acids that are necessary for the detoxification of the body.

The more bad food you eat, the fewer components there are from which your body can produce glutathione; in addition, the glutathione levels already in the body become reduced, the liver is increasingly under stress and can no longer carry out its detoxifying function. When you add stress, polluted air, medicines and radiation, the body cannot detoxify, the immune system starts getting weaker and as a result you get inflammation and small infections, you age faster and get ill more often – even with serious diseases like cancer.

Glutathione is of key importance in the functioning of the immune system; it is the master of detoxification, the main antioxidant which ensures good cell metabolism. When you have enough glutathione, you feel invincible – both psychologically and physically. Research has shown that elevated levels of glutathione influence the reduction of muscle damage and help with faster recovery after injury; there is also more strength and endurance. Glutathione even has a beneficial effect on fat burning and muscle mass growth.

What is glutathione?

Glutathione is a substance that can be found in every cell of the body. The secret of its power is in sulphur. Sulphur is a sticky, smelly molecule that acts like floating paper, to which all the bad substances in the body stick, such as the heavy metals mercury, cadmium and aluminium. Sulphur and vitamin C bind together and help with the formation of collagen, which contributes toward the quicker healing of wounds, firmer gums and a better and younger appearance of the skin, nails and hair.

How to produce glutathione

Glutathione is produced from three amino acids – glycine, glutamine and cysteine; in addition, the mineral selenium and vitamin C are also needed. Selenium can be obtained from onions, garlic, broccoli, tomatoes and Brazil nuts, and vitamin C from all the fresh vegetables and fruit.

The amino acids glycine, glutamine and cysteine are found in the following foods:

- **animal sources**: prosciutto ham, chicken, turkey, duck, eggs and milk protein found in milk, cottage cheese, cheese, yogurt and whey;
- **plant sources:** pistachios, red pepper, garlic, onions, broccoli, cabbage, Brussels sprouts, oats, sprouted wheat and carrots.

An interesting fact: Patrick Holford says in *100% Health* that three servings of Brussels sprouts a day could reduce the risk of certain cancers by a half. It has been shown that 300 g of Brussel sprouts a day increased the activity of the important liver enzyme glutathione by *30%*.

Amino acids build cells, detoxify the body, build the immune system, help with the hormone balance and accelerate the re-shaping of the body. The listed foods also contain precious vitamins and minerals, which help with detoxification. If you want to accelerate detoxification, consume garlic daily, since it contains selenium, sulphur, vitamin C and some of the B vitamins.

As you can see, for the creation of glutathione you need a varied diet containing high quality proteins and vegetables. Usually, things go wrong when you are in a hurry, when you don't have enough time to prepare healthy meals, and you satisfy your hunger on the go. At those times you do not have the components from which your body could make glutathione, and as a result, there is tiredness, lack of energy and a "spare tyre" around your middle.

Detoxification takes place in the morning. This is why it is very important what you eat in the evening as this is the only way you can ensure that precious nutrients reach the cells by the morning, thus helping the body in the detoxification.

The herbal teas which are of great help in the balancing of the thyroid – Simon Ašič's recommendations:

1. For insufficient functioning of the thyroid drink tea made of:

• marigold, mistletoe, common wormwood, yarrow, centaurium, plantago,
• goldenrod, dandelion, mint, juniper berries, angelica, althaea.

6 tablespoons of the mixture of herbs should be covered with a litre of boiling water and left to stand for 10 minutes. The tea should then be strained and drunk 3 times a day, 300 ml each time.

2. For excessive thyroid functioning drink tea made of:

• elder, thyme, mint, St John's wort, (pour one litre of boiling water over 4 spoonfuls of the herb mixture),
• hawthorn, coltsfoot, lemon balm, bramble leaves,
• nettles, parsley, plantain, sage.

Pour boiling water over the mixture. Let it stand for 10 minutes, then strain. Two cups of the tea can be drunk before meals and another cup after meals.

Maria Treben recommends for thyroid problems a tea from marigold, yarrow and nettle. Place a full teaspoonful of the mixture into 250 ml of water. She recommends a litre and a half to two litres of this tea a day.

Note: The Austrian herbalist Maria Treben was born in 1907 in Bohemia (then still part of Austro-Hungary). During World War Two she and her husband were moved to a refugee camp in Austria. Later, Austria became their home. Maria Treben became famous for two books – *Health Through God's Pharmacy* (translated into 24 languages, with over 8 million copies sold) and *Maria Treben's Cures.* She died in 1991, aged 84.

*More about the Fountain of Youth, which is one of the ways to balance the functioning of the thyroid, can be found on page 224.

An old Chinese saying says: **"That which the kidneys and the bladder cannot excrete, has to be excreted by the intestines. That which the intestines cannot excrete, has to be excreted by the lungs. If all this isn't enough, the skin comes to assistance. And that which the skin cannot excrete, leads us to death."**

Lack of fluids and acidification of the body

When the body doesn't have enough fluid, the balance in the body can be disrupted by an inappropriate diet, smoking, lack of exercise and too much stress, and the body becomes acidified and toxified: acids begin to collect in the joints and other tissues in the form of salt, which destroys the cell structure. The body stores other toxins, such as heavy metals, because it doesn't manage to remove them. At the same time, it also stores fluid, which is why the body looks bloated. Problems with digestion and metabolism appear. As a result, the person feels dehydrated and without strength, and has circulation problems, which can result in the hardening of the arteries.

The body becomes acidified because of:

- acids, contained in sweet things and fats,
- uric acids (from foods that contain a lot of purine: meat and beans),
- sulphuric acid (pork),
- nitrous acid (cured foods),
- oxalic acid (asparagus, rhubarb),
- acetylsalicylic acid (aspirin),
- hydrochloric acid (stress, fear, anger),
- lactic acid (tension, excessively strenuous sports),
- nicotine.

Fat cells store water!

If you don't drink enough, toxins stagnate in the body. I know, you will say: "I can't drink in the morning – it makes me feel sick; at work I can't drink because it makes me constantly go to the toilet; I'll drink in the evening." But when you come home you don't drink again because you have so many things to do; and in the evening you don't drink because you don't want to have to get up at night. With time, your body becomes chronically dehydrated and begins to store water in the fat cells.

Consider camels. They store water in their hump, which is not some kind of a water reservoir, but fatty tissue. The human body is also able to store water in fatty tissue. But when it sees that its cells are getting enough water and fluids – it takes from two to twelve weeks – it dismantles the fat stores.

When you are hungry, have a glass of water. It doesn't contain calories or fats but is proven to reduce the feeling of hunger. Water speeds up the metabolism. More water means faster fat burning. Research shows that after two glasses of water, the body needs 10 to 40 minutes before it starts the metabolic processes and then uses 30 percent more energy. Some studies have shown that those who drink six glasses of water a day, reduce their weight without a special diet by as much as three kilograms a year.

The consequences of a chronic shortage of water are:

- rapid skin ageing,
- slow healing of wounds,
- chronic fatigue and poor concentration,
- joint pains – sometimes also swollen joints,
- bloated body – water retention,
- appearance of cellulite,
- a long-lasting shortage of water results in: rheumatism, gout, varicose veins, atopic dermatitis (chronic, itchy skin inflammation), periodontitis (gum disease), stomach and bowel disorders, migraines and in extreme cases also heart attack or stroke.

The liver, kidneys and intestines are very effective at detoxification. But if we overburden them, they give up. We expect the kidneys to do the cleaning, but at the same time we don't drink enough. Without the energy from water, the kidneys simply cannot function properly and they send the metabolic toxins back into the blood system. Intestinal cells are also powerless because they don't get enough roughage from grains, fruit and vegetables. Alcohol additionally harms the intestinal tissue and instead of the toxins going into the sewage system, they go into our blood.

Drinks with hidden sugars:

• Fruit juices – although it is true they are full of vitamins and minerals, they are also full of fructose. Do not include fruity drinks in your slimming journey. Fruit juices have a glycaemic index of around 50. Unwittingly, you consume a heap of sugar.

• Fizzy drinks – half a litre of a fizzy drink contains 50 g of sugar. If you know that 5 g of sugar is 1 spoonful, this means 10 spoons of hidden sugar. Fizzy drinks and light, refreshing drinks have a glycaemic index of around 70.

• Flavoured water – read the label! With 100 ml of such water you consume 12 g sugar. Let us look at one label: in 100 ml there is 4.5 g sugar. This is comparable to a small sachet of sugar we get with our coffee or one full tablespoon of sugar. Horrifying, isn't it? If you drink 1 large plastic bottle of flavoured water (a litre and a half), you unwittingly consume 15 spoons of sugar!

Which water is right?

Drink natural spring water, it is the best. In the second place is tap water. Water should act on the body with what it flushes away, not with what it brings in. Water will cleanse the body of all the toxins collected in the fatty tissue.

At every step, we hear: "Drink bottled water!" If you think that tap water is not good enough, simply attach a good quality charcoal filter to your tap.

Drinks recommended for detoxification:

- water,
- vegetable juices,
- tea – herbal,
- coffee – caffeine accelerates digestion. Drink a glass of water with your coffee as caffeine is a diuretic,
- a glass of dry white wine has a low glycaemic index and can be drunk with your meal without guilt.

Protein drinks that help with detoxification and losing weight:

- **Buttermilk** – contains few calories and lots of protein and minerals that melt the fat (magnesium, zinc and calcium). It is best to drink it in the morning, mixed with fresh fruit.
- **Kefir** – a drink consumed by centenarians in the Caucasus, which improves digestion.
- **Whey** – contains lots of amino acids – the building blocks of new cells. It helps in the regeneration and cleansing of the body, and contributes to better metabolism due to the high content of B vitamins.

Water retention – a result of blocked cells

In order to stimulate cell metabolism, we have to start by consuming good oils, which soften the cell membrane and make it "semi-permeable".

Good fats, such as cold pressed oil from salmon, anchovies, sardines, and plant oils, such as rapeseed, linseed, walnut, pumpkin and olive oil, contain omega-3 fatty acids, which contribute toward the better functioning of the cells. Soya oil and oil from sprouted wheat and rice are also recommended for better cell metabolism.*

We often hear that water retention is caused by salt. Here is a translation of a lecture given by Dr Lenkei,* a Hungarian doctor and the author of a number of books, who educates people about how they should take care of their own health.

**To view the lecture in Hungarian, visit https://www.youtube.com/watch?v=ZXd_39cRwLU.*

You have probably also heard that the use of salt has a harmful influence on your health. A child would ask: "Why? Explain this to me! Where is the salt in our body?" I'll give you an interesting fact. An average person (70 kg) has 250 grams, i.e. a quarter of a kilo of salt in his or her body. Kitchen salt (NaCl). The basis of the human body is salty water – like sea, salty water is everywhere. Let's see what happens with the salt in our body. We have an organ called the kidneys. If you were to cut a kidney in half lengthwise, you'd see that it consists of two parts – the outer part, called the renal capsule, and the inner part. In the renal capsule, there are thousands of small "cleaning devices". Each one is independent and has its own inlet pipe (along which the fluid that needs cleaning – the blood – comes in), an outlet pipe (along which the cleaned fluid – blood – returns to the body) and a third pipe (along which the filtered fluid that we don't need and which we call urine is excreted).

When the blood comes into the kidney, it is divided among the thousands of tiny "cleaning devices", it is then cleaned and returned along thousands of small blood vessels into the organism. From each kidney leads a pipe, called a ureter, which goes to the bladder. Urine collects in the bladder and then, as we know, up to the age of 40 goes into the toilet, and after the age of 40 into our underwear. But the most important part is how the kidneys filter blood.

Everyone has seen pasta being boiled in salted water in a kitchen. The kidneys work similarly to a sieve. When the cooked pasta is poured into the sieve, the pasta stays in the sieve and the salted water runs out. But when blood comes to a cleaning device, the salty water is filtered and goes to the outlet pipe (all the water and salt). The organism takes back the salt from the kidneys and that is what is interesting about the kidneys. The system doesn't work in such a way as to take from the blood what is not needed, but instead everything is strained and then what is needed is taken back. It's as if a cook drained away the salty water and then wanted to get back the water and the salt. This process goes on so intensely that the organism would lose a quarter of a kilo of salt in 4 hours if it didn't absorb it back (take it back). Within an hour, the person would be in a coma and within 2 hours, he would die. Do you understand? It is basically like this: ***the duty of the human organism is not finding a way how to get rid of salt, but how to not lose salt.*** *The organism does this 24 hours a day. Without this, it would lose the salt 6 times a day. In 24 hours, the organism thus "returns" 1.5 kg of salt back to itself. 1.5 kg of salt! But this process isn't perfect and the human organism does lose some of salt.*

So, we aren't talking about the organism being overburdened with salt, but about a shortage of salt. Lack of salt produces characteristic symptoms such as weak muscles, the person is without strength, tired, in a bad mood. Secondly: a person with a lack of salt often has a headache. In my experience, in most cases a headache is a simple result of a lack of salt. If we give these people 2 to 3 g of salt (a teaspoon) and they drink from half to a litre of water, the headache in most cases disappears.

Later, you will understand why. Ladies have headaches more often, don't they? I don't mean the headache in the evening. That's not a result of a lack of salt. In general, ladies use less salt than men, which is why they often have a shortage of salt and a headache. Another sign often noticed by ladies – the main duty of salt is to retain water in the body; if there isn't enough salt in the body, the water simply "runs through" the body. Someone drinks a glass of water and has to go to the toilet immediately. The ladies know this feeling. I often ask them why they don't drink more water. The answer is: "I can't! Not in the morning, because on the bus I can't ... I can't at work because everyone would see me go to the toilet. I'll drink in the evening, when I'm at home." But do you drink then? No, because you would then spend the night going to the toilet. People who lack salt usually don't drink a lot of water. Because they don't drink enough water, wrinkles start appearing. And the pharmacist recommends a moisturising cream.

If someone doesn't drink enough water, something else will happen. Constipation. I'll explain why. When we eat and drink something, the food goes through the gullet and the stomach, winds its way through the small intestine and comes to the large intestine. The most important duty of the large intestine is to sense the water content in the organism. If it senses a shortage of water, in the case of a need the body "sucks up" all the water to the last drop from the intestine. And the large intestine, forgive the expression, doesn't "give a shit" about how that particular individual will excrete the "dried figs". It is the large intestine's duty to provide the organism with enough water. So, when someone doesn't have enough salt in their body, they have a headache and the doctor prescribes them some drugs. They also have constipation. And the doctor again prescribes some drugs.

The only thing I can say about laxatives is: some basic knowledge and common sense is necessary to ask how the laxative "turns" the dried figs into soft faeces. Laxatives irritate the wall of the intestinal tissue, make it water permeable and the water runs into the intestine and the faeces become damp and soft. But the organism was already suffering from lack of water. And we have "stolen" additional water from it. The problem we all have is that we fall for ads. If the ad wonders if you are constipated, the first suggestion should be: "Drink water!" In addition, it would explain the matter a little further and in the end, say that if all this didn't help, take a laxative. Do you have a headache? Have some salt and drink some water! But the opposite happens. Doctors prescribe a painkiller if your body is short of salt. They prescribe a laxative for a person who is already suffering from lack of water. They only make the lack of water worse. Do you understand? I see this example as an unnecessary, inappropriate and irresponsible use of drugs.

Let's take an educational excursion, into the woods, for example. There's a feeding spot for animals. There's a strange object there. What is it? Let's go closer. Let's have a lick. It's salty! It's a salt lick. What's this? Salt for licking is put out for animals, so that they can lick it without any constraints. People aren't allowed to eat salty food, but animals are? Something isn't quite right here, is it? If nothing else, it's contradictory. Let's open a book on managing wildlife. It says that the quality of trophies, fertility and the general state of wildlife depends on whether it has a permanent possibility of obtaining enough salt, enriched with minerals. The human body is no different. Interesting, isn't it? Has anyone seen a sign at a feeding station: "if you have more than two licks of the salt, your life is in danger!" Has anyone ever seen a cardiologist next to a feeding station, taking a wild boar's blood pressure and saying: "Listen, you boar, I don't want to see you near the salt for two weeks!" So animals are allowed?!

At school we learned that salt was a currency, that wars have been fought for salt. Let's use a little common sense here. Add salt to your food without feeling guilty. There are many studies which talk about high blood pressure not being linked to the use of salt. There are also studies about how, in spite of an increase in the use of salt, people are living longer.

We could say that health resembles a garden. Health is like a beautiful garden or a pot plant in a home. A garden with vegetables or flowers. Health behaves like a garden. You don't have to harm the garden – it can be ruined simply by not being looked after. Care and nurture are very important. We don't have to hit a plant with a stick for it to die; it's enough to not water it. If plants outgrow their pots, we replant them, change the soil, wash the leaves, occasionally water them. A garden stays beautiful as long as we care for it. The same applies to an orchard – what would happen if we didn't look after it for a few years? The branches would dry out. No one would harm it, but no one would look after it either. That's how it is with health, too.

Let's draw a rectangle and imagine that it represents all the diseases that can appear in a person. 20 percent of the surface of this rectangle consists of factors harmful to health (smoking, alcoholism, etc.). But up to 80 percent of illness comes without us being aware (due to neglect, lack of nurture). And the health propaganda talks only about the 20 percent!!! A person goes to a doctor and says: "All my life I haven't smoked, I've never had a drop of alcohol, I've never harmed my health in any way. How could I get sick?" If we neglect our health, we lose it, without being aware of the fact. We haven't been taught how to take care of our health. Do you understand? ***That's the key.***

In my opinion, smoking (the 20 percent category) doesn't harm the human organism as much as lack of water.

Let's once more look at a garden. If we don't water it, the plants wilt. If they're flowering, they particularly need lots of water. Let's look at water again. The human body consists of at least 60 percent water. In older people, the percentage is a little lower and in young people a little higher.

A test: an average person, weighing 70 kilos, was sitting in a room, where it wasn't hot and he was neither sweating nor cold. The temperature was just right for him. He sat there dressed, without talking. He just sat there and wasn't doing anything physical while scientists observed how much water he would lose in a day. The result was a surprise. ***Without physical activity or sweating or talking, etc., we lose half a litre of water a day.*** *The person just sat there and with the air he exhaled he lost an additional 0.35 litre of water (the difference in humidity between the air we breathe in and the air we breathe out). Through excretions we lose at least 0.15 litre of water daily.* ***If we add all this up, the result is a loss of 1 litre of water a day.*** *Without sweating, without talking.* ***This is just the minimum.*** *For our body to function normally, we need an additional litre of water. Most people don't drink that much in a day. Simple, isn't it?*

If we don't provide our garden with sufficient amounts of water, it dries out. To put it simply: for every 10 kg of body weight, we need approximately 0.3 litre of water daily. A minimum for a person weighing 50 kg is 1.5 litres of water a day, and for a 70-kg person 2 litres of water a day, and for a 100-kg person as much as 3 litres a day. This is the minimum, if we only sit in a room! ***You don't have to smoke to harm your health – you can harm it also by not drinking enough water!*** *Many people are proud of how little they drink. People aren't cacti! Remember that!* ***Drink!*** *People aren't camels, even though men sometimes try to be.*

In general it applies that this quantity of water drunk daily (the minimum) should be multiplied by 1.5. That is 0.45 litre of water per each 10 kilos of body weight! *If a person doesn't drink at least that much, toxins, fibre, etc. start collecting in the body. The organism ages faster. This is the main reason for ageing too quickly. Think about it. Water needs to be changed in the body for it to be able to refresh itself.*

Health and sickness. It's easy to understand. Although people usually don't see the mutual connection. Health needs to be suitably nurtured! But most people don't even know how much water they need to drink. Drink lots of water. A person can't start to heal while being dehydrated. As a doctor specialising in internal diseases, I have often seen people who were dried out. They were confused. It was impossible to talk to them. An older colleague said to me: "Put him on a drip and wait until the morning!" And when the patient was given lots of water, after a day, the confused person changed completely, he laughed ... We treated confusion with nothing but water!

If we don't look after our health, it starts to weaken and something happens that is not quite yet disease. This goes on, health weakens, disease strengthens. We reach a point when there is "more disease than health". It's a very long journey! This process cannot be changed with medical instruments. The first signs are that the person is no longer happy, but is still not physically ill. He simply isn't how he used to be. Disease doesn't strike like lightning. If for years you don't water your garden enough, it slowly dries out. And we probably don't ask what's happening to the garden, because we know. Illness doesn't happen like lightning either, the organism gives off plenty of signals during the process.

Simply put, illness is like weeds. *When the plants we have planted start to dry out, the weeds become stronger. Weeds are happy in dry ground as well, without nutrients. It's the cultivated plants that need care and nurture, not weeds. If we don't look after the cultured plants suitably, their place is taken by weeds. It's very simple.*

And another thing – herbicides are not a medicine – we want medicine to do away with the disease, don't we? We want to destroy the disease. That's herbicide. Herbicide targets the weeds. If the garden isn't in a suitable condition, we need herbicide for a while. But herbicide, whatever it may be like, is still herbicide. It destroys the cultured plants as well and doesn't re-establish the original state. Does it? It doesn't return the cultured plants to their former condition. The herbicide won't cut off the dried parts of plants, it won't dig the garden and rake it ... The herbicide will only destroy the weeds, it won't restore health. This is the tragedy of health and humankind.

If we only fight the disease, it will be difficult to succeed. We must renew the garden and the cultured plants in order to stop the spread of weeds. If we do nothing, new weeds will come again and again, and we will need 2, 3, 4 ... 10 etc. herbicides, but we will still not have restored health. That's ***why*** *it's not possible to stop the use of herbicides (= medicines) and we need them until we die. While taking the medicines, we must try to restore health. Treatment alone isn't enough! These are two different things. If someone's cancer is cut out, his health won't return. Do you understand? The cancer will come back! It's that simple. It's too simple.*

Finally, let's look into the future. In the future, there will be no patients. Seriously. What is a patient? In Latin, "patienta" means patience, i.e. patient = enduring. Our health is our greatest treasure and in its interest, we are patient. We are patient until things get so bad that we lose patience. We go to the doctor's, where we sit patiently, waiting to be seen, for the test results, for medicines that we than patiently take, while our health is deteriorating. In other areas of life, we are not patients. In other areas, we are partners. What would happen if we were patients at, for example, the hairdresser's? The hairdresser would cut all our hair off and we'd say: "If the hairdresser thinks that this is good, then I'm okay with it. I'll wait for my hair to grow again." Isn't this true? If we go to a restaurant, we are not patients. When we build a house, we are not patients. In all these areas, we are equal partners. We, doctors, also want partners, not patients. You sitting here in this hall, you're not patients. Patients didn't come. They're at home.

Note: This lecture was pointed out to me by Dr Evgen Torhač, a friend of mine, who passes on good information. He researches natural methods, herbs and good information. I respect him. By profession, he is a doctor in chemical sciences, but for me he is a man with a capital M.

For a noticeable change in the quality of your life, do at least the following two things:

- Drink water! Water without fluoride and chloride (0.45 litre per 10 kg of body weight).
- Take vitamin C (2 to 3 g a day).

A disrupted balance between sodium and potassium causes water retention in the body

The solution for draining water is not in not adding salt to our food, but to add potassium. To encourage fluids to drain from our body, it is good to eat vegetables that contain a lot of potassium and manganese, such as:

- **Beetroot** leaves are an excellent source of both potassium and manganese. Add them to liven up your green salad or in a green smoothie.
- **Pulses** like beans and peas.
- **Celery and celeriac**. Most potassium can be found in the green celery leaves and they are an excellent addition to green vegetable juices, while celeriac can be grated and mixed with mayonnaise or pumpkin oil.
- **Cucumber** also helps in draining fluids.
- **Asparagus** – can be tinned or jarred. See page 205.

Herbs and herbal teas stimulate the detoxification of the body and help remove the fluid:

- **Parsley** – contains a lot of potassium, which acts as a diuretic. Soak a spoonful of the root or dried leaves in a litre of water and bring to the boil slowly. Let it boil for a few minutes, then drain and drink 3 or more cups a day. The monk Ašič says that parsley has a beneficial effect on the liver, kidneys and bladder, it cleanses them and drains the excessive fluid. It also helps with cellulite.

Parsley is also recommended when there is an absence of periods or with painful periods. This is because of its high content of potassium, calcium and magnesium. Parsley also contains phytoestrogens and has an influence on the female hormones. Potassium increases the absorption of magnesium and magnesium influences the binding of calcium – these two minerals are also of key importance in the prevention of muscle cramps.

10 g of parsley covers the daily requirement for some vitamins and minerals such as iron, fluoride, manganese, calcium, magnesium, phosphorus and vitamins A, E, C and B1. A single spoonful of parsley daily satisfies all the requirements for manganese, which helps to create a positive mood. A bunch of parsley contains more vitamin C than half a kilo of oranges, which is why it strengthens our immune system. In parsley, there is also a lot of potassium and folic acid. Vitamin A, among other things, strengthens the bones and the nervous system, and the body also uses it for lowering tension when under stress.

Above all, parsley is a diuretic, it detoxifies the body, relieves the kidneys and stimulates the metabolism. Moreover, it strengthens and supports the liver during the detoxification. This is strongly aided by the manganese, which activates the relevant enzymes. Those who regularly consume alcohol should eat a lot of parsley. Alcohol leaches manganese from the body and parsley prevents this or quickly replaces the lost manganese.

Since it is a strong diuretic, it helps with urinary system infections, bladder stones and kidney stones and with the gathering of fluid in tissue. Parsley tea lowers the body temperature and removes the causes that have led to it. Fresh parsley juice calms irritated kidneys, bladder and the urinary pathways. Parsley root tea has the same effects.

Advice: Make a vegetable smoothie from yogurt and a bunch of fresh parsley. This refreshing drink for hot days, which also fills you up, can be consumed as an in-between meal that helps with the detoxification of the body. Due to the potassium, the removal of fluid from the body increases.

• **Mistletoe** – is like a brush for our internal organs. It has an effect on the kidneys, on gall bladder excretions, detoxification and the digestive system glands, which helps with digestion. It strengthens a weak heart and pancreas, helps with balancing the blood sugar and with diabetes, balances the thyroid functioning, improves circulation and has a beneficial effect on the heart and the blood vessels. Mistletoe increases the removal of fluid from the body and is recommended for gout, rheumatism and kidney stones.

The monk Simon Ašič recommends mistletoe tea for a rush of blood to the head and other menopause problems. Maria Treben's help for all hormonal and metabolic problems is drinking two cups of mistletoe tea daily. She also recommends three cups of this tea for excessive bleeding during periods, a strong heartbeat and low blood pressure. Mistletoe works for both excessively high and too low blood pressure.

How to make a mistletoe drink: 1 heaped teaspoon of ground mistletoe (both stems and leaves without berries, picked between October and mid-December or between March and mid-April) should be soaked in half a litre of water and left overnight. In the morning, the tea should be warmed slightly and then strained. You should drink a cup several times a day, but it should not be reheated, which is why it should be kept in a thermos flask.

Advice: As mistletoe berries are poisonous, it is better to buy mistletoe in a health food shop or a pharmacy.

• **Birch leaves** – you can either pick the young leaves yourself or buy them in a health food shop. The tea accelerates urination, it is recommended for gout, rheumatism, joint rheumatism and urinary infections. This tea also lowers temperature. 2 teaspoons of the herb should be covered with 0.5 litre of boiling water. The tea should be drunk several times a day. The monk Ašič recommends birch leaf tea for the reduction of cellulite, in conjunction with bathing in a tea made from birch leaves and bark.

• **Dandelion** – also helps alleviate water retention. Both the leaves and the root have diuretic properties, thanks to the bitterness. Consuming either leaves or the root is beneficial for water retention, kidney dysfunctions and bladder problems, and helps with the cleansing of the gall bladder and liver. Maria Treben says that even the stems are healthful and help with inflammation of the liver. The recommendation is to consume five to six raw stems a day – the blossom is removed and the stem is slowly chewed. For diabetes, Maria Treben recommends up to 10 stems – they can be used while the dandelion is blossoming.

Dandelion tea detoxifies, refreshes, cleanses, stops constipation, accelerates sweating and strengthens the organism. It has an effect on all the excretion functions in the body, particularly the gall bladder. The tea should be drunk first thing in the morning – up to half a litre if possible.

• **Elderberry** – is an excellent diuretic. The berries should be boiled for a couple of minutes and then sieved. The tea can be drunk a few times a day. The young shoots and bark are also beneficial – in his books Ašič states that they are a laxative and help with the functioning of kidneys and the bladder, as well as having a diuretic effect. Tea from elder leaves cleanses the blood and is the best treatment for spotty skin and unpleasant body odour. Elderflower tea has a calming effect and helps with insomnia. Tea made from the flowers has an effect on perspiration and reduces fever.

• **Goldenrod** – goldenrod tea is recommended for chronic inflammation of the urinary tract and for water retention. It has a beneficial effect on the cleansing of the liver and all the other internal organs, while it also acts on inflammation in the mouth and problems with mouth ulcers. Ašič also recommends goldenrod tea for kidney and gall bladder stones, for cleansing the blood and alleviating diabetes problems.

In her book *Health Through God's Pharmacy* Maria Treben says that all psychological feelings are reflected in the kidneys. This is why after a shock due to a sudden death of a loved one or some other tragedy, the kidneys are most affected. Goldenrod has proven to be a healing herb that has the most beneficial effect on the emotional state. This is why Treben says it is necessary to drink goldenrod tea during disappointments and other emotional crises. She says that the angel of healing plants stands right next to goldenrod. We feel the calming effect of this plant during difficult emotional upheavals like a hand that strokes and balances us.

• **Milk** thistle or Cninus benedictus – these are two thistle-like plants that resemble a cleaning brush. The most effective are the milk thistle seeds that can be picked between June and October. A teaspoon of freshly ground seeds can be added to a morning smoothie, made from parsley and yogurt. You must be aware that the detoxification process takes place in the morning and milk thistle can accelerate this. Milk thistle seeds can also be chewed.

Monk Ašič recommends that these two herbs are consumed for problems with the liver, gall bladder (even if it has been removed, so that the food digests better), spleen, stomach, lungs (pneumonia and asthma) and in flatulence. Tea made from leaves, stems and roots of Cninus benedictus (1 teaspoon is covered with a cup of boiling water – drink 2 to 3 cups of freshly made tea a day) also helps with the cleansing of blood, anaemia, high temperature, haemorrhoids, nervousness and insomnia. Both herbs strongly accelerate detoxification. Milk thistle tea (1 teaspoon of the seeds is covered with 250 ml of boiling water and strained after 20 minutes) should be drunk when you have vaginal discharge, problems with your womb and when your periods have stopped. The tea should be drunk three times a day before meals.

A glass of water every hour – 1 litre per 25 kg of body weight.

Protect your body from becoming too acidic by drinking enough water. It is best if you squeeze in a lemon that is rich in vitamin C and flavonoids; this will further support the detoxification. After two weeks of regularly drinking water, the body senses that it is getting sufficient daily amounts of water and no longer clings to water in the tissues. As a result, you lose weight and, above all, lose the bloated appearance.

In addition, you will feel strong and alert, much better than before.

Drinking cold water after a meal is a shock to the body. Cold water solidifies all the fats you have consumed during the meal, which slows down the digestion. The best you can do is to drink warm soup or water after a meal.

In Japan, it is customary to drink straight after waking. Science has confirmed the advantages of this technique. Healing with water produces results with old and serious diseases, as well as with the "new", modern ones. In Japan, this type of treatment is recognised as 100 percent effective with the following complaints:

- headaches,
- body pains,
- heart problems,
- arthritis,
- fast heartbeat,
- epilepsy,
- fat in the blood (triglycerides)
- bronchitis,
- asthma,
- tuberculosis,

- meningitis,
- bladder and kidney problems,
- vomiting,
- gastritis,
- diarrhoea,
- haemorrhoids
- diabetes,
- constipation,
- all eye problems,
- diseases of the uterus and menstrual problems,
- cancer,
- ear, throat and nose problems.

The method of "healing" with water:

1. As soon as you wake up in the morning, even before brushing your teeth, drink 640 ml water.

2. Brush your teeth and mouth and for the next 45 minutes don't consume anything.

3. After 45 minutes, you can eat and drink normally.

4. After 15 minutes (the duration of the breakfast), don't eat or drink anything for the next 2 hours.

5. Those who are old and sick and cannot drink 4 glasses of water at once (until they get used to it), may begin by drinking as much water as they can at once, and then increase the quantity until they reach the 4 glasses.

6. This method heals the sick, while those who are healthy can enjoy even more health.

How many days will you have to drink the water for your condition to improve?

- high blood pressure – 30 days,
- gastritis – 10 days,
- diabetes – 30 days,
- constipation – 10 days,
- cancer – 180 days,
- tuberculosis – 90 days.

During the first week those with arthritis should drink 640 ml of water only 3 times and then from the second week, every day.

This healing method has no side effects, except that you will urinate more often.

It is good if this method is used throughout one's life, not only when treating a disease.*

*Summarised from: Dr Anthony Biz: *Drink Water on an Empty Stomach.*

Chapter 5. The Regeneration Hormone – The Growth Hormone

I see clearly, I know and feel the truth

After less than two hours' sleep, the regeneration hormone starts being released by the pituitary gland. This gland is connected with the third eye, an energy point situated above the bridge of the nose, between the eyebrows.

The growth hormone is directly connected with the feeling of happiness. It stimulates the growth of many different tissues, increasing the number of cells and their volume, which is why this is the only hormone that actually rejuvenates:

- increases the release of fatty acids from fat cells and their use for energy and muscle regeneration,
- breaks down fat and has a positive influence on the thickness of the skin,
- reduces the increase of blood sugar,
- increases the formation of connecting tissue and encourages the growth and renewal of cartilage,
- accelerates wound healing,
- improves sleep,
- lowers the blood sugar level,
- helps with stress,
- increases resistance against diseases,
- cooperates with the sex hormones and helps with the release of the thyroid hormones,
- encourages the production of proteins for muscle growth,
- strengthens the connecting tissue, which is important for healthier joints,
- reduces the body's acidity.

The growth hormone starts being produced at night, roughly 90 minutes after you go to sleep, but only if you eat the right type of foods in the evening. The evening meal is the most important meal of the day and determines whether you will put weight on and age or you will be rejuvenated and lose weight.

The longer you sleep, the thinner, more youthful and full of energy you will be. The growth hormone regenerates and rejuvenates you and helps with weight loss while you sleep.

The amount of the growth hormone in the body declines with age. Sometime around the age of fifty, the body stops producing it completely, unless you help it a little with the right food and good will.

For your body to produce the growth hormone, you need the following nutrients in your evening meal:

- vitamins C, B3 and B6,
- the minerals calcium, magnesium, potassium and zinc,
- the amino acids ornithine, arginine, glycine, lysine, tryptophan, glutamine and tyrosine. The most important amino acids for the production of the growth hormone are arginine and lysine, which can be obtained from eggs, poultry, seafood, spinach and dairy, such as milk, yoghurt and fresh cottage cheese.

When the body gets all these nutrients every evening, the growth hormone can start forming in the same amounts as in a young adult. This means that you can regenerate and rejuvenate every night!

The growth hormone takes the energy for its functioning directly from the fat stores. In the evening, you should avoid all foods with a high glycaemic index. Foods rich in protein and without sugar (low glycaemic index) ensure that the blood sugar level remains balanced, which in turn means that insulin remains balanced, helping fat cells to excrete the stored fat.

If you eat sweet snacks in the evening, insulin is released and the nutrients are stored in your fat cells and literally locked in there for the next 5 hours. The regeneration process during your sleep will be shortened or it may even not begin. On the other hand, missing the evening meal or having a nutritionally poor meal will lead to becoming weaker. Eating only vegetables for your evening meal is absolutely not enough! You must also have protein, such as prosciutto ham, as this is the way to set in motion the regeneration of your body during sleep.

With regard to insulin release, it is also very important not to eat fruit in the evening. The only exception is "sour" fruit, which has a low glycaemic index. This includes blueberries, raspberries, strawberries and cranberries, but you must combine them with protein. For more on fruit and why consuming fruit is not recommended in the evening, see page 103.

For the production of the growth hormone, combinations of different foods are necessary so that you obtain the required vitamins, minerals and amino acids. Here are a few meal plans that help with the creation of the growth hormone:

Menu 1:

- prosciutto ham
- mozzarella
- olives
- 5 walnuts

Menu 2:

- egg
- 5 pistachios
- carrot
- 200 ml yogurt (no sugar added)

Menu 3:

- cottage cheese
- blueberries
- 10 peanuts

Menu 4:

- fish – e.g. trout filet
- spinach
- 5 walnuts

Menu 5:

- cottage cheese
- avocado (the recipe for a spread is below)
- fistful of almonds
- juice of 1 squeezed lemon

Menu 6:

- egg
- pepper
- cup of blueberries, raspberries and raspberries

Menu 7:

- omelette made from 1 egg, milk and spoonful of spelt flour
- cottage cheese and blueberry spread

Menu 8:

- guacamole sauce
- stalks of celery, carrots cut into strips
- handful of walnuts

And the result?

You will be making the growth hormone at night, which will regenerate and rejuvenate you, melt your fat and reshape your body. If you want to reshape your stomach as well, add at least 1 g of omega-3 fatty acid to your evening meal in the form of a supplement, and you will have won.

The evening meal should consist of protein and vegetables, with as few carbohydrates as possible. If you are still hungry, have a few more nuts instead of bread. Sometimes when I have a hunger attack in the evening, I get a carrot from the fridge and nibble on it; or I get a cupful of olives; or just some prosciutto ham and cheese. For the regeneration to happen even faster, you can have a glass of liquid whey.

When cells get an abundance of nutrients, hormones are produced, which stimulate the feelings of happiness. You can also influence these hormones with positive thinking, happy laughter, dancing and fast walking. This is the key that opens the door to hormonal balance – first there has to be the feeling of happiness – do whatever, as long as it lifts your spirits: shout, dance, go crazy, listen to loud music – allow yourself to feel a new wave of energy. When you combine everything together – healthy food and cheerful thoughts, then you are bound to be filled with happiness, health and youth.

The meal plans above are suitable for an early evening meal or as an afternoon mini meal – sometime between 5 and 6 p.m. If you want faster regeneration, eat a few spoonfuls of low-fat cottage cheese, thinned down with yogurt, between 8 and 9 p.m., and add a little avocado.

10 foods that help with the creation of the growth hormone and with the regeneration of the body

1. eggs
2. avocado
3. prosciutto
4. vegetables – spinach, carrots, peas, asparagus
5. sour fruit – lemons, strawberries, blueberries, blackcurrant, raspberries and grapefruit
6. grains – rye, oats
7. fish and seafood
8. mushrooms
9. nuts – walnuts, pistachios, almonds, peanuts (more on page 243)
10. dairy – liquid whey, cottage cheese, yogurt, mozzarella and milk (more about protein on page 240)

Eggs

Eggs contain lots of protein and vitamins B. A study showed that people who ate 2 eggs for breakfast every morning for 8 weeks and kept to a diet, considerably reduced their weight. But people who ate 2 eggs for breakfast and did not stick to a diet, did not lose any weight.

Since eggs are a protein food, they have a glycaemic index of 0; you raise their GI if you fry them – it is thus best to have boiled eggs.

Prosciutto ham

Prosciutto ham is a superfood for quick regeneration. It contains amino acids, which can be absorbed by the body very quickly as the ham doesn't need to be treated by heat. It contains 6 amino acids that the body needs for regeneration and growth. These are lysine, tyrosine, threonine, methionine, leucine, isoleucine and tryptophan, which is the component necessary for the creation of the happy hormone.

In his book *The Vitamin Bible*, Earl Mindell says that if you are often tired, you have difficulty focusing and your eyes are frequently bloodshot, you feel nauseous and dizzy, your hair is falling out or you are anaemic, the reason could be lysine deficiency.

Prosciutto keeps you full for a very long time as it has a glycaemic index of 0. It is recommended for everyone, except those who cannot consume any salt due to health problems.

Numerous health professionals recommend the consumption of prosciutto due to its high B vitamin content, especially B1, and the retention of other vitamins lost during cooking. Prosciutto is suggested for individuals seeking to enhance memory (including school children and adults) and prevent dementia. Its vitamin B3 content is beneficial for diabetics, while vitamin B6 is advantageous for those experiencing stomach, skin, or hair issues, as well as women with menstrual problems. Experts also note that the presence of vitamin B2 in prosciutto is beneficial for individuals with vertigo, eye problems, and weak nails. Vitamin B12, a crucial nutrient found in prosciutto, is often deficient in the elderly, anemic individuals, and those who frequently feel fatigued and irritable, as well as those with a monotonous diet. Additionally, prosciutto is rich in vitamins A and E, with the former supporting healthy mucous membranes and the latter promoting youthfulness.

Asparagus

It contains a heap of vitamins and minerals, even protects the heart and vascular system and helps with regeneration and detoxification. Research has found that sportsmen who consume asparagus, thus obtaining aspartic acid, have notably increased endurance. Aspartic acid plays a part in the protection of the central nervous system.

Often, after consuming asparagus, urine has an unpleasant, specific smell. This happens because of increased detoxification, stimulated by the aspartic acid, which accelerates the activities of the kidneys and the excretion of urine. When aspartic acid (also known as asparagine) decomposes, it produces tartaric acid and ammonia, which have a slightly unpleasant smell when excreted. Don't let this put you off!

Asparagus is a healing vegetable, which stimulates urination, alleviates bladder and kidney problems; according to some theories, asparagus even dissolves kidney stones and increases the excretion of kidney sand. Asparagus is particularly good for people with liver and gallbladder problems.

- Due to vitamin A content, asparagus helps in the renewal of the mucous tissue, with eye health and even improves night blindness.
- Due to B vitamins (B1, B2, B3, B5, B6, B7, B9), it improves your mental wellbeing and consequently you find it easier to cope with stress.
- Due to vitamin B6, food turns to energy more easily – improved metabolism.
- Due to vitamins B7 and E, asparagus has a rejuvenating effect. Both hair and skin are improved.
- Asparagus has a high content of vitamin B9 – folic acid, which has an effect on the rejuvenation of cells. Folic acid deficiency is the most common reason for tiredness, nervousness, despair, lack of concentration and grey hair.
- Asparagus encourages the creation of the happy hormone, as it contains aspartic acid, which is of key importance in the making of the growth hormone.

• Due to B vitamins, asparagus has a calming effect and consequently, you sleep better.

• Due to the excellent combination of vitamins and minerals, it strengthens the immune system.

• Asparagus has a low glycaemic index – only 15. If you consume it as part of your lunch, your feeling of fullness will go on for hours.

• As it contains a lot of fibre, it helps with constipation and encourages the development of probiotic bacteria in the intestines.

• Asparagus contains a lot of potassium. If you have a potassium deficiency, other minerals such as calcium and magnesium cannot bind, which can lead to osteoporosis or high blood pressure.

As you can see, asparagus really is a healthy vegetable. Cook it in a small quantity of boiling water – for only a few minutes – and serve it as an accompaniment to your lunch.

A few other ideas for preparing asparagus:

• asparagus with mushrooms – fry asparagus and mushrooms with some onion and add eggs;
• asparagus moussaka – a layer of potato and then a layer of asparagus. To prevent a blood sugar rise, have some protein, e.g. roast veal;
• cream soup made with asparagus;
• fried asparagus in beer batter;
• asparagus and broccoli risotto;
• asparagus and prawn risotto.

Spinach

Remember Popeye? When he needed strength, he tipped a tin of spinach into his mouth and then he could beat anyone. You, too, will gain strength by eating spinach – that cartoon is telling the truth!

Spinach contains fibre, protein, the minerals potassium, calcium, magnesium, sodium, phosphorus, iron, zinc, iodine, manganese, copper, cobalt and fluoride, as well as vitamins A, E, C, B1, B2, B3, B6, B9, B13 and K.

Due to the high content of the amino acids tryptophan, leucine, lysine, methionine, threonine, valine and tyrosine, it helps in the production of the growth hormone, the thyroid hormone and DHEA. All these hormones help with regeneration and make you feel good. They assist in giving you peaceful sleep, they calm you down and even act against depression.

Vitamins from the B group also increase your energy, calm your nerves and influence regeneration. The combination of vitamins, minerals and amino acids has an enlivening effect on your body and improves your mood, as well as reducing your appetite. Spinach contains the amino acid tyrosine, which encourages the healthy functioning of the adrenal glands (it balances the secretion of cortisol, the stress hormone), thyroid, pineal gland (where the happy hormone and the sleep hormone are produced), and the pituitary gland, where the growth hormone is secreted.

Spinach has the following beneficial effects on your body:

- helps in the renewal of the mucous membranes,
- strengthens the immune system,
- accelerates the metabolism of carbohydrates,
- calms the nerves and strengthens the brain,
- ensures beautiful skin, hair and nails,
- balances blood sugar levels (glycaemic index of 15), and thus helps you feel full,
- alleviates tiredness and apathy,
- ensures good mood,
- accelerates the secretion of the growth hormone, the happy hormone and the thyroid hormone,

- helps in the functioning of muscles and heart,
- lowers blood pressure,
- prevents the occurrence of cramps,
- improves sight and night vision,
- strengthens the libido, increases the ability to orgasm and sexual strength,
- improves the blood,
- helps increase bone density and strengthens teeth,
- releases fluid from the body and helps with weight loss,
- improves lazy bowel syndrome and helps with constipation,
- improves cell metabolism.

Spinach contains the fat-soluble vitamins A and E, which influence the immune system, and carotenoids, which influence eye health and even act against cancer. The vitamins K and B13, and the minerals calcium, magnesium and phosphorous, play a role in healthy bones, which is why spinach is good for osteoporosis, but it should always be consumed together with foods containing calcium – yoghurt, cheese, sour or fresh milk. Our grandmothers clearly knew this, because spinach was always cooked in milk. This destroys the oxalic acid, which washes calcium from the body.

Consuming spinach prepared with milk also has a beneficial effect on improving the blood as milk contains vitamin B12 and spinach the other microelements beneficial to blood – iron, vitamin C and copper. Let us add that copper also contributes to the release of the happy hormone, while also having a beneficial effect on skin pigmentation and prevention of grey hair.

Due to its iodine and zinc content, spinach helps with the functioning of the thyroid hormone. Besides mushrooms, it is one of the rare vegetables that contain nearly everything the body needs for making the thyroid hormone.

Warning: Spinach should not be eaten more than 3 times a week since by eating it too often, you may overdose on oxalic acid. You should not reheat spinach, but always have it freshly cooked. If you have kidney or gallbladder stones or arthritis, consume spinach in small quantities. And above all, listen to your body. If you crave spinach, it will definitely benefit you, but if you feel repulsed by it, don't force yourself to eat it.

Fruits rich in antioxidants

Lemons – the citric acid in lemons stimulates digestive enzymes, improves circulation and reduces blood sugar. In addition, lemon contains a lot of vitamin C, which activates the melting of old fat.

A single lemon can provide as much as 200 mg of vitamin C. When combined with vitamin B6 and niacin, it produces L-carnitine, a vital compound for cell energy metabolism by transporting fatty acids into cells. This process converts fatty acids into energy. Lemons are versatile in cooking, used for enhancing the flavor of salads, meat, and vegetables. However, the most beneficial consumption method is by enjoying chilled, unsweetened lemon water.

Lemons have a glycaemic index of 15.

Grapefruit is a treasure house of medicinal and protective substances

Grapefruit contains a lot of vitamin C, which is inseparably connected with the immune system and acts as a biocatalyst. The flesh is rich in bioflavonoids (plant protective substances), which increase the effectiveness of vitamin C by up to 20 times and contribute greatly to the health of the vascular system. Grapefruit also contains a lot of folic acid, which is very important for cell growth.

Fresh grapefruit contains potassium, calcium, iron, phosphorus, sodium, vitamins B1, B2, B6, B9 – folic acid, vitamin C and a little vitamin E.

Grapefruit has the following beneficial health effects:

- helps with problems with veins, varicose veins and haemorrhoids,
- strengthens the immune system, accelerates the release of hormones,
- prevents infections and colds,
- cleanses the intestines and stabilises the intestinal flora,
- enlivens metabolism and cell growth,
- assists in dieting.

Potassium is of exceptional importance in controlling the fluid levels in the body and for the normalisation of the heart rate. Potassium deficiency can cause both physical and mental stress. This is why it is vital while you are taking anti-depressives as it helps with reactions to stress.

Vitamins B – a combination of B1, B2, B6 and B9 – help with responding to stress, detoxification and weight loss. It is the deficiency of these four vitamins from the B group that leads to chronic tiredness, depression and irritability, which is why it can be said that grapefruit encourages good mood.

Due to its excellent content of vitamins and minerals, it helps with the faster renewal of the intestinal microflora after taking antibiotics, and with the strengthening of the weakened immune system.

Grapefruit speeds up weight loss.

Grapefruit's glycaemic index is only 25, so it is an excellent fruit for weight loss. The problem arises when you squeeze out the grapefruit juice and discard the fibre. The glycaemic index rises to as high as 48.

Let me explain: grapefruit juice makes you put on weight. But if you eat a whole grapefruit as an afternoon snack, if possible accompanied by a reduced-fat cheese or a few walnuts, your excess fat will start to melt faster.

Warning: Excessive consumption of grapefruit juice or flesh can in some people cause heartburn or belching. In this case, grapefruit should always be consumed together with calcium (a glass of yogurt), which binds the excess acid.

Blueberries are a super fruit with no competition!

They contain:

- **vitamin C**, necessary for the creation of collagen, which creates good, youthful skin, firm blood vessels and flexible joints. Vitamin C activates cell metabolism and therefore helps with weight loss;
- **vitamin E** – the youth vitamin, which helps balance hormones;
- **certain B vitamins**, which improve metabolism and act on the nerves;
- **bioflavonoids**, which are strong antioxidants and prevent the ageing of the eyes;
- **carotenoids**, which have a protective effect on the fatty part of cells;

• **potassium**, which encourages the draining of fluid from the body;

• **calcium**, necessary for building bones, teeth and muscles; also necessary for a normal heart beat and functioning of the nervous system;

• **iron**, necessary for good blood;

• **phosphorus**, which helps with the normal functioning of the kidneys;

• **polyphenols**, very strong antioxidants, found in some parts of certain plants, particularly in shells;

• **manganese**, which has an effect on the skin, memory and acts against joint pain;

• **magnesium**, which has a match-like effect on cells – for the creation of energy. It acts against muscle cramps;

• **pectin** – a water-soluble fibre, which regulates digestion.

Did you know that blueberry juice can help you stop smoking?

Raw blueberry juice is one of the best and most natural substances for rinsing and gargling. It heals mouth ulcers, gum infections, tonsillitis and throat catarrh. It gets rid of bad breath, which is why it should be consumed by smokers. If a smoker drinks it regularly, she will not keep lighting one cigarette after another, as blueberry juice is said to create a repulsion against smoking. The longer this treatment goes on, the more repulsed you will be by cigarettes. For this purpose, small sips should be consumed several times a day and before the juice is swallowed, it should be kept in the mouth for a few moments. Blueberry juice is also said to lower blood pressure.

Blueberries act against stress

Due to the high content of nutrients, blueberries are excellent for calming yourself. Vitamin B settles the nerves; vitamin C repairs the damage created by stress; minerals like potassium, calcium and magnesium improve your mood and the “flexibility” of your nerves.

Blueberries are good for diabetics and help with night vision

Blueberries are particularly good for various eye problems. Experts suggest to people who have problems with their vision that they regularly consume blueberries or, even better, various concoctions or extracts made from them as these contain larger quantities of anthocyanins, which improve the clarity of vision and help those whose eyes have problems adapting to darkness. The purple colour – flavonoids – protects the eyes from the damage of free radicals, UV-rays and other types of everyday stress on the eyes.

Blueberries should be consumed in large quantities by:

- those whose eyes often feel tired,
- those who spend a lot of time sitting in front of a computer or television,
- those who read a lot.

Pilots and drivers should also reach for blueberry juice or blueberries. They are recommended both for those who are short-sighted and long-sighted. They are also said to help with macular degeneration and with diabetes for preventing diabetic retinopathy, a disorder that affects the blood vessels in the retina, which may burst and cause bleeding.

Diabetes and age-related macular degeneration are among the most common causes of blindness. Even blueberry leaves have a medicinal effect as an infusion made from dried blueberry leaves lowers blood sugar. Young leaves should be picked before the berries ripen.

Blueberries are also beneficial for the vascular system as the flavonoids in them, together with the vitamin C, strengthen the walls of blood vessels. They also hinder the oxidation of the LDL cholesterol and oxidative damage to the blood vessel walls, which leads to their leaking. Blueberries thus also help in the prevention of cardiovascular diseases. When we eat blueberries, we are fighting lifestyle diseases without being even aware of it.

Blueberries act against inflammation

Bacteria need an environment in which they can multiply. Blueberries turn an acidic environment into alkaline, thus preventing bacteria from multiplying by:

• cleansing the urinary tract,
• having an anti-inflammatory effect on the bladder and kidneys,
• increasing the quantity of urine and helping to drain fluid from the body,
• easing problems with kidney stones,
• healing and regenerating the mucous tissue in the whole of the digestive tract,
• preserving the health of the digestive system, particularly the large intestine, where they prevent the development of harmful microorganisms – the pigment myrtillin hinders the multiplication of bacteria. The dark skin contains a lot of tannin. Half a cup of blueberries (125 ml) contains 2g of fibre.

Due to the high content of antioxidants, blueberries also act as cancer prevention since they have a protective effect against oxidative cell damage.

Blueberries help with losing weight

Blueberries have a very low glycaemic index – only 25. They are an excellent in-between meal. To speed up weight-loss, mix them with cottage cheese. The protein will help the blood sugar to stay balanced, while the blueberries will activate the fat burning in the cells.

You don't have time to pick blueberries? There is a natural food supplement that contains an extract from blueberries, beetroot, blackberries, cranberries, etc. It influences the detoxification of the fluids in the body.

Cottage cheese is a very high-quality source of protein that is easily digested and even helps with constipation, bloating in the stomach and heartburn. A series of amino acids ensures the correct functioning of the liver and the immune system, as well as a healthy fat metabolism. Cottage cheese will help your fat melt away faster. It is very tasty if you mix it with avocado; you can also thin it down with yogurt and add a few herbs or spices.

If you consume low-fat cottage cheese, it will lower the cholesterol and blood pressure; as it contains a lot of calcium, it ensures healthy teeth and bones and prevents osteoporosis. The B-complex vitamins in it have a calming and relaxing effect and prevent a nervous attack due to a changed diet.

Cottage cheese has a GI of 0.

Other dairy products are also excellent because of their composition. Milk, milk protein, cottage cheese, cheese, yogurt and whey all contain the amino acids from which the body creates glutathione (see page 178), which is one of the strongest antioxidants that binds free radicals and influences the detoxification of the body, particularly the liver.

Whey is at the very top of good proteins. It is a milk protein that can be consumed even by people who are otherwise sensitive to milk proteins. It contains many amino acids: leucine, isoleucine and valine, which all help with the regeneration and building of the tissue. Alfred Vogel established through numerous experiments that whey also has a positive effect on problems with the skin, constipation, candida and intestinal bloating, heartburn and insufficient gastric acid, in problems with blood sugar fluctuations and diabetes; it helps improve your immune system, and with a sore throat and a tickly cough. Whey also has a positive effect on skin problems as it contains a lot of B vitamins. It reduces eczema and skin blemishes. Whey can also be used externally for itchy skin or a fungal infection between the toes or in the vagina, as it also contains probiotic bacteria.

Fish and growth hormone

Fish are an excellent source of protein that help with the building of the muscle mass and the release of hormones, enzymes and anti-bodies. The glycaemic index of fish is 0; if you cook it in batter made with white flour, the GI rises slightly because of the flour, which is why it is better to use wholemeal flour. In spite of this, fish is an excellent food for hormonal imbalance and even for weight loss.

Oily fish also contain omega-3 fatty acids that help with the creation of DHEA, which is of key importance in the melting of fat around the stomach. Omega-3 stimulates the production of leptin, which plays an important role in weight management. Leptin is created from fat cells and tells the brain how much energy is available and how to use it. Leptin determines whether you burn or store energy.

Fish contain vitamins from the B group, which improve your mood, vitamin E, which is important for circulation, and a lot of potassium, which is necessary for the maintenance of normal blood pressure and also acts against fluid retention. Potassium binds with sodium, which is why it is recommended that you salt fish before cooking it since this is the only way for your body to be able to bind all the other vitamins and minerals. Sodium binds to potassium, potassium influences the binding of calcium, calcium controls the binding of vitamin B12 and B12 of all the other vitamins from the B group. This is why if you eat food without sufficient salt, neither minerals nor vitamins will bind.

Choose fatty sea fish, which is richer in omega-3 and iodine and has a stimulating effect on the thyroid.

Omega-3 sources*

**Dr Garry Gordon and Herb Joiner-Bey: The Omega-3 Miracle.*

Type of fish	**Quantity in g per 100 g of raw fillet**
Rainbow trout	1.1
Pacific mackerel	1.1
Atlantic herring	1.1
Sardine	1.2
Sole	1.3
Swordfish	1.3
Atlantic salmon	1.4
Brown trout	1.4
Anchovy	1.4
Norwegian salmon	1.5
Bluefin tuna	1.5
Atlantic mackerel	1.9
Dofgish shark	1.9
Albacore tuna	2.1

Omega-3 fatty acids

A diet rich in fish that contain omega-3 fatty acids has a beneficial effect on our health. Research has shown that the brain consists mostly of omega-3 fats. People who consume too little of this fatty acid in their diet or none at all are more prone to depression and have a reduced ability to concentrate.

The beneficial effects of omega-3 fatty acids:

• constituent element of cell membranes,
• stimulating the immune system and preventing inflammation (throat, lungs, joints, etc.),
• helping with cell metabolism,
• alleviating various inflammations and injuries,
• increasing muscle strength and aerobic results in sports,
• protecting against asthma attacks, as they alleviate the inflammation of the lung tissue,
• increasing bone density – recommended for both children and elderly people,
• alleviating arthritis (joint inflammation) – necessary for everyone involved in sports who puts extra stress on their joints,
• improving the metabolism of carbohydrates, which is why they are recommended for people with diabetes,
• preventing a reduction in muscle mass during weight loss, helping with gaining muscle mass instead,
• helping with cardiovascular health by:
• melting clots in the blood vessels (preventing thrombosis),
• alleviating varicose veins,
• balancing cholesterol and blood pressure,
• melting fat in the blood (triglycerides),
• acting beneficially against heart attacks and strokes,
• alleviating gout,
• helping with normal functioning of the kidneys,
• influencing the prostate,
• acting beneficially on the skin – psoriasis and scabies,
• helping with headache and migraine,

- balancing eye pressure,
- improving eyesight
- preventing age-related degeneration of the brain and even acting beneficially on autoimmune diseases, such as multiple sclerosis, Parkinson's and Alzheimer's disease,
- helping with hormonal balance – insulin, DHEA, serotonin.

Researchers have found that children who regularly consume omega-3 fatty acids have better eyesight, motor coordination (handwriting), concentration (improvement even in hyperactive children), speech ability and better school results than their peers who do not consume omega-3.

Proportion of fatty acids in some oils

	Saturated fatty acids	**Omega-6**	**Omega-3**	**Omega-9**
Hemp oil	8%	20%	10%	62%
Saffron oil	9%	77%	0%	14%
Sunflower oil	11%	63%	traces	26%
Olive oil	14%	10%	traces	76%
Corn oil	14%	52%	2%	32%
Soya oil	15%	54%	8%	23%
Peanut oil	19%	34%	2%	45%
Palm oil	51%	10%	traces	39%
Coconut oil	91%	2%	0%	7%
Butter	64%	2%	1%	33%

The omega-3 fatty acids EPA and DPA (also obtained from oily fish) create super hormones that help you feel youthful, act against inflammation, help with the melting of fat around your waist and help you concentrate. Omega-3 fatty acids in vegetable oils (linseed, rapeseed, walnut and evening primrose oil, which contain ALA omega-3 fatty acid) do not contribute towards the better functioning of your joints, do not have an anti-inflammatory effect and do not help with hormonal balance.

Vegetable omega-3 fatty acids consist mostly of alpha-linoleic acid (ALA), while fish are an excellent source of EPA, DHA and DPA. Our body needs mainly EPA and DHA. Even though these two fatty acids can be produced in the body from the alpha-linoleic acid, this process is relatively ineffective – the conversion of ALA from vegetable oils into DHA is very limited, only approximately 4 percent of DHA fatty acid is created in this way. This is why regular consumption of fish is recommended.

If you consume too much vegetable oil (omega-6), this increases inflammation in the body, which can be a reason for an increase in depression and inability to lose weight. If you eat oily fish which contains omega-3 several times a week, the right balance between omega-6 and omega-3 is restored.

Sources of omega-3 and omega-6 fatty acids

	Total fat (g/100 g)	Omega-6 (mg/100 g)	Omega-3 (mg/100 g)		
			ALA	EPA, DPA or DHA	Total omega-3
Nuts and seeds					
Almonds	55.8	13500	0	0	0
Hazelnuts	61.4	7000	100	0	100
Peanuts	51.7	16300	0	0	0
Pine kernels	70.9	39800	0	0	0
Sesame seeds	55.6	24400	0	0	0
Walnuts	69.2	43200	63000	0	6300
Sea food					
Cod	4.1	46	0	756	756
Blue mackerel	3.3	204	34	1108	1204
Oysters	4.0	184	109	1024	1404
European perch	2.3	265	79	460	602
Atlantic salmon*	7.1	592	108	1836	2131
Australian salmon	1.5	48	5	615	626
Tinned fish**					
Sardines	15.7	1839	329	2615	2944
Australian salmon	3.4	86	36	981	1089
Pink salmon	6.8	116	69	1454	1643
Tuna	23.2	10700	930	487	1417

*Fish caught in the north-east Atlantic have the lowest content of heavy metals.

**Be careful with tinned fish – do not consume it more than 3 times a week due to the high content of mercury. The best choice are sardines, while tuna is highest in mercury.

Influence of the good fats on health

Omega-3 and the vascular system

Did you know that omega-3 helps your blood vessels? The human body has 150,000 km of blood vessels. They all must allow an uninterrupted flow. Too much fatty food or too little vitamin C make the blood vessels hard and full of bad cholesterol, reducing blood flow through them.

The fact that **in Slovenia, 74 percent of people have high cholesterol, which is the main cause of cardio-vascular disease that causes death before the age of 65 (heart attack and stroke), is rather horrifying.**

Omega-3 fatty acids help improve **cardiovascular health** by:

- dissolving **blood cloths** (preventing thrombosis),
- alleviating **varicose veins,**
- controlling **cholesterol and blood pressure**,
- **melting fat in the blood** (triglycerides),
- acting against **heart attack and** stroke.

Omega-3 and the brain

Omega-3 fatty acids are necessary for the functioning of the brain and nerve transmitters, particularly serotonin – the happy hormone. Although it has not yet been confirmed that food supplements prevent depression, research shows that omega-3 fatty acid capsules ease the symptoms, particularly in people who do not respond well to antidepressants.

Dosing: Food supplements usually contain at least two omega-3 fatty acids – EPA and DHA, but research has shown that the best effect is achieved with 1 g of each fatty acid. If you want to take higher doses, consult your doctor, particularly if you are taking blood thinning medications. *

*Reader's Digest: *Food Heals*.

Deficiency in omega-3 shows up as silent inflammation:

- muscle pain,
- joint pain,
- frequent headaches,
- dizziness,
- hormonal imbalance,
- cardiovascular problems,
- inability to lose weight,
- in children, attention deficit, behaviour problems and hyperactivity,
- depression and postnatal depression,
- impulsive, aggressive behaviour,
- bipolar disorder,
- schizophrenia,
- Alzheimer's disease,
- several cancers – lung, pancreas, breast, prostate cancer,
- joint problems,
- high blood pressure,
- pre-menstrual syndrome,
- painful periods,
- psoriasis,
- osteoporosis.

Omega 3 and the joints

Joint pains indicate silent inflammation in the body. If you feel "stiff" every morning, you will have to oil your joints, just like hinges on a door. Omega-3 fatty acids act on your joints like WD-40 on hinges. They slow down the effects of inflammation, which is why they are the best choice for people with pains and stiffness associated with rheumatoid arthritis. Their effect is so good that many people who take aspirin or some other anti-inflammatory and pain killing medications are able to reduce the dosage of these drugs.

That which is good for the joints, is also good for the bones. Research has confirmed that women who for 18 months consumed omega-3 fatty acids had more solid bones and fewer breaks that those who did not. *

*Reader's Digest: *1001 Home Cure*.

It has been proven that the omega-3 fatty acids DHK and EPK prevent joint problems. They preserve the flexibility of joints, ease pain and sensitivity and reduce the need for anti-inflammatory drugs. They also have a beneficial effect in rheumatoid arthritis. Experiments have shown that after consuming fish oil for three months, joints are less painful and stiff. Even the regeneration of the cartilage is improved.

In their book *Enter the Zone*, Dr Barry Sears and Bill Lawren say that we should not be afraid of fats as they are urgently needed in the creation of eicosanoids (super hormones) and are very important for the reduction of excessive body fat, as well as for general health.

Hormonal balance and sports

Both the growth hormone and DHEA can be stimulated by exercise. Regular exercise, adapted to the available time and your physical abilities, will bring quick changes both in how you feel and how you look. If you want to remain young, abandon all old-people's habits. Your step should be lively, your walk upstairs brisk, your posture upright – chest out, stomach in, paint a smile onto your face and allow new energy to flood you.

Children know how to be happy!

Every day they play, run around, dance and laugh. And that is not all – children feel that exercise is a basic human need.

Adults should model themselves on children

Exercise alleviates stress and improves every area of our life: health, finance and relationships. Our bodies long for exercise, which stimulates our heart, our blood vessels and our muscles. I am convinced that everyone can find the right motivation, time and form of exercise to suit them.

Exercise in the morning

Morning exercise extends the fat burning that goes on at night. Light aerobic exercise is recommended in the morning, before breakfast, which stimulates the circulation, enlivens us and brings oxygen to our lungs. If you over-exercise in the morning, your body will begin to use muscle mass for producing energy. But the fat will stay stuck to your body.

Morning stretching can consist of nothing more than going out, either in your garden or on your balcony, and having a thorough stretch, standing on tiptoe a few times, breathing in deeply through the nose and breathing out through the mouth. Just look at our pets – first they stretch and then they start their day.

> Dissatisfaction with my appearance, constant criticism, caring for the family, lack of time and overtiredness – this is what I remember when I think of the time when my three daughters were still little. I took care of everyone but myself.
>
> I came to the conclusion that I had to start moving – that it was time to take care of my energy. I began by doing exercises with a ball in the evening, in our living room. The children soon worked out that mummy was an excellent swing. There was a lot of laughter as the children climbed all over me, but if you spend all your day just giving and never taking care of yourself, it is no longer fun but exhausting.
>
> Every night I fell into bed shattered from the weight of my day. I had neither energy nor will power to exercise. I kept putting it off to "tomorrow", which only increased my dissatisfaction. This led me to the realisation that I had to take care of myself in the morning.
>
> The Fountain of Youth exercises were introduced to me by a woman who had beaten cancer. She could have been my mother and I respect her as if she were my mother. Smoothly, she showed me the exercises, but when I tried to do a few repetitions, I saw that I could not lift my legs, let alone hold my weight with my arms. At the age of just over thirty, I was without muscles. How embarrassing!

Often, we only make a change when life pushes us over the edge. Then the warrior inside us awakens and takes us to some new knowledge, new energy and, above all, to the decision that something needs to change. The Tibetan exercises – the Fountain of Youth – are aimed at rejuvenation. They are a true fountain of youth. This doesn't mean that they help us avoid death, but that they improve the quality of our life. The first pleasure will come from putting yourself first immediately in the morning – first we take care of ourselves and then of the rest of the world. The world can wait!

The Fountain of Youth exercises stimulate the energy centres (chakras) into balance

In his book *The Fountain of Youth*, Peter Kelder says that the part of the body in which the chakra works more slowly begins to decay and becomes diseased and in the parts where the chakras spin faster, we may feel nervousness, anxiety and exhaustion. With these exercises, we make the chakras spin like they do in a healthy person who is around 25 years old.

The fastest way to return to health, youthfulness and energy, is to accelerate the spinning of the chakras.

Try the Fountain of Youth! You will be impressed!

The following three things are important with these exercises:

1. breathing – best with your eyes closed;
2. positive thoughts that you can believe;
3. the squeezing of the core muscles.

Start off with three repetitions, the following week do 5 repetitions, after another week add another 2 repetitions – by now you are already doing 7 repetitions, etc. Gradually, you will get to 21 repetitions, which creates the best effect.

The most suitable time to do these exercises is in the morning, at sun rise, as then the energies of the awakening day are exceptionally high. Peter Kelder says that you can exercise either in the morning or in the evening, but it is better to do it in the morning. If you want, you can start doing them in the evening as well, after you have reached 21 repetitions in the morning; again, first you do 3 repetitions and then gradually add more repetitions until you reach 21.

After a while, the body becomes more resistant, the core muscles become stronger, prostate activity increases, as does the blood flow to the muscles, bones and joints, while it becomes easier to cope with stress. Since you are full of energy already in the morning, you are more relaxed throughout the day.

The exercises have an exceptional energetic self-healing significance – the body is capable of healing itself.

During the exercises, the combination of **movement and breathing** is very important, as is the squeezing of the core. This activates the hidden potentials in your body and increases your level of energy. With these three rites, you can re-establish health and youthful strength in your body.

1st exercise – spinning clockwise;

2nd exercise – lying on the back, simultaneously lifting your head towards your chest and your straightened legs to a 90° angle (inhale when lifting the legs, exhale when lowering them back down);

3rd exercise – kneeling, place your hands on the back of your thighs, exhale into your chest and on the inbreath, strongly bend your back backwards (inhale when you bend your back, exhale when you straighten it up);

4th exercise – sitting on the floor, place your hands by your hips, lift your backside and bend your neck backwards – making a kind of a bridge (inhale when lifting, hold the breath at the top and release it when lowering your body back down);

5th exercise – position yourself as if you wanted to do push-ups. Lean on your arms and try to place your feet fully on the floor (inhale when lifting, exhale when lowering).

Imagine that with every outbreath, bad energy and tension leaves your body; and with each inbreath you receive new energy. Breathe in through the nose and out through the mouth.

While doing these exercises, I also control my thoughts. I count the repetitions with my fingers, while thinking happy and grateful thoughts. If you think of all the things you have to do today – can you be relaxed? That is why you should think good thoughts:

- I'm breathing in life and breathing out fear.
- I'm breathing in light and breathing out anger.
- I'm breathing in love and breathing out anxiety.
- I'm breathing in peace and breathing out illness.
- Today, everything is going smoothly and quickly.
- A wonderful day awaits me today!
- I'm grateful for being able to move.
- Energy flows through my body.
- Light shines through my body. I am light.
- I allow miracles to happen in my life.
- All is well.
- My life is blessed.
- I let go of everything my body no longer needs with ease.

When my thoughts wander off to an event or a person I don't like, I say: "I bless you with love and allow you to go." And it works … My life is calm.

After the completion of the exercises, it is recommended that you have a shower. If you use cold water so that you feel chilled to the bone, the rejuvenation effect of the exercises is reduced.

Do something for yourself!

Those who regularly perform the Fountain of Youth really do get younger. They hide quite a few years. And what is best, they go younger "from inside out".

Try it – you won't regret it. You can do the exercises every day, they are free and very effective and simple. The Fountain of Youth – the Five Tibetans – will rejuvenate you and fill you with new enthusiasm and energy. Don't look for excuses about not having the time! Don't say that in 24 hours you cannot find a few minutes for yourself. It's time you put yourself first and in the morning, take care of yourself first and then of the rest of the world.

The daily practice of the five rites is much more than physical exercise. It is the fastest way to return to health, youth and strength and to accelerate the spinning of the chakras. Everyone who tries to raise his consciousness to a higher level, helps to raise the consciousness of the whole of humanity.*

*Summarised from: Peter Kelder: *The Fountain of Youth.*

Exercising in the evening

Increase your muscle mass and you will increase the number of your "power stations" – mitochondria, which turn excess fat into energy. An individual cell may contain up to 1000 mitochondria.

Evening exercise contributes towards regeneration during sleep; by exercising in the evening you also stimulate the production of the growth hormone, which reshapes you while you sleep. In the evening, your exercise can be more intensive, because this will accelerate the metabolism. You start producing more muscle mass, which will create more cell power stations and these will use additional fat.

Go out and breathe the fresh air, inhale new energy that is abundant at every step. It is time for you to change the habits that do not benefit you and introduce new ones, which will fill you with energy and health.

Exercise empties the fat stores in the fatty tissues, lowers insulin levels and increases the release of the sex hormone testosterone and the growth hormone. Exercise not only breaks up old fat but also reduces the storing of new fat. Testosterone takes care of strengthening your muscles. After 45 minutes of moderate endurance exercise, testosterone level rises by about 20 percent, while cortisone levels drop at the same time. With this exercise regime, testosterone values will rise even during inactivity. This will allow you to fight the age-related loss of muscle mass. After the age of forty, it becomes more and more clear who has taken care of themselves with exercise and who neglected themselves.*

*Summarised from: Detlef Pape, Elmar Trunz-Carlisi, Helmut Gillessen and Rudolf Schwarz: *Schlank im Schlaf* (Lose Weight in Your Sleep).

The good news is that the body renews itself. As long as we are alive, our cells function. If we encourage them a little, they will renew themselves faster than they will age, which means that youth can be preserved for a long time.

Overdoing it

> I love riding my bicycle. In the past, convinced that excess calories would be used, I pedalled like crazy. After returning home, I needed quite some time for my "soul" to catch up with me. Now I just smile when an out-of-breath cycling enthusiast overtakes me and I happily ride at my own speed. I know that my cells function best during an easy rhythm, serotonin is produced and it accelerates regeneration throughout my body.

Let us have a look at a few examples of exaggeration:

1. A colleague has a dog – an Alaskan Malamute. This is the kind of dog that needs at least 6 km of action a day. So, every day he went for a quick walk with his dog. In spite of exercising a lot, he did not lose weight. Why?

2. A friend cycles every day – she covers 20 km at her maximum speed and more – but she cannot lose weight.

3. Another friend decided to lose weight. He climbed a hill every day. When I asked him which path he took, he said: "No living soul can catch up with me. I go straight up." And in reply to my question of what his pulse rate was, he said: "200 and more."

In all these cases, the body was using muscle mass. The result is always the same – the body ages because intense exercise produces the stress hormone, muscle mass is used for energy, while the fat stays around your waist. If you wish to reduce the subcutaneous fat and your stomach, you have to gain muscle and work out at medium intensity. It is the same as with a car – the optimum fuel consumption occurs at medium-range RPM.

Your body burns most fat when you exercise at medium intensity

If you want to lose weight, reshape your body and stimulate the production of the hormones that will regenerate you, you can get slightly out of breath during exercise, but you must not overdo it. When you can still talk, your body is already using the fat stores, but when you are so out of breath that you can no longer talk, your body starts to use muscle mass.

When you want to reshape your body and get rid of the "spare tire" around your waist, the fat on your backside and thighs, it is good to exercise lightly in the evening. The body will be using energy from the fat stores and this will also stimulate your body to reshape during the night with the help of the growth hormone.

Calculate the maximum heart rate at which you can still burn fat without touching your muscle mass:

((220 – age in years – resting heart rate*) x exercise factor**) + resting heart rate* = maximum heart rate

Example: If you are 40 years old and you do not do regular exercise:

((220 – 40 – 72) x 0.55) + 72 = 131 – this is the maximum heart rate at which you will still be using the fat stores. If you go beyond this limit, your body will start using muscle mass.

* Assessment of your resting heart rate:

Up to the age of 40	Between the ages of 40 and 60	Over the age of 60	
up to 50	up to 55	up to 60	if you are in very good form
50-59	55-64	60-69	average form
60-69	65-75	70-79	normal form
70-80	75-85	80-90	relatively bad form
over 80	over 85	over 90	very unfit

**Exercise factor:

Fitness condition	Exercise frequency	Exercise factor
completely unfit	no exercise	0.5
unfit	no regular exercise	0.55
moderate fitness	regular 1- to 2-times a week	0.60
endurance fitness	regular 2- to 3-times a week	0.65
good endurance fitness	at least 4-times a week endurance exercise	0.7

Summarised from: Detlef Pape, Elmar Trunz-Carlisi, Helmut Gillessen and Rudolf Schwarz: *Schlank im Schlaf* (Lose Weight in Your Sleep)

Now you have all the information you need for being able to calculate your maximum heart rate – when you go beyond it, you will be burning muscle mass, except when you are doing impulse training – fast cycling or sprinting, but the intense interval should last only a few seconds, as if you were sprinting for 100 metres. This means you can work hard, but not to the point of losing your breath. Think of sprinters – their muscles are strong and dense, whereas marathon runners look like a withered flower.

How long should you exercise for?

All those adds saying you need "only five minutes a day" are lying. Why? For the first 20 minutes, your body only uses glycogen, i.e. the stored energy in the liver and muscles that is available immediately. Only after 20 minutes does fat start being used if the exercise is of medium intensity. For people who are not active, a 20-minute fast walk is considered exercise, but the optimum is 40 minutes a day. An evening walk or gentle running should last between 30 and 45 minutes. That is enough to increase the fat burning rate at night.

With moderate exercise in the evening, the muscle tissue increases and consequently also the number of cells, which burn off the excess fat. One muscle cell can have up to 1000 mitochondria – cell power stations. More muscle tissue means more power stations and this accelerates the reshaping of the body. In addition, insulin sensitivity in the cells increases. The greater the sensitivity of insulin receptors, the better muscle cells can absorb sugar and turn it into energy in the power stations. This is an explanation for the subsequent fat burning, since exercise accelerates metabolism and the body uses stored energy – fat – for a few hours after the finished exercise.

What to eat before exercise

Opinions differ – most say that it is best to consume something that gives you lots of energy – a banana, white pasta, i.e. simple carbohydrates with a high glycaemic index. But foods with a high GI do not lead to good results. In the book *Enter The Zone*, the authors Barry Sears and Bill Lawren mention research which shows that sports competitors who consume mostly carbohydrates force their body into creating excessively high insulin concentrations, because of which their cells constantly and quickly create bad eicosanoids (super hormones that cause silent inflammation). They go on to say that this unfortunate combination prevents the transfer of oxygen into muscle cells, which lowers endurance and the general readiness of the body.

At the same time, hyperinsulinemia causes a constant feeling of hunger; and if after all this a person again eats carbohydrates, she is caught in a vicious circle.

What to eat when you come home from work so that you don't lose the motivation to exercise

Food is important. After eating, you should have more energy, not less. This is why it is important that in the evening you don't eat anything white. Do an experiment: today after 5 p.m. fill up on white bread. You will see that you will lie on your sofa without any energy and with no motivation to exercise.

This is why it is important to eat something that gives you energy. If in the evening you always feel tired, I suggest you eat vegetables, yogurt and nuts – almonds, walnuts or hazelnuts, but avoid cashew nuts as they have the highest level of carbohydrates, as much as 3 times more than hazelnuts and 10 times more than almonds.

Advice: Before exercise, eat a handful of soaked almonds and a piece of reduced fat cheese. You will see that your energy lasts for ages. When you go hiking in the mountains or just mushroom picking in the woods, take some soaked almonds and a piece of cheese with you. This is a wonderful snack that gives you energy.

What to eat after exercise

Some friends make an agreement to play volleyball once a week. After two hours of exercise, they are thirsty and beer is the best thing for quenching thirst. One round and then another – after all, they've just exercised and a couple of beers can't be too much; everyone does it, so it must be good. And then when they come home, they are so hungry they could not give a damn about healthy eating – what they want is bread and something on it … and then perhaps another beer. After all this, they roll onto the sofa, fall asleep and that night their bodies don't reduce fat but put some on instead – beer after exercise achieves nothing but a beer belly!

Beer after exercise?

What chemical reaction happens in your body if straight after exercise you consume alcohol and simple carbohydrates?

Beer and white bread dramatically raise blood sugar. Beer has a glycaemic index over 100. When you add white bread with a glycaemic index of 85, you end up with an energy bomb! After a meal like that all you can do is lie down.

This combination is also common in the mountains. When people go hiking and reach a place where food and drink are served, they first have "a short" and then some home-made food. I won't say I never have a glass of something strong. But I do keep to a very simple rule – immediately after exercise, I eat some protein. When I come to a mountain hut, I first have a handful of nuts that I usually carry with me, so that my body gets some protein, and then have a blueberry liqueur and a home-made pastry.

Even if we take the glycaemic index into account, we can have a glass of beer without feeling guilty, provided we eat a few spoonfuls of cottage cheese first. This way, the glycaemic index will be greatly reduced:

Beer GI 100 + cottage cheese GI 0 = 100: 2 foods = 50 – the metabolism is still blocked. If we want to lose weight, the overall glycaemic index of the meal needs to be below 40.

Glass of beer + cottage cheese + handful of almonds = 100 + 0 + 15 = 115: 3 = 38.3 – that is a bit better. Now, the blood sugar will stay balanced and our body will regenerate in spite of the beer.

Immediately after exercise, have some protein

Fifteen minutes after exercise, have some protein so your body has a chance to regenerate quickly. This leads to a surplus of protein, which is necessary for regeneration and the strengthening of the muscle mass.

The best protein rich meal is without carbohydrates. Here are a few suggestions:

- reduced-fat cheese, a slice of prosciutto ham and some olives,
- plain yogurt mixed with cottage cheese and a few almonds,

- mozzarella and pepper,
- a protein shake that contains all 22 amino-acids and not only isolated amino-acids for increasing muscle mass. A shake containing isolated amino acids will "bulk up" your muscles, but if you stop exercising, your muscles will shrink.

If you exercise for 20 minutes to an hour in the evening, and eat some protein afterwards, you will weigh less in the morning. You will reshape in your sleep!

Protein is the builder of new cells

Protein builds cells: it is a constituent part of hair, nails, muscles, all the organs, and of every cell. Protein encourages the creation of warmth. As it cannot be stored, the surplus protein must be burnt for warmth. Let me rephrase this: if you have some protein with every meal, you will feel warm, you will not be hungry and, above all, you will have energy. Protein regenerates muscles. People who don't eat enough protein may look much older than they are. Protein is a source of B vitamins, calcium and magnesium, which are all necessary for feeling good. Protein prevents attacks of hunger and the "yoyo effect" after dieting.

But a word of warning: protein-only diets are not recommended. If you eat nothing but protein, you will acidify your body. You should always consume protein together with vegetables or fruit as this is the easiest way to maintain a balance between the acidic and alkaline state in the body.

For those who are quite active, the recommended daily consumption of protein is between 1.5 to 2g per kilogram of body weight.

Signs of protein deficiency – **if you lack protein, you may notice the following problems:**

- weakened immune system,
- weakened hair: brittle, thin, dull hair without shine, which may fall out in clumps,
- premature greying of the hair,
- brittle nails – also splitting and slow growth,

- loose, withered skin,
- appearance of stretch marks and cellulite,
- aged appearance,
- flabby muscles,
- prolapsed pelvic floor and urine incontinence,
- problems with hormones, tiredness and inexplicable sadness,
- inability to lose weight.

If you are short of protein, the building stones of new cells, you will become old, wrinkled and incontinent!

The body starts using muscle tissue for its functioning. Do you remember someone who lost weight using the "just eat less" approach and after the diet, looked withered and old? The problem is not just the loose skin on the face, the real problem appears when all the internal organs sag and you get urine incontinence. The solution to incontinence is the same as with all the other muscles – exercise (Kegel exercises) and the right diet, which contains sufficient protein and vegetables.

A woman weighing 60 kg needs around 90 g of protein, and a man weighing 80 kg at least 120 g. There is no point in eating a protein rich breakfast and then forget about protein. You have to spread your protein consumption throughout the day. Too much protein at once can harm the kidneys – which is why it is necessary to drink more – every hour at least one glass of water.

Protein gets digested in the stomach. If you don't produce enough gastric acid, you may get stomachache after eating protein, such as cottage cheese or eggs. In order to get rid of these problems, simply drink after each meal a glass of water into which you have squeezed half a lemon. You will be adding vitamin C this way, which helps in the decomposition of protein into smaller particles. The precious amino acids will arrive where they are meant to – the cells.

Why you may have a protein deficiency

- if you don't consume enough protein;
- if you don't have enough gastric acid (you have a heavy feeling in your stomach after eating). Protein cannot decompose into smaller particles – amino acids. Add vitamin C;
- if you lack vitamin B6. Its most important task is helping in the decomposition of proteins into amino acids;
- if you are under constant stress. Then all the protein, all the vitamin C and B vitamins are used to produce cortisol and none is available for all the rest.

20 g of protein can be found in:	**10 g of protein can be found in:**
60 g soya	200 g soya yogurt
120 g shiitake mushrooms	330 g soya milk
	1.5 eggs
Meat, poultry, sausages:	**Dairy:**
65 g prosciutto ham	250 ml kefir
80 g chicken breast	250 ml sour milk
80 g turkey breast	300 ml milk
90 g non-fatty lamb	300 ml buttermilk
90 g venison backstrap	300 g yogurt
90 g pork fillet	25 g parmesan
95 g rabbit meat	38 g 30% fat cheese
100 g veal fillet	50 g mozzarella cheese
100 g roast beef	60 g feta cheese (40 % fat)
120 g ham without the fatty rind	75 g plain cottage cheese (20 % fat)
123 g low-fat chicken sausage	
Fish:	
80 g smoked salmon	
100 g Atlantic halibut	

100 g salmon	**Grains:**
100 g sardines	65 g wholemeal pasta
100 g tuna	75 g wild rice
110 g shrimps	85 g durum wheat pasta
110 g mackerel	80 g oat flakes
120 g plaice	90 g wholemeal flour
120 g codfish	125 g brown rice
120 g sole	
125 g lobster	
220 g oysters	
Nuts and seeds:	**Legumes, vegetables:**
35 g peanuts	50 g beans or lentils
40 g linseeds	125 g tofu
45 g sunflower seeds	175 g peas
50 g almonds	200 g Brussel sprouts or Savoy cabbage
50 g pistachio kernels	500 g potatoes
55 g sesame seeds	
60 g cashew nuts	

*Summarised from: Marion Grllparzer: Gi-doet.

Note: As you can see, even potatoes contain some protein, but you would have to eat 4 ½ kilos to get the required daily quantity.

If you consume:

- 1 boiled egg – 10 g protein,
- 100 g cheese – Edam with 30% milk fat – 27.3 g,
- trout – 40 g,
- handful of almonds – 8 g.

This way, you will consume 85.3 g of protein. As you can see, it is quite difficult to ensure a sufficient amount of good protein. Add a protein supplement to your food and then you will cover your body's needs.

Glucosamine and carnitine are substances your body can make when it has enough building stones

Glucosamine influences the elasticity of tissues

Glucosamine is a substance produced by the body which influences the flexibility of joints. In addition to omega-3 fatty acids, in order to produce glucosamine your body also needs vitamin C, silicon and the amino acid glutamine.

Glutamine (Gln or Q) is one of the twenty-two essential amino acids. It is the most common free amino acid in the blood (500 - 900 μmol/l) and plays an important role in:

- the functioning of the immune system,
- protein metabolism,
- the appearance of glutathione – a substance that is present in every cell and helps in detoxification,
- preservation of the acidic-alkaline balance, i.e. the normal pH level of the blood,
- stimulates the functioning of the brain and the secretion of the growth hormone,
- plays a key role also in muscle growth and the prevention of muscle decomposition,
- speeds up the healing of wounds.

Glutamine was isolated for the first time from beetroot juice in 1883, but not until 1932 from protein. In spite of the relatively early discovery of this amino acid, the positive effects on the human body have been found only recently. Glutamine is now used in medicine as it accelerates the healing of tissue damage and bone fractures, has a beneficial effect on the inflammation of the digestive system and on stomach ulcers, while also being one of the most sought-after amino acids among recreational and professional sportsmen.

The best natural sources of glutamine are foods of animal origin:

- fish,
- meat (beef, poultry),
- milk, dairy,
- followed by foods of plant origin – spinach, beans, parsley and cabbage.

The biggest users of glutamine in our body are muscles, kidneys, the immune system and the small intestine, and the largest producers the skeletal muscles and lungs. In spite of the fact that the human body produces glutamine independently, during **increased use due to stress factors** production cannot match the requirements and it needs to be consumed in the form of a food supplement.

Carnitine

Carnitine is a "vehicle" which transports fat molecules through the blood to the cell furnaces – the mitochondria, where fatty acids are turned into energy. Carnitine is a substance produced by the human body from the amino acids lysine and methionine. In order for carnitine to be produced, the body also needs vitamin C, vitamins B3 and B6 and iron.

The amino acid lysine uses fatty acids in the right way and turns them into energy. It helps with some problems with fertility. If you are often tired, your eyes are bloodshot, your hair is falling out, you are anaemic and dizzy, the reason could be lysine deficiency.

Sources in food:

- fish,
- eggs,
- beans,
- prosciutto ham,
- spinach,
- cottage cheese,
- whey,
- yogurt,
- oats,
- all foods with a high protein content.

The amino acid methionine is a powerful antioxidant and helps with the decomposition of fats. It consists of sulphur and helps protect the body against harmful substances. Methionine helps drain the fluid from the body, reduces the production of bad cholesterol and prevents hair loss.

Sources in food:

- eggs,
- fish,
- beans,
- garlic,
- onions,
- cottage cheese,
- whey,
- yogurt,
- prosciutto ham,
- spinach,
- wheat germ.

All the above foods also contain B vitamins, which are necessary for the production of carnitine.

When there is a vitamin C deficiency, protein cannot disintegrate into amino acids and iron cannot bind, which is why carnitine cannot be created – this means there is no transport for excess fat and this is the answer why anaemic women cannot lose weight. Supplement your food with the natural food supplement Formula IV from neoLife, which contains everything – from vitamin C, vitamin B12, iron and copper – your body needs all these for the renewal of blood.

The role of carnitine in the body:

- It is a means of transport for fatty acids to travel to the mitochondria, where they turn into energy.
- Prevents the acidification of the body.
- Removes the lactic acid that appears in the muscles – we are all familiar with that special pain after exercise. Immediately after exercise, it is necessary to consume protein so that muscle tiredness and lactic acid are reduced and regeneration increased.

• Metabolises amino acids and helps in muscle regeneration.
• Increases the excretion of ammonia from the body. Most protein causes the appearance of ammonia, which acidifies the body. Carnitine forms uric acid from ammonia and quickly takes it out of the body.
• It is an excellent antioxidant, which prevents the appearance of free radicals. An increased number of free radicals accelerates ageing – this is why we could say that carnitine prevents ageing and increases regeneration.

What about rice milk, soya milk and almond milk, compared to cow's milk? Do they also contain protein?

Product	Glycaemic index	Protein	Carbohydrates	Fats
rice milk	85	0.1	12.6	1.5
goat's milk	25	3.9	4.5	4.3
almond milk	30	3.3	1.1	8.1
cow's milk (full fat and semi-skimmed)	30	3.5	4.63	3.5
soya milk	30	3.6	0.3	2.1
soya yogurt with fruit flavour	50	3.5	15.96	1.8
oat milk	30	1.0	6.5	1.5
coconut milk	40	1.7	3	18
chocolate coconut milk	65	0.6	8.4	2
yogurt – full fat	30	3.8	4.3	3.2
yogurt – reduced fat	15	3.3	4.3	1.3
yogurt – light fruit yogurt	40	3.0	14	0.9

Rice milk has a glycaemic index of 85. It is not suitable for losing weight because you will be consuming a lot of carbohydrates without being aware. 100 ml of rice milk contains only 0.2 g of protein. Since it contains hardly any protein and lots of carbohydrates, it should not be called milk but a refreshing drink or, even better, a calorific drink. It is the most widespread grain milk, but there are also varieties made from barley, rye, spelt and oats. These milks are made from wholegrains. Often vitamins and minerals are added, and the sweet flavour comes from the carbohydrates turning into sugar. Rice milk does not contain lactose or cholesterol.

Oat milk has a glycaemic index of 30 and is an excellent food that helps in the detoxification of the body. Oat milk strengthens the functioning of the nervous system due to vitamin E and folic acid. As it contains minerals – it is rich in iron, calcium and iodine, vitamins A, B3 (niacin) and vitamin C – it is suitable for everyone whose thyroid is underactive. Oat milk is not recommended for those who are allergic to gluten. Due to the low protein content, it cannot be classified as a protein food.

Soya milk has a glycaemic index of 30 and is with regard to protein content the best alternative to cow's milk, since it contains a similar percentage of protein and fat. It is used for making tofu, soya cheese. As soya milk does not contain calcium that our body could easily absorb, it is often added. Soya milk is a healthy cow's milk substitute, suitable also for those with lactose intolerance or an allergy to milk as it does not contain lactose. Since it contains only plant proteins, it is classified as a food that contributes towards the lowering of bad cholesterol. Soya milk also does not contain vitamins B12 and D, which do occur in cow's milk.

Almond milk has a glycaemic index of 30 and is rich in magnesium, antioxidants, vitamin E, selenium, calcium and manganese. Almond milk is an excellent replacement for cow's milk; because of the magnesium it contains, it helps reduce muscle cramps. Almond milk is not suitable for small children as there is a high possibility of an allergy to nuts. The only other warning is connected with chocolate or vanilla flavoured almond milk, which has added sugar and a much higher glycaemic index.

Coconut milk has a glycaemic index of 40. This is not the water found inside a coconut, but the fluid obtained by squeezing coconut flesh through a special sieve, which is then soaked and squeezed once more. Like other plant milks, coconut milk contains healthy unsaturated fats, but unlike the others it also has a very full flavour. It gets its colour and flavour from the high content of oil and sugar and you should not use too much of it.

Cow's milk has a glycaemic index of 30. Due to lactose – a sugar found in milk – cow's milk is unfortunately not suitable for those with lactose intolerance or an allergy to dairy. A glass of cow's milk contains 8 g of protein. If possible, you should buy farm-produced cow's milk that you do not have to boil.

Goat's milk has a glycaemic index of 25. The human organism digests goat's milk in 20 minutes. Goat's milk has 10 percent less lactose than cow's milk and causes fewer allergies. It strengthens the immune system and alkalises the blood. As consuming goat's milk does not increase the production of mucous, it doesn't cause the worsening of respiratory allergies, such as asthma.

Include nuts in your diet

	Glycaemic index	Protein	Carbohydrates	Fats
Almonds	15	18.7	3.7	54.1
Cashew nuts	35	17.5	30.5	42.2
Walnuts	15	14.4	10.6	62.5
Hazelnuts	15	12.0	10.54	61.6
Peanuts	15	25.8	16.13	49.2
Peanut butter	40	25.1	19.56	50.39
Brazil nuts	15	13.6	3.55	66.8
Chestnuts	65	2.42	45.54	2.26

Almonds

Include these super nuts in your diet. Almonds are at the very top as they contain the best ratio between calcium and magnesium, which are very important in detoxification, and influence the correct contraction of the muscles, including the heart muscle; they contain a lot of good fats and the highest value of vitamin E. Almonds have nearly no sugar and a glycaemic index of 15 so they keep you full for a very long time.

Almonds contain:

- protein,
- good fats,
- vitamin E,
- calcium and magnesium ratio 2:1 – i.e. the combination that the body can absorb and which influences the bones, detoxification, etc.,
- potassium, which influences the metabolism and helps with fluid draining from the body.

Don't worry about eating a handful of almonds – you will not gain wait, just the opposite, you will lose it. Since almonds are sprayed, it is good to soak them for a few hours before consuming them and discarding the soaking water.

Cashew nuts

These are the nuts you should avoid!

Cashew nuts contain the highest level of carbohydrate of all the nuts. Although various sources claim that they have a glycaemic index of only 35, I can tell you from my own experience that they cause hunger. If you eat a lot of them, you will soon not like what you see in the mirror. Since they contain 3-times as many carbohydrates as almonds, I believe they have a glycaemic index of around 45.

With regard to their nutritional value, they cannot compete with walnuts. If you are sugar sensitive, stay away from cashew nuts!

Walnuts

Walnuts are the healthiest nuts.

They contain the highest amount of omega-3 fatty acids, are the best plant source of protein, and rich in vitamins B and E.

Good fats have an anti-inflammatory action and it has been proven that they alleviate problems like asthma, rheumatoid arthritis, eczema and psoriasis. The glycaemic index of walnuts is 15.

Hazelnuts

Hazelnuts as an independent food (not in chocolate!) will help your mood. They contain glutamic acid, which alleviates tiredness and increases endurance. As they contain mainly omea-9 fatty acid, it is good to consume them together with walnuts.

Hazelnuts are very rich in the amino acid arginine, which helps strengthen the immune system and improves the functioning of hormones, as well as increasing the flushing of ammonia from the body. Arginine widens the blood vessels, which is why it is also good for heart diseases, high blood pressure and erectile dysfunction. Hazelnuts also have a low GI – only 15 – and are suitable for weight loss.

Brazil nuts

Two nuts for one egg. That is what they say in Brazil and, considering the nutritional value of Brazil nuts, it is probably true. The huge trees growing in the Amazon rainforests are tens of metres high and famous for their slow growth. They produce the first yield after ten or more years and it takes nearly a year for the nuts to develop from the flowers.

Brazilian people are convinced that the divine goodness is stored in these nuts as with their abundance of selenium, which is hard to find in typical western food due to the impoverished soil, they strengthen the immune system.

These nuts are also a wonderful source of magnesium, which helps you with a lot of energy. They have a low GI (15) and are suitable for weight loss. But use good sense – three Brazil nuts constitute a meal!

Peanuts

Peanuts have a glycaemic index of 15 and are full of protein. Worthy of special mention is the amino acid arginine, which has a beneficial effect on the cardiovascular system. Peanuts also contain tyrosine, which is a non-essential amino acid. It influences the maintenance of the mental processes and, indirectly, our mood; it is a component of the thyroid hormone, which plays a special role in the management of the rate of metabolism.

Peanuts contain another amino acid – phenylalanine – which has an effect on the release of the fullness hormone. But be careful! Peanuts contain a lot of aspartic acid, which reduces your libido. Peanut butter has a GI of 40.

Chestnuts

Chestnuts can be eaten both roasted or boiled.

Chestnuts are healthy! They are full of vitamins and minerals:

• **Potassium** helps lower the blood pressure and drain fluid from the body, it also acts against depression.

• **Manganese and magnesium** help alleviate pain in the muscles and joints, prevent muscle twitching and improve memory function.

• **Copper** prevents premature greying and pigmentation changes.

• **Calcium** helps with detoxification and good brain function and is necessary for healthy bones and teeth.

• **Phosphorus** works against tiredness and helps improve psychological strength. In combination with magnesium, it helps with the building of bones.

• **Zinc** improves the immune system and helps with detoxification.

• **Iron** in combination with copper and vitamin C improves the blood.

• **Vitamin B1** prevents muscle cramps.

• **Vitamin B2** improves the nails, prevents greasy hair and hair loss.

• **Vitamin B6** and the other B vitamins act on the metabolism, i.e. increase energy and improve how you feel; they also have an effect on the mental health and the nervous system.

• **Vitamin B9 – folic acid** influences the creation of the happy hormone.

• **Vitamins A and C** are strong antioxidants and improve the immune system. They have a protective action against free radicals, thus contributing to cardiovascular and eye health.

Like hazelnuts and almonds, chestnuts do not contain gluten. This is why they are very suitable for those who have an allergy to gluten. Chestnuts are also used in the food industry in the making of foods for those who are allergic to wheat and those with celiac disease.

Chestnuts do not contain bad fats and do contain a few omega-6 fats. Studies have shown that monounsaturated fatty acids in the diet help to lower overall cholesterol – help lower the LDL (bad) cholesterol and help increase the HDL (good) cholesterol.

In addition, chestnuts contain a lot of dietary fibre. In each 100 g, there is 8.1 g of fibre, which is approximately a quarter of the daily requirement. Dietary fibre helps with lowering bad cholesterol, and with the detoxification of the liver and gall bladder, as well as with digestion.

People who have kidney problems, should be careful when consuming chestnuts.

Because of the large quantity of potassium, chestnuts place a stress on the kidneys and should not be eaten in large quantities by those with kidney failure.

Diabetics should also consume chestnuts in moderate quantities.

Chestnuts contain a lot of carbohydrates and have a glycaemic index of 65. They are therefore not suitable for weight loss.

According to the value of the starch that in the blood turns into sugar, chestnuts can be compared to sweetened jam, blueberry cake or a delicious croissant. Below is a list of foods that contain a similar amount of sugar as chestnuts:

70 white bread	65 rye bread (30 % rye, the rest white flour)
70 croissants	65 corn (tinned)
70 toast	65 raisins
70 risotto (white rice)	65 tinned apricots
70 gnocchi	65 beetroots (boiled, still warm)
70 brown or white sugar	65 macaroni cheese
65 brown bread with seeds	60 pizza
65 maple syrup	60 honey
65 pineapple (tinned)	60 ripe bananas
65 potatoes (boiled in their skins)	60 ice cream
65 chestnuts	60 blueberry cake
65 jam (sweetened)	55 chocolate spread

To avoid blood sugar problems and to lose weight, consume chestnuts together with protein. I remember the times when we had boiled chestnuts as our evening meal. We had them with milk. As milk is a protein, the chestnuts do not cause weight gain – the overall GI is just over 30.

Combinations:

- milk and chestnuts;
- prosciutto or cheese (GI 0) as a starter + chestnuts (GI 65) = 32.25 – you lose weight;
- as a starter, have 300 ml yogurt (or any other protein), and only then eat chestnuts;
- mushrooms (GI 15) + prosciutto or cheese (GI 0) + rye bread (GI 65) + chestnuts (GI 65) = 36.25 – you lose weight (If you eat less or no bread and more prosciutto, you will lose weight faster!);
- chestnut picnic – first goulash, then roasted chestnuts.

Chestnut spread recipe:

Ingredients for 4 people:

- 250 g cooked, peeled chestnuts
- 1 avocado
- 250 g cottage cheese
- 1 dl yogurt
- 1/2 pomegranate
- 2 spoonfuls of sour cream

Mix all the ingredients in a mixer. Add seasoning and a pinch of sweet paprika. Serve on rye bread or wholemeal walnut bread as a healthy breakfast, snack, tasty afternoon mini meal or healthy evening meal.

Since you have added protein (cottage cheese and yogurt), the glycaemic index of the chestnuts is greatly reduced. Calculation: 65 + 10 + 0 + 15 + 35 + 0 = 125: 6 foods = 20.8 – it is a slimming spread!

Protein supplements?

If you know you are not consuming enough protein, you need to supplement it. It can be in the form of a food supplement. When choosing the protein, make sure that it contains all 22 amino acids and vitamin C, vitamins from the B group, zinc, calcium, magnesium, chromium and potassium. These are the essential ingredients for the release of the renewal of hormones. A protein supplement should also contain some carbohydrate since it stimulates the secretion of insulin, which "opens" the cell doors, allowing nutrients in. When you are consuming large quantities of protein, also make sure you are consuming sufficient amounts of water, otherwise you will acidify the body.

Which nutrients are missing if your joints and muscles are aching, when you have cramps or back problems?

Aching legs with muscle pain

If you have aching legs, a stabbing pain in your muscles, the pain moves from your calves to your thighs, or you have a feeling that your muscles are hurting "from inside", your body is telling you that you have a vitamin B1 and magnesium deficiency. You also lack potassium, which influences the binding of magnesium, magnesium influences the binding of calcium, calcium the binding of vitamin B12 and B12 the binding of all the other vitamins from the B group, including B1. If this is the case, it would be good to reach for a good supplement containing all the vitamins and minerals, with an emphasis on B vitamins and magnesium. For the renewal process to be set in motion, it also makes sense to add vitamin C and a yogurt and parsley smoothie, so that you obtain some calcium and potassium.

Muscle cramps

Your body is telling you there is a magnesium deficiency. The signs of magnesium deficiency are the same as those of a vitamin B1 deficiency. The solution is the same as above.

Severe pains in the soles of your feet

This problem often appears in diabetics and hints at a deficiency in metabolic vitamins and minerals. When the body obtains a sufficient amount of B vitamins, magnesium (which should always be in combination with calcium) and vitamin C, the condition improves in a short time. When there is a severe deficiency of vitamins in the body, it makes sense to reach for a food supplement.

Joint pains, tennis elbow and can the body produce glucosamine by itself?

A dull pain is a sign that there are micro injuries at the cell level and the body needs a natural substance to mend this condition. When a great deal of stress is frequently placed on joints, these tiny injuries cannot heal and the inflammation can only increase.

Glucosamine plays an important role in the creation of joints, tendons, ligaments, synovial fluid, bones, nails, skin, heart valves, blood vessels and the mucous excretions in the digestive, respiratory and urinary systems. The body produces it by itself, but this process decelerates with age. If we give the body the right ingredients, we can encourage the renewal and production of glucosamine. We make it every night if we provide the body with sufficient omega-3 fatty acids and vitamin C, which create cartilage, while vitamin C also ensures the renewal and flexibility of the connecting tissues. Don’t forget that we also need protein as it builds new cells – if there is none in the evening meal, the regeneration does not begin.

For the renewal of cartilage, silicon and selenium are also needed. They can be found particularly in vegetables with hard leaves or tubers. Research has shown that cruciferous vegetables, such as broccoli, cabbage, swede, radishes and cauliflower help with the renewal of the connecting tissues due to their high content of silicon and selenium. In addition, these vegetables also contain sulforaphane, which helps with the detoxification of soft tissue, including connecting tissue.

Our body communicates with us, trying to tell us that we are deficient in nutrients

Problem	Deficiency	Solution
Withered skin, appearance of cellulite	Protein and vitamins B6, B9 and B12	Vitamins B6 and B12 and folic acid participate in the formation of substances that build the connecting tissue. Consume eggs, cottage cheese, whey and prosciutto. In order not to acidify your body, always eat vegetables with these foods.
Age spots	Vitamin E	The best solution is wheat-germ oil with added vitamin E, which can also be found in all nuts.
Allergies	Problems originate in the intestines – increase detoxification	You need probiotics, omega-3, calcium, magnesium and vitamins from the B group. Consume more whey, fatty sea fish and linseed and hemp oil.
Asthma	Vitamin E, omega-3, B vitamins and probiotics	Foremost, start consuming garlic since it dissolves mucous. I recommend you have a few sips of sage tea every day, some kefir or whey and wheat germ oil with added vitamin E.

Bad body odour	Vitamin B12, zinc and probiotics	The problem is in detoxification. Work up a sweat every day. Go to a sauna, exercise and include yeast, eggs, kefir, pumpkin seeds and mushrooms in your diet.
bad breath	probiotics, vitamin B3 and zinc	Exclude all white grains: white bread, pasta, rice, and cakes and pastries. Drink sour cabbage water, whey or kefir and at least three times a week eat fish, eggs and avocado.
Bags under eyes	Water retention, bad functioning of the kidneys – as a result of stress and negative feelings	Who is getting on your nerves so badly? Who do you have to listen to? Drink goldenrod tea. It calms your emotional state, cleanses the liver and helps with flushing fluid from the body.
Brittle and split nails	Protein, calcium, magnesium, iodine and iron	The simplest way of obtaining all these nutrients is with mushrooms, fried with a lot of onions, with eggs.
Brittle, slow-growing nails	Zinc and protein	Protein and zinc can be found in all seafood – you should eat sea fish several times a week.

Bruising broken capillaries	Vitamins C and E	Consume lemons, rose hip tea and wheat germ oil with added vitamin E.
Cold hands	Iodine; could also be the reduced functioning of the thyroid	Iodine and all the other vitamins and minerals that stimulate a lazy thyroid can be obtained from mushrooms – can be pickled mushrooms.
Cracks in mouth corners	B vitamins	Consume more eggs, cottage cheese, prosciutto, spinach, walnuts and peanuts.
Dandruff	Vitamins B12 and B6, zinc, selenium and omega-3 fatty acids	At least once a week, consume sea fish, such as sardines, as this way you will be consuming some copper, iodine, protein, zinc and vitamins B. Vitamin B12 can also be found in eggs, while some zinc and selenium occur in mushrooms. Consume linseed and salmon oil.
Decreasing libido	Vitamin E	Change your partner – I'm joking! No, you don't have to change your partner, just get yourself back to normal. If you spend your days sitting, your sex organs do not get much blood and you cannot expect to be particularly lively in bed in the evening. A decreasing libido indicates acidification of the body. You

		are particularly deficient in oxygen. Consume wheat germ oil as vitamin E influences the blood supply to the small capillaries.
Dry mucous tissues	Vitamin A and red pigments – carotenoids	Consume more red peppers, tomatoes, carrots and drink carrot juice. Advice: As red pigment is fat soluble, you should always consume some oil – can be linseed oil, fish oil or wheat germ oil.
Dry skin	Vitamin B	The vitamins from the B group can best be obtained from consuming one boiled egg a day and cottage cheese, cabbage, walnuts and mushrooms.
Dry, dull hair	Protein, omega-3 fatty acid, vitamins A and E, iodine, silicon and vitamins B	As you are deficient in a number of nutrients, I recommend a good dietary supplement. Alongside it, you should also eat healthily – nuts, red peppers, mushrooms, eggs and with every meal have a glass of plain yogurt.

Eye problems: • night blindness • bad adjustment to darkness • bloodshot eyes • inflammation • burning eyes • sties	Vitamins A and B2	Vitamin A can be found in fish, egg yolks and in all yellow, orange and red fruit and vegetables. Vitamin B2 is found in milk, cheese, fish and eggs.
Gaining fat on the stomach	Stress, evening meals poor in nutrients, omega-3 deficiency	Consume foods with a low glycaemic index, in the evening eat protein and vegetables and supplement your diet with a high-quality omega-3 source.
Greasy hair	Lack of B vitamins	Eat an egg every day and don't eat anything with white flour – cakes, bread or pasta.
Hair problems: • greying • falling out • thin hair	Protein, vitamins B, copper, zinc, selenium, iodine and omega-3 fatty acid	At least a few times a week, consume sea fish, such as sardines, as this will give you some copper, iodine, protein, zinc and B vitamins. Selenium can be found in Brazil nuts – but have only up to five a day so that you do not overdose on selenium.
Hot flushes in menopause	Vitamins E and B6, omega-3 fatty acids and zinc	Consume wheat germ oil since this is the best natural source of vitamin E. Consume cabbage, mushrooms, linseed oil and fish oil. Eat sardines a few times a week.

Insomnia	Nutritionally poor evening meals do not provide enough protein, which is necessary for the production of the required hormones (sleep hormone and growth hormone)	In the evening, consume prosciutto and olives; almonds and cheese; yogurt and avocado with cottage cheese. See also: The Growth Hormone on page 199
Joint calcifications	Vitamin C; improper storage of calcium; another possible reason is not enough gastric acid, which is why calcium cannot decompose properly	After every meal, drink a glass of fresh lemon water without sugar. Supplement your diet with vitamin C.
Joints – painful	Omega-3 fatty acids, vitamin C, silicon and protein	The reason is silent inflammation. You need omega-3 in the evening. Three times a week, have sardines in the evening, with fresh vegetables, e.g. fresh red pepper.
Menstrual problems	Vitamin B12, calcium, magnesium and vitamin E	Same as above; include nuts, such as almonds, in your diet. They have an excellent ratio between calcium and magnesium.
Muscle cramps	Magnesium and vitamin B1	Several times a week, consume prosciutto, almonds and spinach or kale.
Nervousness, irritability	Lack of B vitamins (B12, B3), calcium, magnesium and omega-3	Consume eggs, milk, yogurt, cabbage of all kinds, walnuts, almonds and peanuts. Omega 3 fatty acids can be found in all cold pressed oils.

Osteoporosis	Acidified body, calcium, magnesium, vitamins B and omega-3 fatty acids deficiency	Vitamin B6 will keep you young, prevent the decomposition of bone cells and consequently osteoporosis. Omega-3 fats, in combination with calcium and magnesium, increase the forming of bone mass.
Pins and needles in hands and feet	Magnesium, vitamin B1 and vitamin E	Several times a day consume prosciutto and almonds; besides magnesium, almonds also contain vitamin E.
Pneumonia, problems with lungs	Vitamins B, zinc, copper, calcium, magnesium, selenium, vitamins A and E and omega-3 fatty acids	Essentially, the reasons are silent inflammation and toxicity. Pneumonia indicates that your "soul is tired" and urgently needs a rest. You need at least 1 g of omega-3 fatty acids a day – preferably in supplement form. Consume nuts, such as almonds and walnuts (due to the vitamins and minerals), and several times a day drink 200 ml of whey. Several times a day, have a vegetable smoothie made with carrots and consume a carotenoid supplement. Selenium in connection with the vitamins C and E and carotenoids blocks the chemical reactions in which

		free radicals appear, which damage the cells.
Ridges on nails	Iron	Consume red meat; but for iron to bind, you also need copper, which you can get from beans and mushrooms, and you should have a glass of fresh lemon water because of the vitamin C.
Shaking hands	Vitamin B and magnesium	Both vitamins B and magnesium can be found in nuts – include walnuts, hazelnuts and almonds in your diet and always have a little yogurt with them.
Skin peeling by the nail bed	Carotenoids – vitamin A and amino acids	You need more protein – at least twice a day, have a glass of green smoothie to which you have added red pepper or carrots, and a plain yogurt.
Split hair	Vitamins B and omega-3	All cold pressed oils contain omega-3 fatty acids; consume fish oil, linseed, hemp or walnut oil and in the evening, eat a meal containing protein.
Spotty skin	The problem originates in the intestines, the body is detoxifying through the skin – deficiency in probiotics and vitamins B	Exclude all white grains, such as white bread, pasta, white rice and cakes and pastries. Consume whey, yogurt, kefir, cabbage and garlic, which will additionally help with detoxification.

Stretch marks	Protein and zinc	Best way to consume protein and zinc is to have an egg a day, together with pickled mushrooms.
Vitiligo (patches of skin without pigment)	Probiotic bacteria and antioxidants	Avoid meat, dairy and citrus fruits. Add vegetables that are red (carotenoids), purple (beetroot, blueberries) and green (cruciferous vegetables: radishes, black radishes, broccoli).
Waking up between 2 and 4 in the morning	The reason is again the evening meal – not enough protein and fibre	The evening meal should always be eaten 2 hours before bed. Consume a combination of protein and vegetables, such as a boiled egg and gherkins; prosciutto and olives; fish and vegetables. If you eat tinned fish, let it be sardines. Always have some vegetables, you cannot have too many of those.
White spots on nails	Zinc and silicon	The highest level of zinc can be found in seafood and of silicon in the hard parts of vegetables. Mushrooms contain both zinc and silicon.

Wrinkles	Protein, vitamin C, vitamin E and silicon	In the evening, consume prosciutto, olives and almonds. Silicon and vitamin C are elements that help with skin renewal and with the regeneration of joints and gums.

Nutrients for fast regeneration

Hormones are fat soluble. If your diet does not include enough good fats, this will first be reflected in your hormonal balance. When you stick to the rule “away with fats”, you are well on the way to your hormonal balance being destroyed.

Away with bad fats – that is true! But all fats are not bad. Milk fat is good – we are talking about unprocessed milk; farm produced butter is a good fat; lard is a good fat; coconut butter is a good fat; ghee is a good fat. Keep to a very simple rule – the price of fats always says everything.

Good fats of plant origin are cold pressed oils – pumpkin, olive, linseed, argan, rapeseed, etc. All these oils contain unsaturated fats. The price of oil also says everything. The French say about the rest of Europe that we stick to the following rule: “No oil is good enough for my car, but the cheapest oil is good enough for my salad.”

Every cell has a membrane, 75 percent of which is fat and 25 percent protein. If you want to renew your body, give it enough high-quality protein and good fats.

Good fats

Omega-3 fatty acids

Did you know that omega-3 fatty acids are of key importance in the creation of the hormones that influence weight loss?

- DHEA, which ensures you lose weight from your waist, is created on the basis of omega-3 fatty acids and amino acids.
- Omega-3 fatty acids help during weight loss because they prevent the decomposition of the muscle mass and help build new muscle mass.
- Omega-3 fatty acids improve the metabolism of carbohydrates (helping bread, pasta, rice and other carbs to turn into energy).
- Omega-3 fatty acids are a constituent part of the super hormones. They help to regenerate the body; they also act on the cardiovascular and immune system and the mechanisms that decide about body fat.

By consuming omega-3 fatty acids, you will lose weight faster, become more and more flexible, you will be able to do up your belt more easily and your clothes will look better on you. More about omega-3 fatty acids on page 216.

Vitamin E

Vitamin E is called the "youth vitamin". It brings oxygen to the lungs, blood, brain and sex organs – it brings oxygen to every cell. Since vitamin E protects oxygen, it helps cells to breathe.

Vitamin E consists of a family of tocopherols and tocotrienols.

Vitamin E is fat soluble and consists of a series of elements. Eight principal members of the vitamin E family are divided into two groups: the tocopherols and tocotrienols. In each group, there are alpha, beta, gamma and delta members. Alpha-tocopherol was discovered first. The quantities on the label usually refer to this member only. But research has revealed other family members that play a hitherto underestimated role. The other vitamin E family members extend the life span of the red blood cells and improve the utilisation of vitamin A.

Vitamin E:

• acts on the fatty part of the cell – the membrane – and improves metabolism;
• acts against chronic fatigue;
• strengthens the heart and blood vessels;
• lowers the oxidation of cholesterol;
• slows down blood clotting and the appearance of blood clots;
• improves circulation (against cold feet) and concentration;
• helps with bronchitis and asthma;
• helps with painful periods and menopause problems (balances the hormones);
• prevents the oxidation of fats – the appearance of age spots;
• helps with muscle ache after hard exercise (lactic acid is excreted, which causes the pain, but vitamin E decomposes the acid);
• helps get rid of spots;
• acts against loose skin – oil can be smoothed onto the cleansed skin as a mask;
• protects the eyes and acts against bad eyesight;
• influences male sexual strength;
• helps with female and male infertility;
• with regular use, nails become firmer, hair more manageable and skin more flexible;
• increases the flexibility of connecting tissues;
• improves the transfer of glucose, thus influencing the metabolism of sugars and is of great help to insulin – the pancreatic hormone.

Vitamin E is the vitamin of youth. It rejuvenates us.

It acts as a constituent part of 144 metabolic enzymes:
• acts as a strong antioxidant,
• prevents the aged appearance of the skin,
• ensures the flexibility of cell membranes,
• accelerates blood flow through the small capillaries,
• takes care of toxins leaving the body.

The vitamin E that has already been used, i.e. has oxidised, is renewed with the help of vitamin C. This is excellent news for those who are under stress, have high cholesterol or blood sugar. This is why you should always consume good fats, such as vitamin E and omega-3 together with vitamin C!

Vitamin E deficiency

If you start getting pins and needles in your hands, the body may be telling you it is short of vitamin E. The same happens with nerves and the brain when they become short of this vitamin. There is also a vitamin E deficiency if you often bruise, have broken capillaries or age spots. The first indicator of a vitamin E deficiency is tired skin.

Food sources: The highest amount of vitamin E can be found in wheat germ oil and in the following foods:

- unrefined sunflower oil,
- milk,
- mackerel,
- nuts, such as hazelnuts and almonds.

Note: You can recognise natural vitamin E under the name d-alpha-tocopherol, and artificial vitamin E under dl-alpha-tocopherol.

Research has shown amazing effects of vitamin E. Professor Eric Rimm from Harvard University examined all the studies on vitamin E, carried out until 1997, and came to the conclusion that by taking at least 100 mg of vitamin E daily for two years, the number of deaths from cardiovascular diseases can be reduced by 30 to 40 percent. Taking a smaller dose was not proven to be successful.

Nutrition experts agree that for protection against cancer and cardiovascular disease we need vitamin E. Sadly, we cannot obtain enough through food. An example: in order to consume 100 mg of vitamin E, we would have to drink at least half a litre of sunflower oil or two litres of olive oil. There is not much of this vitamin in fruit and vegetables. This is why it has to be taken as a food supplement.*

*Summarised from: Dr Ulrich Strunz and Andreas Jopp: *Die Vitamin-Revolution*.

Vitamins that help in cell metabolism

If you don't consume sufficient amounts of vitamins in your diet, you feel tired, without motivation, you are constantly hungry, your body demands sugar and the fat keeps collecting.

Signs of a vitamin C deficiency:

- appearance of crow's feet,
- low immune system,
- chronic tiredness,
- depression and low concentration,
- bleeding and inflamed gums,
- proneness to allergies and asthma,
- slow healing of wounds,
- haemorrhoids and varicose veins.

Vitamin C activates the metabolism

Vitamin C plays a part in over 15,000 metabolic processes. Only when your body has a sufficient amount of this vitamin does the metabolism start to function normally. Since vitamin C is a very fragile vitamin, it is excreted from the body very quickly. To prevent your teeth from falling out (scurvy), eating 1 orange a day (60 mg) is enough, but to ensure good metabolism, this dose is too low.

Vitamin C:

- is actively involved in the creation of hormones,
- takes part in the formation of neurotransmitters, which pass information from one cell to another,
- is involved in the formation of collagen (strengthening the connecting tissue, tendons and bones),
- actively involved in the burning of fat since it takes part in the formation of carnitine, which ensures that fatty acids are transferred to the "cell furnaces". This is the only way of obtaining energy from fatty acids,
- activates the detoxification of the liver, which filters harmful substances from the blood,
- binds with heavy metals, such as iron, lead and other harmful substances.

Vitamin C activates old fat – vitamin C ensures slimness

- vitamin C creates new collagen fibres and preserves youth – collagen gives structure to skin, bones, joints and gums,
- helps preserve the flexibility of blood vessel walls,
- gets rid of redness of the cheeks,
- alleviates varicose veins and acts against atherosclerosis (blocked veins),
- helps in the binding of iron, thus helping to improve the blood,
- strengthens the immune system and stimulates the production of antibodies,
- helps with quick thinking,
- creates the happy hormone (acts against depression),
- helps with weight loss,
- acts on male fertility as it accelerates sperm motility and prevents sperm sticking together.

In his book *100% Health*, Patrick Holford mentions a more than 10-year long study at the Los Angeles university that included 11,000 Americans, which showed that a daily dose of 300 mg of vitamin C – compared to the American average of 70 mg – reduces the number of heart attacks in men by 50 percent and in women by 40 percent. In addition, the average life expectancy increases by six years.

Dr Linus Pauling's and his successor Dr Mathias Rath's research showed that we need at least 1000 mg of vitamin C daily. Translated into oranges, this means that we would have to eat 20 fresh oranges a day to consume this amount of vitamin C.

Since there are many users of this fragile vitamin in the body – for example, a 20-minute long period of stress (anger, crying, a quarrel, nervousness, fear) uses 300 mg of vitamin C, 1 cigarette uses 100 mg of vitamin C – it makes sense to add it in the form of a natural nutritional supplement, which is gradually released into the body.

Vitamin D

Vitamin D is produced in the skin exposed to UV rays in natural light. Even sun creams with a very low protection factor block the body's ability to generate vitamin D. The healing rays of natural light cannot pass through glass. This is why our body doesn't produce this vitamin when we sit at home or in the car.

Over 40 percent of the world's population has a vitamin D deficiency – 48 percent of girls, aged 9 to 11, 60 percent of patients in hospitals, 80 percent of patients in home care and in homes for the elderly, and 76 percent of pregnant women, which shows up in their children (81 percent of new-borns have insufficient amounts of vitamin D for normal development), who are much more susceptible to a later development of type 1 diabetes, arthritis, schizophrenia, etc.).

Warning signs of a vitamin D deficiency:

- worsened sight and smell,
- insufficient tear fluid and dry and red eyes,
- night blindness,
- dry, itchy skin,
- frequent inflammation of the mucous tissues – colds and pneumonia,
- acne,
- miscarriages
- infertility and reduced production of testosterone,
- increased risk of the cancer of the lungs, prostate, breasts, cervix and large intestine. A sufficient amount of vitamin D and calcium reduces the appearance of cancer by 77 percent – this study was carried out for 4 years at Creighton University School of Medicine, Nebraska.

Signs of a vitamin D deficiency:

- worsening of diabetes and reduced functioning of the pancreas,
- osteoporosis, osteopenia, osteomalacia – these bone diseases always appear due to a vitamin D deficiency and consequently due to a calcium deficiency,
- psychological conditions, such as depression,

• vitamin D deficiency is also connected with Alzheimer's and Parkinson's disease,
• various diseases connected with the immune system: psoriasis, rheumatoid arthritis, gluten intolerance,
• increased heart trouble with high blood pressure, the metabolic syndrome – syndrome X, infertility, behavioural irregularities, irregular tooth development, caries,
• inability to lose weight and a sudden weight gain – especially on the stomach,
• incorrect functioning of the adrenal glands is also connected with insufficient amounts of vitamin D; even the causes of PMS originate in the deficiency of this vitamin.

Vitamin D and the adrenal glands

The calcitriol in the adrenal glands is regulated by the enzyme tyrosinase, which is necessary for the production of dopamine, adrenaline and noradrenaline. These play a part in stress situations. If there are excessive amounts of these substances, our body becomes tired, which can lead to chronic fatigue and depression.

Vitamin D is unique in comparison to other vitamins

It is created automatically – we only have to allow the sun to shine on our skin and not be covered in sun protection cream. The risk of getting diabetes or cancer is reduced by up to 80 percent through sunbathing (2 to 3 times a week for half an hour).

A hint: We all know that sunbathing between 11.30 and 15.00 is not advisable, especially without protection. As with everything else, the rule "Use your common sense!" also applies to sunbathing.

Food sources:

• egg yolk,
• fish,
• fish oil,
• butter,
• milk.

The bodies of those who have insufficient amounts of vitamin D in their blood absorb lead more quickly. Perhaps therein lies the answer why people suffering from a vitamin D deficiency have all the above listed problems.

The B group vitamins

Even normal, happy people can become depressed when they have a deficiency in vitamin B3 (pulses, cabbage), B6 (cabbage), B8 (eggs), and folic acid – vitamin B9 (egg yolks, cabbage).

The B group vitamins are of key importance for good hormonal functioning, for the mental state and for energy. If you are deficient in the group B vitamins, you cannot lose weight, you feel tired, exhausted, and cannot think straight – you have low concentration and are often nervous and irritable.

B vitamins:

- are involved in the metabolism of fats and carbohydrates,
- help in the creation of energy,
- build protein into muscles,
- help with the creation of serotonin, the happy hormone,
- vitamin B5 acts as a precursor to good cholesterol and is involved in the formation of the sex and growth hormones, which literally reshape you while you sleep.

Food sources of B vitamins:

- **B1** – egg yolks, milk – helps alleviate depression and anxiety attacks,
- **B3** – niacin – eggs, avocado, fish, spinach – it acts against depression and is necessary for the creation of the sex hormones,
- **B5** – pantothenic acid – nuts; it is a natural substance for reducing tension, is needed for the creation of the hormones the body secretes during stress or during longer periods of emotional stress, depression or anxiety,
- **B6** – cabbage, eggs, yeast – helps with the natural creation of antidepressants,

• **B8** – choline – eggs, walnuts, mushrooms – sends nerve signals to the brain and has a calming effect,

• **B9** – folic acid – spinach, broccoli, eggs – when there is a deficiency, you feel chronically tired, even depressed,

• **B12** – eggs, milk, meat – a deficiency results in anaemia; it affects the stability of your mental state.

Vitamin B1

Who has not experienced feeling lousy after a night of partying? Your muscles ache, you have a headache, people talking loudly get on your nerves, your brain is not functioning well and you cannot think fast. A hangover. So you understand – this is how a person who has a vitamin B1 deficiency feels.

Vitamin B1 is involved in raising your mood and in good brain function.

The body needs vitamin B1 for building nerves, for the proper functioning of the muscles, the eyes and the digestive system. It is needed in the metabolism of carbohydrates and has an effect on how energetic you feel. When you are deficient in vitamin B1, you go grey quickly, your hair may be falling out, and you have a feeling of sadness and sleepiness.

Vitamin B1 deficiency may cause muscle cramps and a very low tolerance for mental challenges. A person lacking B1 very quickly loses patience and reacts violently.

Warning signs of a vitamin B1 deficiency:

- slow healing of wounds,
- low pain threshold,
- premature greying,
- muscle cramps and pins and needles in your hands and feet,
- stabbing pains in the heart and heart palpitations,
- insomnia,
- frequent headaches,
- reduced abilities and the feeling of tiredness,
- worsened concentration and reduced attention,

- forgetfulness,
- inexplicable sadness,
- water retention,
- constipation
- raised bad cholesterol.

If you have difficulty remembering 5 consecutive numbers or often forget where you have left your keys, wallet or telephone or where you have parked your car, then that is probably a sign that you lack vitamin B1. It is also possible that you are consuming enough of it, but because you are also drinking coffee and alcohol, taking hormonal tablets or you are under stress, B1 decomposes too quickly.

Vitamin B1 has an important influence on:

- growth,
- reduction of the secretion of gastric acid,
- raising the pain threshold,
- healing shingles,
- improving the mental state,
- feeling energetic,
- speed of thinking,
- regeneration of the myelin sheath in the brain.

Food sources:

- brewer's yeast,
- wheat germ,
- sunflower seeds,
- oat flakes,
- bananas,
- hazelnuts,
- pistachios,
- peas,
- egg yolks,
- peanuts,
- milk,
- most vegetables,

- lean pork,
- soya.

Vitamin B1 is absorbed together with the other B group vitamins. It is most effective in combination with vitamins B2, B5, B6, B9 and B12.

Vitamin B3

Vitamin B3 – niacin is a vitamin for the soul. The body needs B3 to make serotonin. It is necessary for creating energy. When there is a deficiency of B3, most serotonin disintegrates into vitamin B3 and this results in insomnia, distractedness, despair, fear and neurological disorders that can lead to depression.

Vitamin B3 deficiency may lead to a rise in bad cholesterol or triglycerides.

Warning signs of a vitamin B3 deficiency:

- tiredness,
- muscle weakness,
- skin changes,
- proneness to getting a sun allergy with red and rough skin,
- bad breath,
- mouth ulcers,
- ulcers on lips,
- headache,
- insomnia,
- distractedness
- despondency
- irritability
- oversensitivity of gums
- digestive problems – diarrhoea and nausea.

Vitamin B3 plays an important part in:

- cell breathing and cell energy,
- brain metabolism,
- heart functioning,

- muscles and connecting tissue,
- control of cholesterol,
- functioning of the digestive system,
- sleep,
- mood,
- metabolism of carbohydrates.

Food sources:

- lean meat,
- liver,
- fish,
- poultry,
- eggs,
- brown rice,
- milk,
- vegetables,
- mushrooms,
- spinach,
- avocado,
- peanuts,
- salmon,
- almonds,
- peas,
- dark chocolate.

For many people, chocolate is a solution to being sad. Chocolate raises the serotonin level and offers a quick feeling of happiness. Unfortunately, reaching for chocolate soon results in an increase in body fat.

Vitamin B6

Vitamin B6 is the vitamin for being in a good mood and having a youthful body. You are deficient in vitamin B6 if you are under a long-term mental and/or physical stress. During this time, all the B vitamins are used for the metabolism of protein and consequently the creation of the stress hormones, while there is not enough for the other 120 metabolic processes.

Vitamin B6 activates the cell production of energy

Did you know that contraceptive pills lower vitamin B6 concentration by a fifth?

Vitamin B6 is water soluble and does not collect in the liver. It is excreted from the body within eight hours of consumption and, like the other B complex vitamins, has to be regularly provided through healthy food or supplements. If you consume too much of it, i.e. between 2 and 10 mg a day, it could cause neurological problems. The recommended daily amount is between 1.6 and 2 mg.

Vitamin B6's duties:

- helps prevent various disorders in the functioning of the nervous system and skin problems,
- stimulates the correct synthesis of the liver acids and acts against ageing,
- reduces muscle cramps at night,
- improves the immune system,
- controls the amount of fluid in the body,
- and the most important duty is to help in the disintegration of protein into amino acids.

Warning signs of a vitamin B6 deficiency:

- tiredness,
- gloominess,
- tension,
- irritability,
- distractedness,
- feeling of numbness in the hands and feet,
- arthritis,
- muscle weakness,
- hair loss,
- cracked corners of the lips and inflamed corners of the eyes,
- weakness of the immune system.

When do you need more vitamin B6?

• When you are under stress: vitamin B6 makes your nervous system and you happy,

• when you take contraceptive pills, you will probably need higher amounts of vitamin B6,

• if you eat lots of protein, you need additional amounts,

• if you are a diabetic, as B6 can even reduce the need for insulin,

• if your immune system is low;

• if you are in menopause – vitamins B6 and B12 and folic acid take part in the creation of the substances that build the connective tissue. Vitamin B6 will keep you young, prevent the disintegration of bone cells and osteoporosis.

Food sources: eggs – yolks, liver, walnuts, peanuts, spinach, cabbage, yeast, brown rice, wheat germ.

An interesting experiment was carried out in Iowa state among some prisoners, which showed how drastically human behaviour changes when people are short of vitamin B6. After only a week, the volunteers who had consumed food without vitamin B6 developed headaches, they became increasingly aggressive or depressed, irritable or apathetic, without energy and could not sleep.

At the end of the second week, they got psoriasis, red skin, eczema and cracked lips. The third week, they also got diarrhoea, nausea and vomiting. The concentration of protein in their urine increased. Their muscle mass diminished. The fourth week, they became anaemic, their immune system was partly destroyed, which is connected with a pronouncedly small number of the white blood cells, antibodies and killer cells. The experiment had to be stopped. They rewarded the prisoners with the promised reduction in their jail sentence. The experiment clearly showed the consequences of a vitamin B6 deficiency after only four weeks.*

*Summarised from: Patrick Holford: *100% Health*

Vitamin B8 – choline – quick thinking vitamin

Vitamin B8 is responsible for a stable mental state. It passes directly into the brain cells, where it forms a chemical substance that helps with memory; it also plays a part in the excretion of toxins from the body:

- accelerates brain development and strengthens memory,
- influences concentration,
- ensures the normal functioning of cells,
- influences fat metabolism,
- lowers blood pressure,
- is a transmitter of nerve signals and prevents fat collecting in the blood,
- prevents muscle aches and exhaustion,
- alleviates psychological problems,
- acts against skin inflammation,
- helps increase the ability to remember.

Warning signs of a deficiency vitamin B8:

- high blood pressure,
- raised values of the bad cholesterol.

When there is a choline deficiency, brain activity decreases. There can be a weakening in the memory function, vomiting, vertigo and hair loss. Until recently it was considered that eggs raise cholesterol, but now it is clear that eggs contain choline which acts against cholesterol. We are talking about boiled eggs, not suffused with burnt fat.

Food sources: eggs – yolks, liver, walnuts, peanuts, mushrooms, cabbage.

It is absorbed together with vitamin B12. The damp, oily protection of the nerves (myelin sheath), for which vitamin B8 is responsible, can dry out in the case of deficiency, which leads to lower concentration, while in old age it can contribute towards Alzheimer's disease.

Vitamin B12 is the vitamin of eternal youth

Vitamin B12 influences the binding of all the other vitamins B. Without it, there is no absorption, no binding. Those who are anaemic, need vitamin B12, vitamin C, iron and copper in the same meal. The simplest solution is a supplement, which contains all of these.

Functions of vitamin B12:

- helps with the formation of the myelin sheath in the brain,
- improves concentration and memory,
- reduces irritability,
- influences the absorption of all the other vitamins in the B group,
- plays a part in the creation of red blood cells,
- prevents the risk of a heart attack,
- prevents the fragility of bones and back pain,
- preserves a healthy nervous system,
- prevents dementia,
- increases energy.

Warning signs of a vitamin B12 deficiency:

- first come neurological problems – numbness of the limbs,
- tingling, burning feeling in the limbs,
- trembling, dizziness, muscle weakness,
- vision disturbances, problems with tasting and smelling,
- tinnitus,
- sleep problems,
- forgetfulness,
- lowered concentration,
- dementia,
- irritability and depression,
- confusion,
- psychoses,
- balance problems,
- urinary and bowel incontinence,
- impotence,
- lack of energy and quickly getting tired,
- premature hair greying.

Vitamin B12 deficiency lowers the sperm count and affects the sperm's motility; girls short of vitamin B12 are anaemic, have problems with irritability, find it difficult to get pregnant or have an early miscarriage.

Food sources: eggs, liver, fish, cheese, milk, brewer's yeast.

It is absorbed together with calcium. It is not surprising that there is a lot of vitamin B12 in eggs, which also contain calcium and protein, which makes the absorption of B12 that much easier.

When you lack vitamins B (B-complex), people cannot talk to you, because you cannot hear. All you hear is voices that get on your nerves. But when you have a sufficient amount of vitamins B, you listen, you are focused, you learn quickly and you are generally happy and in a good mood. You are brimming with healthy energy. A person with enough vitamins B is a happy person!

Advice: If you take a supplement, make sure it contains the full spectrum of natural vitamins and minerals:

• **Vitamin A** influences the eyes and the visual field; encourages growth, healthy bones, hair and gums; stimulates the immunity system and shortens the duration of infections.

• **Vitamin D** is needed for the utilisation of calcium and phosphorus, which are needed for strong bones; together with vitamins A and C, it helps prevent colds; it helps in the healing of the inflammation of the conjunctiva. Signs of a deficiency of this vitamin appear as a bad degeneration of the teeth.

• **Vitamin E** reduces tiredness; increases circulation and improves concentration; helps alleviate muscle spasms in legs and after physical exertion.

• **Vitamin C** plays a part in the creation of collagen, which is important for the growth and renewal of cells; it heals wounds and bleeding gums; helps reduce the amount of cholesterol in the blood; strengthens the body's immune system and helps in the treatment and prevention of colds; accelerates the absorption of iron, thus improving the blood; reduces the effects of numerous substances that cause allergies; helps lower high blood pressure; prevents scurvy.

• **Thiamine (vitamin B1)** is connected with clear thinking; it is necessary for the functioning of the nervous system and the metabolic processes. The signs of a deficiency in this vitamin are nervousness, joint aches, periods of palpitations, muscle weakness, etc.

• **Riboflavin (vitamin B2)** is necessary for beautiful and healthy skin, nails and hair; it stimulates clear thinking; it also helps with the creation of blood and hormones.

• **Niacin (vitamin B3)** also acts on the brain, since it influences the circulation. The signs of a deficiency in this vitamin appear as tiredness, irritability, muscle weakness.

• **Vitamin B6** acts on the blood, brain, skin and concentration. A deficiency is perceived as irritability and excessive tiredness.

• **Choline (vitamin B8)** affects the functioning of the brain, concentration and the memory.

• **Folic acid** protects the heart and plays a part in the formation of new cells. A lack appears as growth problems, depression, mucous membrane inflammation, memory problems.

• **Vitamin B12** influences the nerves and memory. The signs of a deficiency are excessive tiredness and severe nervousness – irritability.

• **Biotin (vitamin B7)** has an effect on the health of nails, hair and scalp; it is also needed for metabolism – food turning into energy.

• **Pantothenic acid** is needed for the creation of hormones that the body secretes during longer periods of emotional stress.

• **Iron** prevents anaemia and tiredness; gives skin elasticity; encourages growth and increases resistance.

• **Zinc** accelerates the healing of wounds; encourages growth and mental vitality; helps with colds and the renewal of the mucous membranes; it has an important role in the functioning of the brain; it is irreplaceable in the creation of the proteins that affect the regeneration of the body.

• **Iodine** encourages growth; influences energy; encourages mental flexibility and helps a lazy thyroid.

• **Copper** has a beneficial effect on the blood; it helps with the pigmentation of hair and skin.

• **Chromium** helps balance a desire for sweet things and prevents a sudden fall in energy; encourages growth.

• **Manganese** is required for the normal building of bones; it helps with tiredness and memory; reduces nervous irritability.

• **Selenium** acts like a natural medicine; it is needed for rejuvenation (antioxidant) and acts against skin ageing.

Minerals are vital for your hormonal balance

Minerals activate cell metabolism and help with the feeling of hunger

Even though we promise ourselves to eat more healthy food, we are most lacking in the essential nutrients when we need them the most. Stress, both emotional and physical, exhausts our mineral stores. As a result, on days when everything is upside down, we reach for something sweet.

Calcium helps in detoxification and in the decomposition of fats

Calcium is the most present mineral in our body. It is an essential mineral, necessary for the solidity of the skeleton and teeth, as well as for a good physical and mental state. Calcium is the main building block and important for the functioning of muscles, the heart and nerves. It prevents high blood pressure and helps with blood coagulation. If we consume too little with our food, our body starts taking it from our bones, which results in weakened collagen in our bones.

Warning signs of a calcium deficiency:

- insomnia,
- muscle cramps,
- back ache,
- palpitations,
- muscle twitching and aches,
- bad body odour,
- weak nails,
- osteoporosis,
- mental instability.

Brittle bones (osteoporosis) cannot be noticed on the skin or felt in any other way. We only become aware of it when we break a bone. This is why it is important that we consume a sufficient amount of calcium every day – approximately 1200 mg – around 1 l of milk, 1 l of yogurt and some cheese and vegetables. But because we know that we do not consume all this, we have to ensure that our body gets the amount it needs on a daily basis.

Functions of calcium:

- Calcium binds acids and turns them into salts. They are excreted via the kidneys and bladder. When we are short of calcium, our body becomes acidified. This is why calcium plays an important role in protection against cancer – particularly large intestine cancer.

- Calcium reduces gastric acid.

- Calcium is required for the renewal of the brain's myelin sheath. People who are short of calcium immediately notice this by their mental instability.

- Calcium increases the binding of vitamin B12, which ensures the binding of all the other B group vitamins.

- Calcium plays a part in the metabolism of iron.

- Calcium is needed for the transfer of nerve impulses – if there is not enough calcium, you find it difficult to remember certain things and you have a very low patience threshold.

Natural sources of calcium:

- linseed,
- sesame,
- salmon,
- milk and dairy,
- cheese,
- mozzarella,
- legumes,
- almonds,
- walnuts,
- broccoli,
- cabbage,
- Brussel sprouts,
- parsley,
- leek,
- nettles,
- wild garlic.

The first condition for the calcium from food to be absorbed is good gastric acid. Those who have do not have enough gastric acid should have a glass of lemon water with every meal, for vitamin C. This makes calcium change its structure – it ionises and in this form, the body can absorb it. Calcium which has not been ionised can cause a great deal of trouble in the body – inflammation, kidney stones, and joint calcification. This is a sign that you are very short of vitamin C. Supplement your diet with gradual release vitamin C.

Magnesium – the mineral of constant energy

Magnesium plays an important role in the solidity of your bones and teeth and for the functioning of your nervous system and muscles. When you are short of magnesium, you feel nervous and have frequent muscle cramps.

Magnesium is a metabolic mineral – this means that it acts like a match – without it there is no energy. Magnesium is of key importance in the functioning of the mitochondria – the cell power stations that produce energy.

One muscle cell can have as many as 1000 of them. If you imagine them as small furnaces, magnesium is necessary to light them, for the creation of energy. Also needed are vitamins from the B group and vitamin C.

Magnesium is indispensable for the effective functioning of the nerves and muscles. It is known as an anti-stress mineral.

Warning signs of a magnesium deficiency:

- weakness, tiredness,
- low concentration,
- inability to lose weight,
- muscle cramps and twitching of the face muscles,
- restless arms and legs – a tingling feeling,
- weak nails,
- problems in the functioning of the heart, stabbing pains in the heart,
- raised blood pressure,
- insomnia,
- nervousness.

Magnesium is also needed for the transmission of the nerve signals, flexibility of tissues and metabolism.

Duties of magnesium:

- helps with the creation of energy and fat burning,
- helps combat depression,
- helps prevent heart attacks,
- ensures that the cardiovascular system is in good condition,
- prevents early childbirth and false contractions,
- prevents tingling and stabbing in the soles of your feet,
- prevents cramps,
- helps with digestion,
- alleviates premenstrual syndrome,
- prevents calcium deposits in the wrong places and the appearance of kidney and gall bladder stones,
- together with calcium acts as a natural sedative and helps with allergy to the sun and all other allergies,

• influences the flexibility of connecting tissues,
• takes part in the metabolism of calcium, vitamin C, phosphorus, sodium and potassium. If you are short of these elements, you feel chronically tired,
• influences the formation of the hormone dopamine, which influences your mood and prevents water retention,
• encourages the use of insulin – the hormone that causes hunger attacks – consequently, you do not crave food.

Research has shown that if you consume 200 mg magnesium a day, you will put on less weight, feel less bloated and feel less chest pain.

When does your body need even more magnesium?

When you are under increased physical or emotional stress. A young person who is involved in sports and is also at university must supplement magnesium. If she also goes to parties and does not shy away from alcohol, there it is very likely that she will be short of magnesium. Since magnesium is a metabolic mineral, it is necessary for the metabolism of carbohydrates. People who consume an unbalanced diet with sweet snacks and white bread, have a greater need for magnesium.

Magnesium helps bind calcium, potassium, sodium, phosphorus and vitamin C. If calcium is wrongly deposited on joints, a supplement of magnesium and vitamin C is needed.

Natural magnesium sources:

• grains,
• figs,
• pumpkin seeds,
• hazelnuts,
• Brazil nuts and cashew nuts,
• almonds,
• pine kernels.

Magnesium activates energy production in the cells

Did you know that magnesium is needed to turn blood sugar into energy? If you are short of magnesium, you cannot lose weight, you feel exhausted, you cannot think straight, your concentration is low, you are often nervous and your muscles twitch, you may also have cramps in your legs.

Calcium and magnesium supplement

If you supplement your diet with calcium and magnesium, make sure that there is twice as much calcium as magnesium and that vitamin D3 is added. D3 is required for the transfer of calcium from the intestines into the blood (it acts like a vehicle, transporting calcium).

Calcium, in combination with magnesium, has the following beneficial health effects:

- protects against osteoporosis and preserves strong bones,
- prevents growing pains in children who are growing fast,
- acts on the nervous system (in combination with vitamin B it helps with depression),
- ensures a steady pulse,
- recommended for pregnant women – calcium for the baby and magnesium for preventing spasms of the womb and premature contractions,
- alleviates painful periods,
- a necessary supplement for those involved in sports as it affects the bones, muscles, nerves and vascular system,
- research has shown that in women who consumed enough calcium and vitamin D, the values of bad cholesterol fell and of good cholesterol rose.

Advice: Magnesium and calcium supplements should never be taken after a meal as they reduce the release of gastric acid. These minerals bind and absorb best in the evening, before sleep; they should be combined with vitamin C.

Iron

Iron is the mineral of solid health

I have already mentioned that vitamin B12 is important for the blood. It binds iron, in combination with vitamin C and copper; iron forms haemoglobin, which is responsible for the transfer of oxygen around the body. If there is a deficiency of iron, there is also a deficiency of oxygen; as a result, anaemia shows up as tiredness, lack of motivation, weakened immune system and inexplicable weight gain.

Warning signs of an iron deficiency:

- anaemia,
- tiredness,
- dizziness,
- pallor.

Foods that contain iron: beef, lamb, game, sardines, dry apricots, crabs, tuna, egg yolk.

You utilise iron badly if you are under stress, your temperature is raised, you take hormonal tablets, or you drink caffeine and alcohol.

If you want iron to bind, you also need vitamins B12 and C, as well as copper. Vitamin C is found in lemons, blueberries, beetroot and blackberries, and copper in nuts, liver, legumes, mushrooms, peas and tomatoes.

Problems often appear when people consume an unbalanced diet. White bread and chocolate spread have neither iron nor vitamin C, and even less copper. In connection with copper, it is also worth mentioning that when there is a deficiency, the person ages quickly, greys prematurely, has problems with nerves, fertility and skin and skin pigmentation.

Iron can also help you feel better:

- encourages growth and increases resistance against illness,
- prevents tiredness,
- improves blood quality (anaemia),
- gives elasticity to the skin,
- iron is a constituent part of carnitine – the natural substance in the body that serves as a transport vehicle for fat molecules. Carnitine takes fatty acids to the cell furnaces – mitochondria. If there is not enough iron in the body, carnitine cannot form and there is no transport for excess fat. This is the reason why anaemic women can never lose weight. More on carnitine on page 238.

Chromium prevents hunger attacks

You need chromium to prevent hunger attacks since it balances insulin – the hunger hormone

It is needed in the body because together with insulin it acts in sugar metabolism. It helps protein get where it is needed. Chromium is insulin's main partner and helps it carry out its duties. When there is not enough chromium, the body needs more insulin; but insulin leads to unstoppable hunger and sugar cravings.

Research done by the U. S. Agriculture Department showed that nine out of ten people eat a diet that does not provide enough chromium.

Through food, most chromium is obtained in brewer's yeast, wheat germ and calf's liver.

How often do you eat these foods?

Chromium:

- prevents hunger attacks and the resulting falls in energy,
- slows down diabetes,
- stimulates insulin,
- helps prevent high blood pressure and even lowers it,
- encourages growth,
- prevents atherosclerosis – a chromium deficiency causes plaque and clots in blood vessels.

When the body has a sufficient amount of chromium, sugar cravings are considerably reduced or even disappear altogether.

In their book *The Carbohydrate Addict's Lifespan Program*, Drs Richard and Rachael Heller say that the extreme factors of physical stress, such as lack of sleep, intensive exercise and physical exertion can exhaust the body's chromium stores. They go on to say that chromium is of crucial importance in the balancing of the blood sugar. The body replaces reduced chromium values by releasing additional insulin, which results in a greater or more frequent desire for food.

The authors recommend consuming chromium in the form of a dietary supplement, but with a warning to all those with diabetes – since chromium can cause a reduced need for insulin, they should consult their doctor before taking it.

The mineral potassium helps with weight loss!

Potassium, together with sodium, regulates the fluid in the body. A disrupted balance between potassium and sodium causes fluid retention. Potassium acts within cells and sodium in the lymph. If you look bloated and have bags under your eyes, you should increase your consumption of potassium so that the balance between it and sodium gets back to normal.

Potassium:

- is necessary for transmitting nerve impulses,
- regulates pulse and blood pressure,
- necessary for muscle contractions,
- helps with the proper functioning of kidneys,
- necessary in the metabolism of carbohydrates and the release of insulin from the pancreas;
- turns blood sugar into glycogen, which is used by muscles for energy and this is why a deficiency in this mineral causes tiredness and muscle weakness,
- helps maintain the cardiovascular system in good form and regulates the fluid in the body.

A deficiency in potassium can result in muscle cramps, weakness, oversensitivity, tiredness, vomiting, bad reflexes and problems with concentration, heart arrhythmia and even heart attacks. Potassium's regulation of the transfer of nutrients through cell membranes decreases with age; this explains some of the damage in circulation, and despondency and general weakness in the elderly.

Natural sources of potassium:

- avocado,
- almonds,
- spinach,
- red pepper,
- oranges,
- tomatoes,
- pineapple,
- raspberries,
- currants,
- fish,
- beans,
- walnuts,
- parsley,
- chives.

Advice: Every morning, make a green smoothie from a bunch of parsley, half an avocado, a pinch of salt, a few celery leaves and yogurt. Add a spoonful of a protein shake that contains all the vitamins and minerals. This refreshing drink will fill you up, give you energy and accelerate detoxification.

Chapter 6. Hormonal Challenges Through Life

I trust the flow of life – I am

In this chapter, we will look at the hormonal challenges that appear in the following periods of life:

1. Growing up
2. Pregnancy
3. Inability to get pregnant
4. Breastfeeding
5. Menopause

You will go through all these periods of hormonal fluctuations without any special problems if you keep to the principle of eating according to the glycaemic index. This is the foundation of taming hunger attacks and preventing weight gain.

The first hormonal challenge – growing up

It has only been ten years, but your child is already getting her **first spots**. Puberty is knocking on the door. **The "cocktail" of hormones is starting to bubble.**

Nervous outbursts are not an unusual occurrence, mood fluctuations appear almost hourly. Your child is still a child and at the same time an adult in a child's skin and later (at the age of 16) a child in an adult's skin. This is a stormy period, which we have all been through some years ago and now it is our child's turn.

The nerves and brain

1. B vitamins, particularly B12, are the "food" for nerves. If someone is deficient in this vitamin, they are like a "bomb" ready to explode. The slightest thing sets them off. If a young girl is to get enough B vitamins she has to eat an egg a day. In addition, you can offer her a supplement containing vitamins, minerals and good oils. Your daughter will calm down and communicate in a more peaceful way.

2. What the brain urgently requires are the omega-3 fatty acids since the brain surface to a large extent consists of these oils. How many times a week do you eat fish?

3. In order to function well, the brain also needs calcium. This mineral is necessary for transmitting signals from the brain to the nerves. Calcium appears in the largest quantities in dairy and/or you can take a calcium supplement. The only thing you should be careful of is that the proportion of calcium and magnesium is 2 : 1, and that vitamin D3 is added for better absorption, as well as vitamin C. This combination will also have an excellent effect on the muscles and bones since calcium, magnesium and vitamin C build connecting tissues and strong bones.

4. Concentration – the oxygen supply, which increases brain circulation, can be accelerated with vitamin E. This vitamin is necessary for young girls who have stomach cramps during their period. Vitamin E supplies blood to the smooth muscles and consequently, cramps stop.

Cellulite – the curse of the modern world. Fifty years ago, no woman had cellulite. Girls should consume lots of vegetables, particularly the hard varieties (cabbage, turnip, broccoli, beetroot, radishes, etc.) in order to consume enough silicon, which influences the firmness of the connecting tissues. **Vitamin C** also affects the connecting tissue, acting on collagen, which is necessary for firm skin.

What acts against acne?

The problem lies in insufficient detoxification. The toxins that the body should be removing via the kidneys and intestines are coming out through the skin. The condition of the intestinal microflora can be regulated with the addition of garlic and probiotics. Since garlic reduces the power of probiotics, it is wise to consume one in the evening and the other in the morning.*

*See also: *Detoxification on page 177 and Healthy digestion on page 181.*

When I entered puberty, I grew very quickly. At the age of 12, I was already as tall as I am today. I started putting on weight at the same speed – when I was no longer gaining height, I gained width. I ended up with 70 kg and more, which is rather a lot for my height. For the first few years, I wasn't too bothered about this, but when I went to the secondary school, I began dieting. Since I didn't know any better, I followed the principle "eat less". I denied myself food; in fact, I made myself ill.

For breakfast, I would eat a slice of white bread and drink a cup of milk; for the morning snack, I maybe had a pot of plain yogurt; lunch – I must be honest here, because I've never spoken about this before. I often came home from school starving and ate so much that my stomach hurt. Then I went to the toilet and threw up the whole lunch. I ate nothing the whole afternoon and then maybe had something little in the evening. I wasn't too thin, but I was obsessed with food. If I now look back – my only goal was to lose weight. How I did it, wasn't important.

The true reason for my eating disorder was that I denied myself love.

This resulted in anaemia, mainly because of a shortage of nutrients. Blood represents joy. This was an indicator that joy wasn't flowing through my veins. The doctor prescribed iron tablets. I took them for 6 years, but I remained anaemic. No one told me that I needed copper, vitamin C and vitamin B12 for the iron to be able to bind. My blood improved only when I started taking a supplement containing iron, B vitamins, copper and vitamin C.*

I concealed my vomiting. When I was talking to my daughters one day and told them that I had an eating disorder, their reaction was: "You were such a psycho!" I'm not afraid of criticism. I'm saying this because you may have a growing daughter. Be careful! Talk to her because she won't tell you about her problems on her own. When a young girl has problems, she may be constantly angry, she may shout at you, she may wrap herself in silence. If she is angry, she is short of B vitamins, because sufficient amounts of these mean calm nerves; if she is wrapped in silence, she feels she is not understood and accepted.

You will achieve nothing or you will even do more harm if you approach her by saying: "What's bothering you? What's wrong with you?", especially if you say this in an irritable voice. We know that even a thicker separating wall appears in response to this. It will be much more helpful if you calmly state:

- "I see something has been weighing you down lately."
- "I see you've been angry recently."
- "I see something is bothering you."

Say calmly that you feel it and see it. If you say calmly **"I see"**, it makes communication easier. Children learn to communicate from us; let's show them that it's right to talk about our feelings.

The foundation of the body is a cell. The body needs three micronutrients:

- fats,
- protein,
- sugar.

Every cell has a membrane that consists of 75 percent fat and 25 percent protein. A diet containing little fat slows down the cell metabolism. The body of a young girl needs a constant and sufficient supply of good fats so that cell membranes can function properly. Sadly, many young girls eat a lot of synthetic fats that reduce the permeability of cell membranes.

The more a girl reaches for modern food, the more synthetic fats she eats and the less protein. Today's food thickens and solidifies cell membranes. Fats, sugar and protein can no longer enter cells and instead get deposited on the outside wall in the form of fat. Since sugar as energy cannot enter the cell, the girl feels tired. In order to resolve this problem, her body releases more insulin into her blood. And insulin means unstoppable hunger and sugar cravings.

The building blocks of hormones are amino-acids, which can be obtained with a combination of animal and plant proteins (e.g. meat and green beans).

But often, girls decide to go on limiting slimming diets and do not eat meat, which means they are not getting the much-needed protein and a sufficient amount of B vitamins. In this case, they should have a good supplement– with just one drink a day, they will get all the building blocks, vitamins and minerals.

When a young girl feels tired over a long period and is putting weight on, it is very likely that she is deficient in vitamin B6, which is the key vitamin for metabolism – of both protein and carbohydrates.

Signs of a B-group vitamins deficiency:

- dry skin on which eczema may appear,
- skin impurities, acne,
- excessive skin pigmentation,
- cracked mouth corners,
- premature greying, hair loss and thin hair,
- greasy hair that is splitting,
- itchy eyes, light sensitivity, deterioration of sight,
- trembling hands,
- anaemia,
- lack of concentration,
- restlessness, depression, fear,
- hyperactivity and irritability,
- disturbed sleep.

Contraception

Research has shown* that almost 70 percent of girls between the ages of seventeen and twenty take contraceptive pills. It is a well-known fact that hormone pills flush B vitamins out of the body, but these vitamins are necessary for the metabolism of carbohydrates. If in addition a girl consumes unhealthy food, she may quickly start putting on weight.

Nowadays, girls also often reach for alcohol. If you notice that your daughter is increasingly irritated, ask yourself if she is deficient in vitamin B1. Does she eat enough healthy food? Since young people often eat outside the home and at home reach for the food that is in the fridge and white bread, it often results in them not getting enough vitamin B1. If in addition to this they consume sugary foods and drinks, they are sacrificing the last vitamin B1 stores for the sugar to metabolise. And since sugar badly damages the intestinal flora, the intestinal bacteria no longer create their own B vitamins.

When you add alcohol to this kind of bad nutrition, the measure is full. Alcohol uses up most of the vitamin B1 and the nerves remain completely unprotected. Vitamin B1 with vitamin B12 and calcium with magnesium and omega-3 fatty acids renew the myelin sheath that protects the nerves and ensures good brain function. The daily menu should include one egg and dairy, while at least omega-3 fatty acids should also be added.

*Summarised from: Michel Montignac: *La méthod Montignac illustrée pour les femmes.*

The time of growing up is very important for a young girl. Overnight, she turns from a little girl into a young lady. A hormonal explosion takes place in her body and needs to be supported with the right nutrients and a sufficient amount of water. A young girl's body tries to communicate that something is missing – and you, her parents, can notice this.

Nutritional deficiency:

Research has shown that in the impoverished diet of girls there is a shortage of calcium, magnesium, iron and vitamins such as A, B6. B9 and E, which are at the time when their body is undergoing considerable changes urgently needed.

How does the body communicate a deficit of nutrients?

When a girl is deficient in vitamins – particularly those in the B-group* – you can notice the following:

- **greasy hair** – lack of B vitamins;
- **split hair** – deficiency in B vitamins and omega-3 fatty acids;
- **dandruff** – lack of good fats;
- **brittle bones and frequent fractures** – deficiency in vitamin A, calcium, magnesium, vitamin C and omega-3 fatty acids;
- **low concentration and frequent headaches** – lack of B vitamins and omega-3 fatty acids;

- **hyperactivity** – deficiency in B vitamins and protein;
- **cracked mouth corners**– lack of B vitamins;
- **sties** – B vitamins deficiency;
- **spots** – this problem originates in the intestines – lack of probiotics, B vitamins and vitamin E (more on vitamins on page 262);
- **excessive bleeding during menstruation** – this is thought to cause anaemia. But my observations indicate that just the opposite is true – anaemia causes strong bleeding; when the blood improves, the bleeding is reduced. In order to improve the blood, the body needs more iron, copper and vitamin C. For the necessary binding to occur, there also has to be vitamin B12;
- **painful menstruation** – indicates a severe lack of good fats – mostly vitamin E;
- **sore breasts** – also indicate a lack of good fats – omega-3 and vitamin E.

If I return to my story – I had problems with my skin, greasy hair and painful menstruation; I had cracks in the corners of my mouth and I erupted very easily. Now I know that, in addition to everything else, I was very short of B vitamins.

How could I have very quickly solved my problems? I needed healthy food that contained sufficient amounts of B vitamins and protein. The solution could have been very simple – a cooked egg and some vegetables every day. And a lot of hugs.

Even a few small changes in the direction of a healthier life will produce long-term benefits

Providing the right conditions for the health of growing children is particularly challenging these days. We have got them used to sugar and they have become addicted. We will not be able to change our habits overnight. It takes three weeks (21 days) for a child to create a new habit. Your daughter will get used to new tastes in three weeks. A simple solution – eating according to the principle of the medium glycaemic index is suitable for the whole family. See also page 100.

• Breakfast is one of the main meals. If your daughter cannot manage to or doesn't want to eat in the morning, prepare a fruit smoothie with protein for her. An excellent combination is frozen fruits of the forest (blueberries), milk, cinnamon and a spoonful of protein powder.

• **Your daughter should eat every 3 hours**. This will ensure that her blood sugar stays level and she will not be reaching for something sweet. If she eats regular meals, there will be no desire for constant snacking between meals.

• If your daughter is picky and only wants to eat sweet things, she is most likely sensitive to the sugar in food. Blood sugar fluctuations are caused by roast potatoes, white bread, everything made from white flour and everything that tastes sweet. Eliminate all white foods – white bread, white flour, white pasta, white bread rolls, white rice – and replace them with wholemeal flour, brown rice, rye bread. You decide what to buy.

• **Cream cheeses and fruit yogurts are desserts**. Buy plain yogurt, mix in some frozen fruits of the forest and that is a healthy snack.

• **Ice-cream – who can resist?** Your daughter can have ice-cream. Let her enjoy it. But think what she can have with it to stop her blood sugar going wild. She can have anything with a low glycaemic index. This includes strawberries, carrots, walnuts, hazelnuts, almonds, cucumbers, pistachios, milk, yogurt, reduced-fat cheese, cherries, etc. You can find a list of foods according to their glycaemic index on page 86.

• **Don't buy fizzy drinks** (even when they are on special offer). Flavoured water and fizzy drinks are all full of sugar. 100 ml of Coca Cola contain 11 g sugar, which is equivalent to two tablespoons. Flavoured waters are also full of sugar, 100 ml contain on average 4 g of sugar, nearly a tablespoon. So, what should your daughter drink? Have you thought of tap water?

• **And what about popular foods – pizza and gnocchi?** Of course, your daughter can eat these, just make sure that they are accompanied by vegetables and protein. This will ensure that her blood sugar stays level, her sugar craving is reduced and her mood doesn't fluctuate. But buy crisps and similar snacks only occasionally.

• **Always have two vegetables with your lunch: cooked and fresh**. Allow a choice, for example, broccoli and lettuce, roast courgettes and a cabbage salad; fried mushrooms and green salad, etc.

• **After 5 p.m., young girls should not eat sugary things, white bread, etc**. Instead of chocolate and biscuits, let there be a basket of fruit and nuts on the table. Growing children will reach for snacks that are within their visual field. Offer them protein: cottage cheese spread on brown bread, blueberries with cottage cheese or bread and prosciutto ham. If the snack is not healthy, make your daughter at least drinks a glass of milk to balance her blood sugar. My daughters like a cheesy bread roll for their afternoon snack. They accompany it with a glass of fresh, raw cow's milk and their blood sugar remains balanced – and, above all, this stops them from reaching for something sweet in the evening.

• For young girls, and for you too, it is important that the evening meal consists of protein and vegetables. We have been made to believe that various crisps, chocolate confectionary and chocolate spreads are a healthy meal and that we are bad parents if we don't let our children eat them. Make a spread from cottage cheese, sour cream and avocado, add a few herbs and serve it on wholemeal bread.

• While growing up, girls need twice as much protein as adults. Protein is a component necessary for the production of the growth hormone, which is responsible for growth and proper development.

A time of great changes

During this stormy period of growing, hormonal upheavals and seeking their own way, young girls should support their bodies with a sufficient quantity of B vitamins, good fats and protein. At home, it is wise to reduce the amount of white and processed foods and include wholesome foods and good protein. *You can find recipes and ideas* on page 112.

If your daughter starts putting on weight, you should talk to her about healthy eating. You will not be helping her by talking about how her body is still developing and that puberty is not a time to be losing weight. She may resort to drastic measures and understand your advice as a hint that she cannot expect any support or understanding from you.

Try to understand your daughter. By offering her sensible advice, you will build a good relationship based on trust. Tell her every day that you love her, that you are proud of her and happy that she is your daughter. Praise her as often as possible – that which you give attention to, grows. At least once every day give her a hug and a kiss. Tell her she is wonderful and that you are happy she is part of your family.

I know it is difficult sometimes. But don't forget that you were once that age and you also wanted to be heard. Since we want the best for our children, let us give them the best. I don't mean material goods, but emotional support and healthy food. With that we can really give them the best foundations for a healthy and happy life.

The second hormonal challenge: Pregnancy/problems with getting pregnant/losing weight after giving birth

A future mother should be aware that her body is a temple and that she will be helping God with the creation of a new life. A woman is a goddess. The functioning of the sex glands is influenced by the pineal gland. It is an endocrine gland, situated at the bottom of the skull. The 7th energy centre is connected to the pineal gland. It is connected with the creation of something new and the relationship with God. In order for the pineal gland to function well, a generally healthy lifestyle is needed: the body must be given healthy food, enough sleep, exercise in the fresh air and lots of positive thinking – including prayer. This improves the overall health and particularly the health of the sex organs.

When a woman wants to prepare her body for the greatest miracle – a new life, she must be aware that her womb is like soil. When the soil is too acidic, plants cannot grow. Equally, a woman must ensure that her body is not acidic. It can be acidified by sour thoughts, like fear of failure, despair or being resigned to her fate, and by a nutritionally poor diet.

First, let us look at problems with conception

One year, when at the end of the school holidays I was buying the last items needed for school, I came across a young woman at the till, who told me how lucky I was to have children. I politely asked her if she had children and she replied with sadness that she and her partner were trying.

Stress is the main reason for the low motility of sperm and a weak ovulation. The stress hormone causes menstrual cycle problems, such as irregular periods or even a cessation of periods, or regular periods without ovulation. Research has shown that vitamin B12 deficiency lowers the number of sperms and influences their motility. A young woman deficient in B12 will find it difficult to get pregnant; often, there is an early miscarriage.

In his book 100% Health, Patrick Holford says that one of the main reasons for infertility is a wrong diet. A study carried out by the University of Surrey made young, infertile couples give up alcohol, processed foods and the grains they were allergic to; they received supplements of vitamins and minerals for which tests showed a deficiency. As many as 81% of the women got pregnant and gave birth to healthy children. There were no miscarriages, premature births or babies born with defects. The vitamins and minerals help the body to process and use hormones; a deficiency in one of them can result in infertility.

I recommend a diet high in protein, which contains a large amount of B vitamins: eggs and cabbage salad, seafood, cottage cheese and avocado and, of course, lots of the antioxidants found in blueberries, pomegranates, raspberries and all the fruit whose appearance makes you think of a cell.

Superfoods for fertility:

- eggs,
- avocado,
- almonds,
- wheatgerm,
- turnip and kohlrabi,
- tomato,
- pomegranate,
- linseed,
- blueberries,
- raspberries.

In addition to the above, men should also daily consume garlic and figs (fresh figs if possible), which resemble the scrotum.

A woman's body shows nutrient deficiencies in the following ways:

- sore breasts – vitamin E deficiency – the best source is wheatgerm oil;
- painful menstruation – vitamin E deficiency;
- infertility – lack of good omega-3 fats, vitamin E, B vitamins and vitamin C;
- low sperm motility – B vitamins deficiency – mostly B12, low vitamin C and vitamin E;
- spontaneous miscarriages – B vitamins deficiency.

Vitamin E is beneficial for the blood supply to the womb; the best sources of vitamin E are almonds and avocado, or you can take a vitamin E supplement, such as wheatgerm oil.* If a woman has repeated inflammations, she should ask herself what is making her so angry, and consume as much probiotics, vegetables and garlic as possible to alkalise her body. She can use a supplement containing probiotics,* garlic and calcium.

The functioning of the thyroid and the sex glands is closely connected. A lazy thyroid can be stimulated with the supplementation of iodine, B vitamins, magnesium and calcium. A livelier thyroid results in a faster metabolism, which accelerates the burning of fat and turns it into energy. Another consequence are more active sex glands. It has been proven that overweight women find it harder to get pregnant and it is therefore advisable to eat following the principle of a medium glycaemic index, described on page 100.

Before getting pregnant, a woman should ensure a sufficient amount of folic acid, which binds with vitamin B12. In food, this combination is present in all dairy – it is best to consume the already fermented products, such as yogurt, whey, cottage cheese and kefir; in addition, for a hormonal balance the body also needs omega-3 fatty acids.*

Men: How can a tired, apathetic man expect his sperm to be lively? Vitamins E, C and B have a beneficial effect on mood and energy. When there are enough of these vitamins, not only do men themselves become livelier, but also their sperm. Vitamin E increases blood flow through the blood vessels; vitamin C is good for sperm motility, also making sure that the man has more energy; for better sperm, which consists of proteins, it is recommended that he should consume good protein in the evening and/or supplement his food with a good quality protein supplement from soy or whey.

An increasing number of men have erectile problems. Vitamin E and higher amounts of garlic are very helpful for better circulation. It has been proven that after regular consumption of garlic, erection problems gradually subside.

Men, start moving – you sit too much! Sitting makes blood vessels lazy, which is why at least 3 times a week you should go for a brisk walk, a jog or a bike-ride.

When the body is balanced, everything falls into place

A couple trying to get pregnant should ensure a calmer lifestyle and supplement their diet with good fats, vitamins, minerals and protein. I know it is difficult to see all the women who find it easy to get pregnant, happily wheeling their pushchairs and running after their children. I know you have negative feelings: anger, jealousy, rage. You want a child so badly, but every month with yet another period comes a new disappointment.

This struggle can either bring the two of you closer or drive you apart. You are looking for the culprit. You tell yourself you are not good enough. AWAY WITH THOUGHTS LIKE THAT! Bitterness and despair can only block the processes in your body.

Fill your mind with thoughts of hope, belief, love and peace!

- Creative energy is running through my body.
- My body is a temple.
- I allow for whatever is in the divine plan to happen. I go with the flow. I am calm.
- A healing peace is entering my cells and my soul.
- I am one with God. Divine energy flows through me.

• More and more divine creative energy is running through my healthy cells.

• I am harmonised with the divine energy. The creative energy is touching me.

• I am safe here and now.

• Love is flowing through me.

• I am grateful for my female body.

• I am grateful for everything I have had and will have. God is here with me.

• I go with the divine flow.

• I admire all the mothers of the world.

• I bless all the mothers of the world.

• I allow my feminine energy to express itself.

Since we live fast these days, I recommend that in addition to the above, you sit down comfortably a few times every day and close your eyes. Take several deep breaths and slowly exhale. Concentrate on breathing with your diaphragm and then say:

• "I see the goal," – and the goal will slowly appear before your eyes – you can see yourself as a happy parent, caressing your child. If this brings up too many bad feelings, it is better to choose something that brings you happiness, contentment and joy.

• "I see love," – an image of your love will appear before your eyes – feel the touch of the beloved person, remember all the moments when you have laughed together and enjoyed each other's company.

• "I see peace," – and the image that calms you the most will rise in front of your eyes. Feel yourself calmly floating in water. You just are. You feel happiness. You know that everything is alright.

• "I see happiness," – and the image of your happiness will appear. If you can see yourself being a happy mother, there is a way to achieve that. God did not give people wishes without there being a chance of them coming true.

When you calm down a few times a day, you are encouraging the production of endorphins,* which stimulate the hormones of happiness, and these will help all the processes in your body to run in harmony. In addition, you should carry out the The healing prayer of decoding unconscious emotional patterns (more about on page 43).

Here is a quote from Smiljan Mori: "We must be aware that God gives each of us the lessons we can take, but we have to try at least a little." He and his wife could not get pregnant for a few years. They went through the Calvary of artificial inseminations, bleeding, miscarriages and became very depressed. Today they have a daughter and a son – one is their biological child and the other their love child.

*Endorphins are released when we feel happy. It can be from a touch, music, looking at a child or a beloved person, making love, enjoying good food and company or the satisfaction brought on by an achievement. Whenever we feel happiness via any of our senses, endorphins are released.

A healthy pregnant woman

Instead of wishing away nine months of pregnancy, I'd have cherished every moment and realized that the wonderment growing inside me was the only chance in life to assist God in a miracle.

Erma Bombeck, who died prematurely of cancer

All feelings, thoughts and emotions are transmitted via hormonal messages around the body of the future mother. And since the child growing beneath her heart is a part of her, the unborn baby receives these messages. When I was young, I read about people who under hypnosis spoke about the time they had spent in the womb, about their mother's feelings and even about how their mother experienced the world. Often, the mother had experienced an emotional shock and her children then had psychological problems for which they did not know the reason. Under hypnosis, they realised which events from before their birth had marked them so strongly. This is why it is so very important that the future mother is as calm as possible.

In Vladimir Megre's series of books *The Ringing Cedars of Russia*, you can read the advice of the Russian hermit Anastasia,* who says that the future mother should for the whole nine months stay on the family estate and give birth there. She should follow the messages from her body. She should eat what her body tells her to; it is best if she reaches for fresh fruit from her surroundings. The Earth and the plants feel what she needs and in this way she can provide her baby with all the nutritional support, while she lives in peace with herself and with the people she loves for the whole nine months. Monika Kastelic quotes the author in her degree dissertation:

> *This is why it is important that we plant plants with our own hands, not with machines. Plants planted with love will contain information about the person and the fruits will be healing for this person. And so the pregnant woman walks among the trees, bushes and the other plants she has planted with her husband. With her loving look, she will encourage a flower she likes to grow faster; she will look with disapproval at the weeds in the garden and they will start wilting. And when she is hungry, she will pick a ripe strawberry or apple. Without thinking about it, she will satisfy her hunger with fruit. Her body knows best which substances it needs. And since she has already tasted these fruits, her body already knows their composition, in what proportions the substances are present in a particular plant. In the winter, she also has on the table dried fruits, roots, nuts, bunches of herbs, honey, pollen and so on. She takes food from the table without thinking, whenever she becomes hungry. The goat they have lets them milk her only rarely, when she feels that her milk might benefit the human without harm. In addition, flowers grow on the estate and the ripened fruit releases ethers into the air. The air is full of scents that feed the soul. Experts are already emphasising the right diet for pregnant women and the importance of foods for the baby's health. At her family's estate, the pregnant woman has access to organically produced foods. Moreover, she is guided in her diet by the biggest expert who knows best what she needs – her body. She is living in a pleasant environment and in fresh air, which is also important. A woman as healthy as this can only give birth to a healthy child. The baby should be born on the estate, in the presence of the father, maybe also a midwife, who guides the childbirth.*

*The baby will come into this world accompanied by familiar sounds in the home environment, which is also less stressful for the mother.**

*Monika Kastelic: The Vedic Anti-System of Education and the School of the Academician M. P. Shchetinin; degree dissertation.

This will one day be the case – I am convinced of this. But now, the future mother goes to work, furnishes the home and the tempo of her life is as fast as everyone else's. Only when her pregnancy is nearing the end, when she can no longer go on like this, does she calm down.

The diet of a future mother is important for the baby's health. What kind of food the mother was eating during pregnancy may become apparent immediately at birth or not until the child is growing up or even later, as osteoporosis. Gestational diabetes may be caused by a bad diet. The signs are uncontrollable weight gain and the foetus growing too fast.

It has been proven that the unstoppable craving for food is caused by insulin, the hunger hormone.

Insulin "forces" the body to consume food, rich in carbohydrates – sweet things and small snacks.* The only solution to uncontrolled weight gain in pregnancy is eating according to the medium glycaemic index, see page 100.

*Dr Richard F. Heller and Dr Rachael F. Heller: *The Carbohydrate Addict's Lifespan Program: A Personalized Plan for Becoming Slim, Fit, and Healthy in Your 40s, 50s, 60s, and Beyond.*

Pregnancy and fast weight gain

When I first became pregnant, I had no other problems than restless arms and legs. Pins and needles in my limbs occurred mainly in the evening. I didn't know how to help myself. Now I know this was due to a magnesium deficiency. I did not consume nuts. When you add magnesium, the restless legs syndrome simply disappears. Braxton Hicks contractions also disappear. More about magnesium on page 282.

The second and third pregnancy triggered severe hunger, which made me put on a lot of weight. I was constantly hungry. In the morning, during the whole day, in the evening and through the night. Although I was eating healthy food, I was also including white bread, white pasta, the odd desert, etc. Eating foods with a high glycaemic index raised my blood sugar, the body secreted insulin, which stores the surplus energy in the fat cells and causes constant hunger and with it, uncontrolled weight gain. Towards the end of my pregnancy, I felt like an elephant – I was huge.

Your diet is important already before pregnancy and even more during it.

- Drink water! Limit coffee and tea to a maximum of one a day.
- Avoid cured meats, processed meat products and everything that contains preservatives.
- Consume fish, fruit, vegetables and nuts. You can supplement your diet with natural nutritional supplements.*

A future mother should be taking folic acid at least 3 months before getting pregnant as it is necessary for the development of the foetus even at the stage when most women don't even realise they are pregnant. During the very first week, the baby is developing its vital functions (all the internal organs, the heart, brain, etc.). In the third week, the head and spine begin to develop, while between the 24th and 27th day the spinal canal closes. If during this period there is a shortage of folic acid, the spinal canal may not close and defects in the spinal area or head can appear. Many miscarriages are set off by congenital defects in the foetus. A pregnant woman who is anaemic should add vitamin C, which is necessary for iron absorption. She should also add vitamins B6, B9 and B12. Vitamin A is necessary for the placenta to form and for the development of the foetus, as well as for the baby's sight; vitamin B12 is also needed for the growth and development of the foetus. The signs of a B vitamins deficiency are fluctuating moods and nervousness in the mother to be.

Vitamin B6 alleviates problems during pregnancy. In their book Die Vitamin-Revolution, Dr Ulrich Strunz and Andreas Jopp say that billions of protein cells must be created for the growth of a foetus. An enormous quantity of vitamin B6 is needed for this, which the foetus draws from the mother's blood, down to the last reserve. This is why it is no surprise, the authors go on to say, that many pregnant women have a deficiency and that mothers with a severe shortage of this vitamin often give birth to babies that are too small. They also say that many pregnant women suffer from nausea. A study involving over 350 pregnant women showed that even between 50 and 100 mg of vitamin B6 daily can completely remedy this situation. Some pregnant women get gestational diabetes and raised blood sugar levels. Vitamin B6, which takes part in the regulation of blood sugar, did very well in research into gestational diabetes.*

When a foetus is growing, it needs calcium for building bones, blood vessels, the brain, etc. A calcium and magnesium deficiency is felt by the pregnant woman as something "crawling" throughout her body; particularly in the evening, she finds it impossible to settle down because she has restless legs and arms. A deficiency can also appear as a pain in the legs (beneath the knees) and muscle cramps (deficiency in magnesium and vitamin B1). Calcium and magnesium also prevent heartburn.

Omega-3 fatty acids have a beneficial effect on the development of the foetus's brain, nerves and eyesight. These fatty acids are also good for the mother as they control her blood pressure and prevent post-natal depression.

The foetus needs good protein for its development, as proteins are the building blocks of the skin, hair, nails, all the internal organs and the immune system. Pregnant women who want the best for their child should eat some protein with each meal. More about protein on page 234.

If a pregnant woman gets ill, it is recommended she takes natural antibiotics, such as garlic and lactic acid bacteria that she can obtain from kefir or probiotics in the form of a natural dietary supplement.* This combination also prevents vaginal infection and improves digestion. It alleviates haemorrhoids and varicose veins and lowers the blood pressure. To reduce a fever, pregnant women should use natural substances against fever and inflammation, such as blueberries, cranberries and beetroot. They can also take natural supplements.*

Exercise: Don't forget exercise! Childbirth is a muscle activity. Go for a walk every day for at least half an hour; use a stationary bicycle or a stepper machine; swim or attend an exercise class for pregnant women. Pilates is also allowed, but you should be supervised by a trainer. Be careful about pains in the lower abdomen – if they appear, you should immediately stop exercising and consult your doctor.

Enjoy your pregnancy! Take care of your health, don't worry too much about your body changing – as a mother, you will be much better looking than ever before!

Being a mother

Another message from Anastasia in Vladimir Megre's book Rites of Love is that when we live in the womb we are comfortable and feel pleasant and calm. At the physical level, we are getting everything we need. The absence of the problems typical of everyday life enables us to feel the entire universe. In the nine months of pregnancy, we receive from that which created the world all the information about the beautiful universe and the purpose of humankind. Our world in the womb is wonderful and boundless. But suddenly, we are roughly pushed out of this state of bliss. All women know that this is when the contractions start and that they are unavoidable. But we don't think about the feelings the baby might experience during this time. Very few women in the modern world know that they can fondle their baby during contractions, talk to it, keep it company and invite it to come into this world, rather than frightening it. And then it doesn't feel the pain. The baby hears its mother and father calling and interprets the pressure of contractions as caressing and a call, it wants to learn about the unusual and wants to come out into the world. Anastasia goes on to say that it is very important that the baby wants to be born. After such a birth, the baby will retain all the divine information. But when a woman is afraid of contractions, the baby in her womb also feels fear. When the woman is hurting and thinking only of herself, the pain felt by the baby is doubled, it feels neglected and, what is even worse, helpless and unprotected. The baby reacts to the state of its mother, her feelings and the father's feelings in equal measure. When the husband is talking to his pregnant wife, the foetus cannot make out the words and doesn't understand the meaning of the words but only feels the feelings of its parents. Through his parents' feelings the baby feels the space outside the womb.

The period of breastfeeding is a period of giving and receiving love – the baby gives you all the love back.

The birth of a child is the most beautiful thing in the world. When a little baby is born, you are overcome by a wave of emotion, complete happiness, rapture, gratitude. I have the fondest memories of the time when my girls were little. The time of breastfeeding and those tiny eyes locked on yours, the first smile, the first footsteps – incredible, so many beautiful memories.

Breastfeeding is not just feeding your baby; it is a transmission of energy, it is giving love. The mother's milk not only feeds the body, it also contains information and emotions. The mother's milk is inseparably connected with her feelings and the taste of her milk changes accordingly. Many women know that while feeding the baby they should not be disturbed by conversation and thought, particularly not about bad things. They should focus on the baby and feeding it, they should talk to the baby in their head.*

When a breastfeeding mother experiences severe stress, she may stop producing milk. When a mother is breastfeeding her child, she should think of nothing but the baby and should not pay attention to any other thing. Together with her milk, she can pass on to the baby the awareness and eons-old wisdom, all the way back to the original sources.

**Monika Kastelic: The Vedic Anti-System of Education and the School of the Academician M. P. Shchetinin; degree dissertation.

Since the female hormones must settle after childbirth, the mother should have peace for as long as possible. In the past, midwives knew that the woman should rest. For the first six weeks after childbirth, women used to take care only of the child and themselves. "For the first six weeks, the woman has death under her bed," midwives used to say. It was the midwives who cooked and took care of the family, while the young mother was left alone by everyone, getting spoilt by her family.

Nowadays, things are different.

When a new baby is born, everyone wants to see it immediately. With my first daughter, I wasn't yet aware of the importance of peace. Relatives, colleagues, friends kept coming round. The moment we came home from the hospital we had visitors. After about a week of this, my daughter and I were so irritated that she started getting colic. Then we said NO to everyone.

Peace is the foundation. With my younger two daughters, we forbade visitors in advance – people were welcome only when my daughters were three months old.

A happy mother radiates her happiness over the whole of her family; equally, an unhappy mother infects her whole family with her unhappiness.

When a new mother is in balance, her hormones soon settle. Post-natal depression tells her that her body is out of balance and that she is deficient in both peace and basic nutrients.

The hand that rocks the cradle, rocks the world

A woman is a goddess. A woman fills her family with her love, and the family is the basic cell of society. When during the first years of its life a child feels secure, she will take this into the world; when she feels love and acceptance during her first years, love and acceptance will be what she takes away with her; when she feels peace during the first years of her life, she will carry it with her all her life.

Experiments on rats have shown that the chemical markers on the gene that manages the experience of fear literally change when the mother rat licks her baby. It has been proven that this baby rat feels less fear throughout its life. In his book *Beyond Willpower*, Alex Loyd says that this is proof that a mother's love can programme the brain for life.

Affirmations that will help you stay calm and balanced:

- With every breath, I become calmer.
- My calm energy is transferring to my child.
- I am aligned with the divine energy.
- I am at peace with the world.
- My emotional state is always balanced.

• I admire all the beauty of this world.
• Everywhere around me there is beauty and divine harmony.
• Everything is taken care of. I am safe here and now.
• My children are safe here and now.
• I admire all the mothers of the world and I am grateful for being a mother myself.
• I can. There is strength inside me.
• Love flows through my body and touches my child.
• I prepare healthy meals with love.
• Everywhere around me I see happiness. I am happy here and now.
• I pay attention to my health, joy and playfulness.
• Beauty is all around me. This beauty is reflecting in me.

A destroyed balance

Before 1890, the proportion of the fatty acids omega-6 and omega-3 in the diet was 1:1. Now, it is 25:1. This drastic increase in the proportion of omega-6 fatty acids is thought to be the reason for an increase in depression.*

*Reader's Digest: *Food Cures.*

• In Europe and America, depression is 10 times as common as elsewhere in the world.

• Women who do not consume fish get post-natal depression twice as often as women who do.

• A sufficient amount of omega-3 daily is 1 to 3 grams.

Once, a woman with two children contacted me. After each childbirth, she had post-natal depression. She asked me: “Can post-natal depression be helped by supplements?” My answer was: “Omega-3 and vitamin E are of key importance. A calcium and magnesium supplement helps with the hormones, as do B vitamins.” When she supplemented her diet, her condition soon improved. Now she has 3 children and did not get post-natal depression after her third child.

In addition to omega-3, a new mother also needs sufficient amounts of B vitamins and calcium

The myelin sheath around the brain consists of omega-3 fats, vitamin B12 and calcium. Firstly, if you are deficient in calcium, vitamin B12 does not bind. As soon as you are deficient in B12, and consequently also of all the other B vitamins, you react wildly to the world. You erupt at the slightest noise made by your children and you shout at them; of course, you regret it later, but when it happens you are unable to react differently. I understand you. You are deficient in key vitamins and minerals. When you get a sufficient amount of vitamin B, you will react calmly to all the children's mischief, you will feel you can cope and, above all, you will be in a better mood and full of energy.

The highest level of B vitamins is in cottage cheese, eggs and nuts, and these foods also include calcium. Calcium binds with magnesium (nuts), magnesium binds with potassium and potassium binds with sodium.

B vitamins calm babies

The worse the vitamin B6 deficiency in a breastfeeding mother, the lower the concentration of this vitamin in her milk. A study carried out in 1993 proved that a deficiency in basic nutrients affects the mood of both babies and adults. The study found that the concentration of vitamin B6 in the baby's blood is connected with how often it cries, whether it is sad and whether it sleeps through the night. Young mothers are thus advised to ensure a sufficient amount of B vitamins in their diet, and this will take care of the baby's nutrition.*

*Summarised from: Dr Ulrich Strunz and Andreas Jopp: *Die Vitamin-Revolution*. See also: *The Regeneration Hormone on page 199.*

The old wisdom that says "He has no salt in his brain," or "His brain has gone sour," are true. When there is a sodium deficiency, potassium doesn't bind, and consequently magnesium and calcium don't bind, which is why B vitamins don't get absorbed and the brain cannot function properly.

Parsley and celery – vegetables that contain a lot of potassium

At least once a day, have a smoothie made from parsley and yogurt, to which you also add a handful of soaked almonds and a pinch of salt. This way, you will obtain potassium, calcium, B vitamins, protein, magnesium, vitamin E and sodium.

Losing weight after childbirth

My three pregnancies, a wrong diet and not enough exercise left negative consequences on my body. I didn't see myself as attractive, I didn't feel good in my skin, I didn't feel happy – even though I had everything – three healthy children, a husband who loved me, a home and a dog.

Until I began to look for happiness inside, I could not see it outside.

What did I do? To begin with, I began repeating 100 times a day:

I love myself and I value myself, I love myself and I value myself ... And that is why:

- I can express my feelings,
- I exercise in the morning,
- I drink enough water,
- I make healthy meals for myself,
- I eat healthy meals (and above all I am not a rubbish bin).

Until I felt happiness and contentment inside, no one else could have given me those feelings.

The solution for losing weight after childbirth is eating according to the glycaemic index

If you want to lose weight, eat every 3 hours. Healthy mini meals are of key importance for the blood sugar to remain in balance. They:

• provide calories for the energy needed for the metabolism,

• fill your stomach and reduce hunger,

• do not contain carbohydrates that elevate insulin,

• provide the basic nutrients necessary for good health,

• facilitate excellent metabolism as the body doesn't send severe hunger alarms.

Since you are eating every two and a half to three hours, you never get desperately hungry. You feel wonderful and have plenty of energy all the time. When you eat according to a medium glycaemic index, you will never find yourself collapsing with exhaustion in the evening. Finally, you will be motivated late in the day to do something pleasant, which you have until now been putting off because of tiredness. You will be happiest because you will feel good in your skin again. And your happiness will show in your relationship with your partner and the rest of the family.

Healthy slimming takes place in cells, and cells must feel an abundance of nutrients before they start burning the fat stores. In order for weight loss to begin, you need:

• **vitamin C**, which forms collagen fibres and these contribute towards your body becoming firmer (preventing flabbiness);

• **magnesium** – acts like a match in a cell – if you have enough, you will burn old fat;

• **iron** – acts as a "vehicle" for transporting fat molecules along the blood to the cells;

• **B vitamins**, which influence fat metabolism;

• **amino acids** – these are the smallest protein particles, which the body needs for creating new cells;

• **omega-3 fatty acids** – good oils influence the permeability of cells.

You need chromium to stop you from constantly battling with your stomach and hunger. **Chromium** is a mineral we obtain from unprocessed foods, which is very difficult nowadays since everything is quickly grown and refined. You obtain some chromium from eggs and mushrooms. Let pickled mushrooms and a boiled egg be part of your daily diet.

Why diets following the principle "just eat less" don't work

Cells act similarly to a car engine. Just think – can a car run on water today, oil tomorrow and petrol the day after? Although our cells are more adaptable than a car engine – today they run on water, tomorrow on fruit and the next day on chocolate, they do remember things.

When you are starving – this includes the food-combining diet and all the "eat less" diets, as well as mono diets – your cheeks sag, your breasts sag, your backside sags, the only thing left is your stomach! That is a sign of an improper diet. After you finish such an unhealthy diet (starvation), where your cells no longer know when the next meal is coming – perhaps yesterday's lunch was the last food ever – they store everything; your fat cells inflate like risen dough and gradually you start putting weight on after a glass of water and a look at the fridge. When your body feels abundance again, it will lose weight, in the opposite case it will keep storing.

If you want to reshape your body, you need some protein with every meal. Protein influences the regeneration of tissue and the firmness of your body. But you must always eat fruit or, even better, vegetables with the protein so that too much protein doesn't acidify your body.

- Food rich in protein helps with weight loss since consuming protein makes us feel full sooner. Protein plays an important role in the building and regeneration of the body.
- Protein helps preserve muscle mass.
- Protein prevents blood sugar fluctuations, which in turn stops you getting desperately hungry and into a bad mood.
- Protein encourages the creation of warmth. Since the body cannot store it, surplus protein must turn into warmth.
- Protein is the basic building stone of hormones – including the hormone of slimness (the growth hormone).

• If you are short of protein during a diet, your skin will become loose, you will look old and ill.

I am not telling you to constantly eat meat – which is how many people understand the notion of protein. High quality protein occurs in yogurt, cottage cheese, kefir and whey; and for those who cannot digest dairy, good sources of protein are nuts and pulses. Out of all the nuts, almonds and peanuts contain the most protein, and out of pulses you will get most protein from green beans and soya.

5 mistakes you should not make – I did…

1. "Mum, I've had enough," and I opened my mouth and shoved away everything the kids could not eat.

2. I became a rubbish bin, for example, I ate all the bread crusts.

3. I ate simple carbohydrates – e.g. pancakes, made with white flour. Since they dramatically raise the blood sugar, I was hungry after an hour.

4. In the afternoon, I would eat fruit and fruity dairy spreads – together with the children, of course. More about why it is not good to eat fruit in the afternoon, see on page 103.

5. Chocolate cereals, fruit purees, semolina and rice pudding are all good for a baby's growth; but for their mothers, who are no longer growing, they result in an expansion in the other direction – width.

What being overweight has taught me

Above all, this is a time to start loving yourself. No one else would sort out your problems but you. Criticising yourself will not get you anywhere. I have learnt that you have to put yourself first, as that is the only way to look after everyone around you with pleasure.

Contraception and hormone replacement therapy

Contraceptive pills, patches, hormonal coils, etc. All these act on the hormonal balance in the body. Even though you may be assured that they contain minimum amounts of hormones, these are still hormonal supplements. This group also includes hormonal replacement therapy during the transition to the menopause.

In the book *100% Health*, Kate Neil says that the widespread prescribing of synthetic hormones to women is the biggest medical swindle of the last 100 years.

The problem with synthetic hormones is that progesterone, which naturally occurs in the body, has a precisely determined chemical composition: only a particular molecule can set in motion a specific string of information, crucial for a normal course of pregnancy, menstruation, bone density and other functions hormones control in every woman.

But sadly, and almost without exception, every contraceptive or hormone replacement drug, be it a tablet, patch or coil contains synthetic prostagens – molecules that resemble the real progesterone but are still different. They are like a key that unlocks the lock but does not quite fit. This brings considerable confusion into the body's biochemistry. It is not unusual for the body to become more toxic; a series of unwanted effects appear, particularly an increased likelihood of the development of some diseases, such as breast cancer, against which the natural hormone serves as a protection.

Similar applies to oestrogen or rather oestrogens, a group of hormones naturally released by the glands. Many pharmaceuticals, including contraceptive pills and hormonal therapies, contain synthetic oestrogens that mimic the effects of the naturally occurring molecules in the body.

In 1995, *New England Journal of Medicine* published the results of a study that included a high number of women. The results showed that in menopausal women who were for five years or longer treated with replacement hormones, the likelihood of getting breast cancer was 71% higher. It transpired that the risk increases with the duration of the therapy.

A similar study was carried out by the School for Public Health at Emery University and published in 1995. The research involved 240,000 women, who were studied for eight years. The results showed that the susceptibility to ovarian cancer of the women who had received oestrogen hormonal therapy was 72% higher.

Research has thus shown that a long-term replacement therapy with oestrogen and/or synthetic progestin increases the probability of breast cancer.

A woman using hormonal contraception is also at greater risk of blood clots, stroke or heart attack. She may also be deficient in the following vitamins and minerals:

- vitamins B1, B2, B3, B6, B7, B9 – folic acid and B12,
- vitamin C,
- magnesium,
- zinc,
- iron.

These are metabolic vitamins and minerals that hormonal pills wash away. As a result, you may put on weight and feel chronically tired. If you add stress and alcohol to the hormonal treatment, which additionally wash away B vitamins, you lose your will to live and what is worse – it all shows up in your psychological state and you start crying at the smallest emotional upheaval. You become ripe for mild antidepressants. And then you enter the vicious circle. Research has shown that depression is twice as common in women as in men and the reason for this may well be contraception.

The solution? Natural contraception according to the Billings Method. This method, which compares a woman to the earth – there are wet periods, when the woman is fertile – the time of ovulation; and there are dry periods – after ovulation, when the woman cannot get pregnant.

Ovulation always happens 14 days before the onset of menstruation. At that time, the chance of conceiving is the greatest. Women know when they are ovulating by the transparent mucous excreted from the vagina. During this time, they should refrain from unprotected sex.

After ovulation is over, the mucous becomes thicker and the vagina dry and this is the time when the woman cannot get pregnant. And the time for unprotected sex. *

*You can find more information in the book by Evelyn Billings and Ann Westmore: *The Billings Method*.

The third hormonal challenge: Menopause

A transition from one period to another is natural – just as it is natural that seasons change, it is natural that the woman's ability to give birth transforms to other levels. Now it is time for her, now it is the time for a woman to listen to her inner guide and arrange her life to suit herself. It is time for the Wise Woman.

The Wise Woman is calm; she is at peace with herself and the world. She feels inner strength, she feels that she can start sharing her wisdom. In a nice way, she adds value to the Earth and all its inhabitants.

On her website, the Red Tent, Ana Drevenšek says:

> *The menopause is another important transition in a woman's life. It brings the cessation of the cycle, which also means the cessation of the woman's ties to material creativity. During this time, the woman may experience intense shocks as her life wants to put itself in order, cleanse itself and take the right direction. This is why this period brings great transformations and specific life changes that shock and confuse many women. If during this time the woman has the support of her female circle, she goes through the menopausal transformation much more easily and much more easily assimilates the changes happening to her.*
>
> *At this time, the woman becomes more focused in her spiritual essence and increasingly more susceptible to the spiritual dimension of life (when before she was not susceptible at all or not to such an extent). In a way, a woman already has one foot on the other side – she becomes the connection between the Earth and the spiritual world. Now, the woman crowns herself as a* ***Wise Woman, Medicine Woman, Witch, Shaman****. She becomes a source of wisdom, a spiritual leader and guide.*
>
> *This is a very significant time for the mature woman and if she cannot fully experience the importance of the change that is happening to her, this period may be very stressful – some women experience the cessation of the cycle as the farewell of her life force, as a sign of ageing and failing strength. The woman may feel weak and less worthy, which is just the opposite of the gifts brought by the menopause. The menopause brings a new enrichment of life, a deepening, a spiritual dimension. Women should*

be glad about this transition since they are crowned as queens, wise women, respected and cherished members of the women's circle and society in general.

The Wise Woman should celebrate this period. When a woman is no longer in her fertile period, her purpose is not over; this period can take a woman who doesn't take time for herself and her equilibrium on a stormy journey.

A woman in her late forties. She has plenty to cope with because of the hormonal changes – the menopause. One moment she is hot, the next cold, and there are all those mood swings. At home she has two teenagers, who are also ruled by their hormones. Moreover, her husband is undergoing the male menopause, when he becomes aware that he is getting old, but won't admit it. All he sees is that his wife is different, that she is suffering from the change. Since the woman wants to feel better, she goes to her doctor and has a moan. The doctor prescribes her mild hormonal tablets, which unfortunately wash away her B vitamins and so her emotional state starts getting worse as well – her mood swings become even more pronounced. One minute she is laughing euphorically, the next she is crying without a reason and then she shouts at the children. Gradually, she is ready for antidepressants, which don't solve the situation.

In addition, she has ageing parents that need her help. Yet another burden!

But that is not all, there is also her job. More demands and pressures, often she has young bosses who have come from university with a head full of ideas, forgetting that only people who are content and happy achieve good results. The pressure they put on their subordinates has just the opposite effect to the one desired – people try less hard than before.

She is feeling tired, old, overburdened, sad, she cries a lot and because of all the stress she starts to gain weight, which makes her even more unhappy with herself. Her dissatisfaction makes her reject her partner, who becomes jealous and perhaps even accuses her of being unfaithful. A vicious circle. Often, women get divorced at this time. The hormonal disruptions are only a result of all this.

When her life takes her to the edge, she sets off on a journey of seeking – searching for her balance. Until she seeks love and balance outside herself, she will not find them; but when she allows herself to be what she is, those she knows often accuse her of having become a little strange, of socialising with strange people, of going round the bend. These opinions may push her back and she goes on being docile, quiet and obedient; or she says: "I need this for my soul!" and continues on her journey. It is possible that some people will leave her life; but there is no harm in that since they had not added anything to it anyway. The Wise Woman should follow her intuition and inner guidance.

How should the Wise Woman take care of her health and happiness?

The Wise Woman should always act in the feminine way. The least stress unbalances her. And this is where the answer lies to the question of why women so often get breast cancer. For years and years, they have been piling one emotional pain after another in the centre of their heart. This is where lies the thymus – an endocrine gland which feeds all the other hormonal centres. The thymus looks after the immune system and facilitates rejuvenation. It produces defence cells that can destroy all abnormal cells.

The thymus feeds solely on love. A woman who wishes to preserve her youth, should take care of her feeling of love, this is the only way in which she can preserve the energy flow through her heart chakra.

When a woman no longer feels love, her thymus becomes more and more rigid and does not let energy through.

Fundamentally, women should feel love for themselves. They should deliberately calm down several times a day, take a deep breath and say: "I see love. I see happiness." They should find in their memory all the times, events and places where and when they had felt complete love. They should seek the pictures that remind them of those events. They should focus on nothing but love. The hot flushes that are unbearable only reflect the swings and roundabouts in their life – they are simply a message that women are not balanced.

If a woman wants to preserve her health and happiness, she should preserve her gentle feminine nature. Grace, arranging things, wisdom, adaptability, patience, gentleness, kindness and tolerance are the virtues of all Wise Women. Such women should not compete with men but support them. They are capable of finishing things. They enjoy their feelings, are able to cleanse them and do not allow their feelings to control them. These women are caring, not only to others and their surroundings, but primarily to themselves; they exercise, relax, sleep, eat and enjoy loving sex the way it should be enjoyed.

If the woman preserves her nature, she doesn't have to do anything else. If she doesn't have a partner, she should not try to get one. The Earth is not trying to make the Sun shine on it, she simply allows it to shine. If we transfer the attraction between these two universal bodies to the human level, the woman (symbolising the Earth) does not strive for the man (the Sun) to notice her. The Earth simply dances around her axis in order to show the Sun all her beauty and greatness. And she has been doing this day after day, for millions and millions of years, and yet the Sun has not tired of it.

*Summarised from: Tao In Society: How to get Health, Happiness and a Good Relationship;

If you look at the ancient peoples and their traditions, you see that they knew how to connect to the divine through sound, singing and words and in this way strongly increase their energy. I am certain that you have already heard about the syllable OM from the East. OM has magical power on both the conscious and subconscious mind and is connected to the eternal intelligence. It corresponds to the word Amen, which is used in Christian and Jewish worship, but it originates in Egypt, where Amon-Ra was the god of sun. This is a name for the cosmic force that has created life in the universe and the earth and means "so be it".

It is not so much the word that is important, but the sound – its value lies in the sound vibration rather than in the meaning. Everyone who pronounces the word OM will, due to its vibrations, be awarded with special gifts, irrespective of his or her mother tongue. But it is also true that this applies only to those that are capable of receiving these high vibrations.

The use of the word OM – called also the seventh rite (the Fountain of Youth or the Five Tibetans exercises) – can in an individual who is ready to accept strong and high vibrations, trigger exceptional results. If we pronounce it correctly, its vibrational frequency strongly stimulates the pituitary gland (the centre for the production of the growth hormone and rejuvenation). But you should not stimulate the pituitary gland unless you are living at a higher level already. Just like a seed does not grow in infertile soil, supreme vibrations cannot flourish in a consciousness that is not ready for them.

*Summarised from: Peter Kelder: The Ancient Secret of the Fountain of Youth.

During menopause, you should also eat according to the principle of a medium glycaemic index. With every meal, you should have additional vegetables that contain a lot of natural vitamin E. These are cruciferous vegetables: broccoli, cauliflower, cabbage, turnip, kohlrabi, radishes and black radish.

Even the shape of these vegetables is reminiscent of the womb.

Cruciferous vegetables act as a body cleanser. They contain the substance sulforaphane, which gives these foods a strong smell during cooking. I recommend you consume them fresh, uncooked. If you cook them, every minute of cooking raises their glycaemic index. More about this on page 107.

Cruciferous vegetables have a particular influence on the tissues that are stimulated by hormones, i.e. the soft tissues. They protect against breast cancer, uterine and vaginal cancer, prostate cancer, large intestine cancer and lung cancer. The substances in cruciferous vegetables remove damaged cells from the body.

Natural vitamin E protects the cell membranes against attack from toxic substances – it protects against free radicals, and also:

- flushes toxins from the body,
- protects the nucleus of cells,
- influences hormones,
- influences the creation of blood and new cells,
- benefits the nervous system.

During the menopause, enrich your diet with omega-3 fats and B vitamins. Research has shown that the best is a good multivitamin and mineral supplement, but B6, magnesium and zinc stand out particularly.* Support your body with herbs and positive thinking and a conscious search for nice memories.

Vitamin E must be natural – if you are taking a supplement, be careful of the chemical name of the natural vitamin E – d-alpha tocopherol, d-beta tocopherol, d-gamma tocopherol and d-delta tocopherol. Artificial vitamin E is denoted by the name dl-alfa-tocopherol.

What should you do when your period is late, when your menstrual cycle is irregular or when you are bleeding excessively and having hot flushes?

Advice given by the herbalist Jožica Okrogelnik from Slovenia:

Make an infusion from a mixture of lady's mantle and capsella and add marigold and lemon balm. Let it stand for 10 minutes, strain and drink three cups a day. Also recommended are sitz baths in tea made from lady's mantle.

• **Lady's mantle** protects you. It balances the hormonal activities. It contains plant oestrogens. The monk Simon Ašič recommends drinking this tea for all women's problems: vaginal discharge, excessive bleeding, stomach problems, menopause problems. Maria Treben recommends lady's mantle tea also for a prolapsed uterus – four cups a day, as well as a sitz bath in the tea.

• **Capsella** has flowers in the shape of hearts. Where there is a heart, there is harmony. The flower tells us it acts on the heart chakra – the thymus, which feeds all the hormonal centres in the body. This herb also contains natural plant oestrogen. The monk Ašič recommends it for problems with bleeding and cramps: it regulates strong menstruation – 8 days before your period, you should have 1 to 2 cups of the tea/infusion a day. It helps with vaginal discharge and eases contractions. Maria Treben recommends for problems with the womb that you finely chop capsella, cover it with brandy and put it out in the sun for 10 days. Use the liquid to massage the lower part of your abdomen a few times a day.

• **Marigold** regulates your periods. 2 to 3 cups of the tea a day should be drunk a week before your period starts. It also has a beneficial effect during the menopause, since it regulates the loss of blood. Marigold has a calming effect.

• **Lemon balm** is recommended for irregular periods and for depression. The monk Ašič says that lemon balm creates nice thoughts and drives away dark clouds, as well as giving the body new strength.

• **Red clover** – the flower: the herbalist Jožica recommends 1 red clover flower crumbled onto rye bread, spread with butter. Red clover contains natural oestrogens.

• **Thyme** is recommended when you miss a period. Make a fresh infusion with a teaspoon of thyme and drink in sips. Have 2 to 3 cups of this tea a day.*

• **Milfoil tea** is recommended when there is internal unrest and for hot flushes. Maria Treben recommends sitz bats in milfoil tea when you have fibroids. You should have sitz baths until the medical tests come back negative.

For **excessive bleeding**, Maria Treben recommends making tea from the following herbs:

- 25 g arnica flowers,
- 50 g valerian roots,
- 25 g Iceland moss,
- 25 g lemon balm,
- 25 g milfoil,
- 25 g sage.

Make an infusion with 250 ml of boiling water and one heaped spoonful of the herbs and let it infuse for 3 minutes. This tea can also be drunk when the periods become normal.

Oregano is recommended for irregular periods. Add oregano to every sauce and to all dishes made with butter – oregano has a calming effect on all internal organs, particularly on the intestines, liver, gall bladder, lungs and stomach.

Parsley is recommended for irregular and painful periods. It is best to consume fresh parsley since the water-soluble minerals are destroyed with cooking.

Advice: Make a smoothie from fresh parsley leaves – you can use a whole bunch, add half an avocado, which contains a lot of vitamin E, a pinch of salt and some plain yogurt.

Parsley contains potassium, magnesium and calcium; salt increases the absorption of potassium, while potassium binds magnesium, magnesium binds calcium from the parsley and yogurt, and vitamin E helps with circulation and hormonal disturbances.

A few thoughts for an easier transition into the Wise Woman period:

- I trust the process of life.
- I am safe here and now.
- I feel love at every step.
- I see love.
- I am love.
- God's peace flows through my heart.
- I see peace.
- I see happiness.
- I accept myself.
- My cells are increasingly young. Healing divine energy flows through me.
- I am free. I love life.
- Inside, I carry a child's soul. A soul is eternally young.
- In my eyes, there is a glow.
- I am amazed at life, I am amazed at each new day.
- In me, there is wisdom. I express myself freely.
- The Holly Spirit fills me with strength and courage.
- My energy renews itself every day.
- I am in contact with God. I am guided by God's wisdom.
- Wherever I go, I am accompanied by angels – I am safe. Angels are all around me.
- I am one with God.

Chapter 7. The Happiness Hormone Serotonin and the Sleep Hormone Melatonin

I trust the creator of life – I am one with everything

In the pineal gland, the happiness hormone is released during the day (if we feel happy, of course), and in the evening, the sleep hormone melatonin starts secreting, which ensures we calm down and fall asleep. The gland is the size of a pea. Such a small centre influences so many processes in the body!

The pineal gland is connected to the crown chakra, the energy point situated in the geometrical centre of the brain. The seventh chakra is connected with the capability to imagine, with creative energy, with intuition and spiritual realisations. When you are full of negative energy or under stress, the energy flow through your body is reduced, which lowers the production of the happiness hormone, the pineal gland functions less efficiently, influencing all the processes in the body. Because of the reduced flow of energy through the body, the release of the sleep hormone melatonin is also disturbed, which is why you find it difficult to fall asleep in the evening and, what is most important, you are not producing the growth hormone. This is why during stress, you may age very quickly.

In order to interrupt this vicious circle, positive energy and thoughts are needed. Thoughts are energy and can be chosen from moment to moment. It is your choice what you will give your energy to.

- I give my attention to nice things. I respond calmly to the world around me.
- Today is a wonderful day!
- I am grateful for being able to exercise.
- Divine energy flows through my body.

It is you who chooses what you will do today in order to feel good; you choose which place you will put yourself in – first or last. If you are in first place, if you love yourself, then you know how to take care of yourself, you know how to say no, you know when you have had enough, you know how to listen to your feelings and your body. When you love yourself, you take care of your own feeling of satisfaction and joy without guilt, because you know that feeling good is your right – and then your body is flooded with happiness hormones. No one else can do this instead of you.

Positive feelings are transferred via hormonal messages – the mood hormones – to every cell. Serotonin is the happiness hormone, the good mood hormone is called dopamine, while endorphins are pleasure hormones. Even just smiling sets of messages of happiness in your body and if you consciously turn on all your senses and direct them to beautiful things, then the happiness hormones tell your brain that you are well:

• Place your attention on **smells** – smell a flower, the fresh morning or the freshness of the forest, smell fragrant fruit or a baby's skin. What smells good? Aromatherapy stimulates the feeling of happiness and the release of the happiness hormone with essential oils. In the evening, light a perfumed candle or put a few drops of an essential oil into an aroma diffuser and enjoy. It is enough to simply be.

• What can you **touch** that makes you feel good? Caress your child or pet, hug your partner and touch your body with love. Touching, stroking and massaging stimulate happiness. It is not surprising that experts claim that at least four hugs a day are needed for survival, eight to maintain a good emotional state and twelve to progress. I grew up on a farm where there was no hugging. Now, when I come home, I hug both my parents. My mum hugs me back really closely and it makes her feel good, but my father embraces me awkwardly and it is clear this is not something he is used to. My girls also hug them and sometimes they laugh about my dad pushing his head into their shoulder.

• **Taste** – which food or drink makes you feel good? For me, it is coffee. Coffee smells good and I like it. But if the only thing that you connect happiness with is cakes, you may end up having weight and/or excessive toxins problem. Sugar blocks metabolism and so it makes sense to find happiness in something healthy.

• **Hearing** – which music lifts you? If we just hear someone laughing, it puts us in a good mood. Think of a laughing child, whose laughter sounds like a mountain stream – even if you are in a bad mood, you start laughing. The sound of water is calming, as is the sound of trees and the sound of the sea creates good feelings. Which news make you feel good? I think that watching or reading the news just before bed is not the best thing for us since bad news do not bring good feelings. Consequently, no happiness hormone is released. And the production of the growth hormone is reduced. If we want to become younger, we should only listen to nice things in the evening.

• **Sight** – what can you see that is beautiful? You can always find something that makes you feel good. Blossoming flowers, a magical morning, a dreamy sunset that has coloured the whole sky, ripe wheat undulating in the wind, autumnal leaves, the whiteness of snow, etc. There is so much beauty in this world, all you need to do is to notice it. You don't have to go to remote places, it is enough to ask yourself: "What can I see that is beautiful?" and our consciousness will find an answer.

One day, my daughters and I were driving to Ljubljana. It was a gloomy autumnal day and nothing beautiful could be found outside at a first glance. I asked them: "What do you see that is beautiful?" The answer was "Nothing." "Look more closely – you can always find something beautiful!" I encouraged them.

My daughters began to observe nature and suddenly found lots of beautiful things: a sunflower in the field, beautiful leaves on the trees, the nice people we met, etc.

Quarrels and difficult conversations in the evening also cause bad feelings in the body. Quarrels cause ageing. If a relationship (marriage, job or family) is not giving you good feelings, make sure that at least in the other areas you bring in good energy and take care of your hormonal balance.

Recommendations for the creation of good mood hormones

A conscious search for nice memories. Thoughts are energy and this is a way of interrupting negative thoughts. Oxytocin starts being released in the body, which is the hormone of love. It is released copiously when we are in love, during sex, touching, fondling and kissing and whenever we feel pleasure. Research has shown that we always relax when we think about a loving relationship.* Oxytocin's effects are:

- it strengthens relationships,
- it strengthens parental ties,
- it brings love, joy and peace,
- it strengthens the immune system,
- it reduces stress,
- it lowers blood pressure,
- it opens cells,
- it acts against addiction and alleviates withdrawal symptoms,
- if stimulates the production of the human growth hormone,
- it strengthens trust and wise reasoning,
- it regulates appetite, healthy digestion and metabolism,
- it encourages the healing of wounds,
- it encourages relaxation.

*Summarised from Alex Loyd: *Beyond Willpower.*

• **Exercise your body!** Even a 20-minute exercise session three times a week influences the release of the happiness hormone. Exercising outdoors in itself brings on feelings of pleasure. If you like dancing, that is a form of exercise that includes both music and singing. **Singing** also encourages the release of the feelings of pleasure. If you like going to the mountains, you will find beautiful flowers along the way and the natural scents will fill you with renewed energy, if you add good company and happy conversations the pleasure hormones in your body will appear in abundance.

Every year, I and a group of women walk to the church in Brezje in Slovenia. Five hours of walking, chatting, laughing, good atmosphere and wonderful company. A commentary by one of the husbands: "My wife came home in such a good mood that I think these walks should happen more often."

• **Turn off the television!** Research has shown that those who spend a lot of time watching television, develop a feeling of loneliness.

• **Limit coffee to a maximum of 2 cups a day**. Caffeine slows down the secretion of serotonin and other pleasure hormones.

• **Consume sea fish**, which contain omega-3 fatty acids and these influence the release of the happiness hormone. Hormones are fat soluble. Research has shown that in the countries where they consume a lot of fish, for example Japan, Taiwan and Finland, depression is a lot less common than where fatty fish is on the menu less frequently.*

• **The amino acid tryptophan** has a calming effect, reduces headaches and tension and helps with sleep. For tryptophan to turn into serotonin, it needs vitamins B3 and B6 and zinc. The highest amount of tryptophan is in protein foods, such as cottage cheese, milk and fish, which also contain high amounts of B vitamins and calcium. Zinc is in mushrooms and seafood.

• **Sleep**. Lack of sleep causes the secretion of the stress hormone, which blocks regeneration. When you don't get enough sleep, you are tetchy! Have a rest!

*Reader's Digest: *Food Cures*.

Conclusion

Hormones connect our thoughts, emotions and body. The most important hormonal centre is in the middle of our body – in the heart area. The thymus gland lies here. It is interesting that thyme, the word for the herb, is very similar. During the Roman empire, thyme was put on the chests of soldiers leaving for battle. Thyme was supposed to increase the soldiers' courage, strength and resoluteness. It has a beneficial effect on the lungs, heart, ability to breathe and accept energy. Thyme fills the body with warmth and a feeling of pleasure.

The heart chakra feeds all the hormonal centres with energy. When it is functioning well – when we feel happiness, love, peace, courage, when we have a feeling of strength (I can do anything) – everything functions well. Then we are healthy, full of energy, get enough sleep in a few hours and start a new day with eagerness. Just the opposite happens when we are unhappy or worried and we don't know how life will continue. Then, the flow through the heart chakra is reduced or even stopped, and the energy potential of the other energy centres is also reduced. That is when you get ill; and you get disease in the part of your body where you are most wounded.

I wish you all the best. I wish you happiness, perfect health, strength and courage, I wish you enthusiasm at any time of day and any time of life. Turn to happiness like a sunflower turns to the sun! Feed your thoughts with the feelings of happiness, peace and love!

I see PEACE

I see LOVE

I see HAPPINESS

My story

I grew up on a large farm in a small village in the Selca Valley in Slovenia. The village only has 10 houses. When still living at home, I wanted to go somewhere where there were lots of people. Sometimes you have to move away to see from a distance what you had in the past. Now I gladly go home – I like how people take an interest in one another. In the past, this used to irritate me.

The first big milestone happened when my mother became ill. I was 11 at the time. Afraid that my mother would die, I learnt how to cook and helped in the household and on the farm to the best of my abilities. My mother gave in to her illness, my father withdrew. I expressed my dissatisfaction through anger. At that time, I rejected God. I started deliberately destroying myself – by smoking.

Then I met my (ex) husband, fell madly in love and loved for both of us. I was a woman who loved too much – but only others, I was very cruel to myself. Later, I learnt to love myself, to take care of myself. Now, I am grateful for this lesson.

The next big blessing are my three daughters. Being a mother is beautiful. Now they are grown girls, and I can see how each of us went through a period when our emotions were controlled by hormones. We successfully passed this period. I love you, I am proud of you. You are the reason for me to live my mission and show you that it is worth following your heart, even at the expense of safety. I like being with you – Sara, Pia and Anja, thank you!

So, here I am. One long learning period. I could have resorted to anger, disappointment, bitterness, accusations, fear, illness. I could have followed darkness, but life led me to light.

I remember a period when I was constantly chatting to someone, I never wanted to be alone. Now, I am glad of being alone – because I know and feel I am not alone; I know that I am supported by all the forces of the universe. I allow light to flow through me and touch people. I am at peace with myself and the world around me.

I wish the same for you.

Minka Maria Izida

europe books

www.ingramcontent.com/pod-product-compliance
Lightning Source LLC
LaVergne TN
LVHW070907210926
848482LV00017B/1015